D0763539

The Unitarian Controversy
Essays on American Unitarian History

Conrad Wright

Skinner House Books

Boston, Massachusetts

Copyright © 1994 by the Unitarian Universalist Association. All rights reserved. Published by Skinner House Books, an imprint of the Unitarian Universalist Association, 25 Beacon Street, Boston, MA 02108-2800.

Note: Every attempt has been made to avoid sexist and racist language in this book. In the interest of historical authenticity, the documents quoted are printed in their original form.

ISBN 1-55896-284-0

Printed in USA.

99 98 97 96   /6 5 4 3 2

Library of Congress Cataloging-in-Publication Data

Wright, Conrad.
    The Unitarian controversy : essays on American Unitarian history / Conrad Wright.
        p.   cm.
    Includes bibliographical references and index.
    1. Unitarian controversy.   2. Congregational churches— Massachusetts—History—18th century. 3. Congregational churches— Massachusetts—History—19th century. 4. Unitarian churches— Massachusetts—History—19th century. 5. Massachusetts—Church history. I. Title.
BX9833.5.M4W75   1994
289.1′744′09034—dc20   94-39098
                                                 CIP

For Conrad, Nielson, and Elizabeth

CONCORDIA UNIVERSITY LIBRARY
PORTLAND. OR 97211

Preface

In the course of the Unitarian controversy from 1805 to 1835, the congregational churches of the Standing Order in Massachusetts divided, and the liberal wing became a separate denomination. The essays reprinted here deal with this crucial period of Unitarian history from a variety of perspectives—institutional, legal, sociological, and theological. At the same time, they are closely interrelated, with themes and interpretations carried from one essay to another.

They are representative of some important revisionist history, which has marked Unitarian historical writing in recent decades. The focus on the first generation of American Unitarians is in itself significant, since much of the story of the denomination has seemed, both by scholars at large and by Unitarians themselves, to be of little interest until Emerson and the Transcendentalists appear on the scene. The concern for institutional and sociological analysis is a change from the concentration on theological debate characteristic of an earlier generation of scholars.

On specific matters, there is an interpretation of the church–parish relationship of the Standing Order that challenges the conventional, confused view; a clarification of the almost universally misunderstood Dedham case (1819); a novel technique for analyzing the relationship between religion and social structure; an explanation for the first time of how the election of Henry Ware as Hollis Professor really happened; and a suggestion that our traditional image of William Ellery Channing is significantly incomplete.

These pieces are reprinted by courtesy of the organizations sponsoring the publications in which they originally appeared. "The Election of Henry Ware" and "The Controversial Career of Jedidiah Morse" are from the *Harvard Library Bulletin* (1969, 1983). "Piety, Morality, and the Commonwealth" was a Russell Lecture at Tufts University, printed in *Crane Review* (1967). "Ministers, Churches, and the Boston Elite, 1791–1815" and "Institutional Reconstruction in the Unitarian Controversy" were prepared for conferences sponsored by the Massachusetts Historical Society; the first of these was published in *Massachusetts and the New Nation* (1992) and the second in *American Unitarianism, 1805–1865* (1989), both edited by Conrad Edick Wright. "The Dedham Case Revisited," is from the *Proceedings of the Massachusetts Historical Society*, Vol. 100 (1988). "Unitarian Beginnings in Western Massachusetts" and "The Theological World of Samuel Gilman" are from the *Proceedings of the Unitarian Universalist Historical Society* (1989, 1973–1975). "The Channing We Don't Know" was published in the *Unitarian Universalist Christian* (1980/81).

Contents

The Election of Henry Ware

The election of Henry Ware as Hollis Professor of Divinity in 1805 occasioned bitter controversy at the time and has always been recognized as a crucial episode in the history of Harvard College. It was the first phase of what Professor Morison has called "a college revolution,"[1] which was completed a year later by the election to the presidency of Samuel Webber. Since both men were liberals in religion, replacing Calvinists, these related events and the angry response they called forth had lasting consequences for the college. But they had larger implications as well, since they precipitated the Unitarian controversy, which profoundly altered the ecclesiastical landscape of New England. Before a generation had gone by, the congregational churches of the Standing Order in Massachusetts were divided into two denominations, the orthodox or Trinitarian Congregationalists on the one hand, and the Unitarians on the other.

Yet there has always been some obscurity about the precise sequence of events leading up to Ware's election, and especially about the situation within the Corporation, the chief governing body of the college, which was initially responsible for the choice of a professor; and the familiar accounts would seem to be misleading in significant respects. It has generally been assumed that in the Corporation, then made up of six men, there was a rigid division along theological lines, repeated balloting over a period of time, and perhaps a series of tie votes, until finally the liberals exerted enough pressure to force a change of one vote and to carry the day.[2] No doubt the basis for this interpretation is the state-

1

ment by Dr. Jedidiah Morse—a member of the Board of Overseers and in a position to know something of what went on in the Corporation—that the members of the Corporation "were at one time equally divided between two candidates," and that "the choice was finally, after several weeks, determined by the change of an individual vote."[3] This comment is correct as far as it goes, but as much cannot be said for some of the conclusions extrapolated from it. That the two candidates were the Reverend Henry Ware of Hingham and the Reverend Jesse Appleton of Hampton, New Hampshire, was at best an ill-kept secret. But precisely what the lineup within the corporation was, who supported which candidate, who it was who changed his vote, and what his reasons were, Morse's statement does not reveal.

It is possible to reconstruct the sequence of events within the Corporation with some confidence, however, because of the existence in manuscript of two accounts by direct participants, together with certain ballots in the handwriting of the Fellows of the Corporation themselves. The existence of these materials is not a new discovery—one of the inside accounts was known to President Quincy in 1840, when he wrote his *History of Harvard University*—but they have never been analyzed in such a way as to fit disparate fragments into a coherent account. What they reveal very clearly is that, while theological and ecclesiastical factors finally were expressed in the outcome, considerations of a very different sort played an equally crucial part in the deliberations; that there was actually a good deal of give-and-take, as well as some intransigence, in these discussions; and that a compromise proposal, though it lost by one vote, drew support from both factions.

The two inside accounts are (1) extracts from the diary of the Reverend John Eliot, as copied into the commonplace book of his brother, Ephraim Eliot[4]; and (2) a narrative account prepared by Professor Eliphalet Pearson in January 1805, which stops short of the crucial meeting on February first of that year, when the election finally took place.[5] These materials tell a story that could never be reconstructed from the official records of the Corporation, which do little more than indicate that the subject was under discussion, with no mention of trial ballots or defeated motions.

The story begins in August 1803 with the death of Dr. David Tappan, who had been Hollis Professor since 1792. Tappan, a Calvinist but not a dogmatizing one, was respected and liked by many whose religious views were more liberal than his. In the terminology of the day, he was a "moderate Calvinist," but he nevertheless retained the confidence of the "Arminians" or "rational Christians" who were moving in the direction of Unitarianism. One of the liberals characterized Tappan thus in his diary:

> From education, from his connexions, and from the general course of his studies, his sentiments were calvinistical. But never were "orthodoxy and charity" more closely allied, than in him. Indeed, his calvinism was of the moderate kind; and, though he was firmly fixed in his own opinions, far from being dogmatical or pertinacious, he was desirous of correcting his own errours, and was willing, that others should enjoy their sentiments.[6]

President Joseph Willard, like Tappan, was a moderate Calvinist; and apparently he hoped to replace Tappan with a man of similar views. Professor Pearson's assertion in his narrative account that Willard was opposed to the election of Henry Ware, and that "he would sooner cut off his hand, than lift it up for an Arminian Professor," is detailed and circumstantial enough to be credible, even though an assertion to the contrary was made in the public press at the time.[7] Willard's difficulty apparently was that he could think of no candidate among the Calvinist clergy who was anywhere nearly as plausible for the position as Henry Ware, who was understood to be a liberal. He therefore procrastinated; and more than a year went by with no discussion in meetings of the Corporation even of possible candidates, let alone any nomination. In September 1804, some criticism of the delay began to appear in the Boston papers. Presumably these comments were not wholly disinterested. They may well have come from those who felt that Ware was an obvious choice, and who wondered whether there might not be more than met the eye in the failure of the Corporation to act.

On September 25, 1804, before he could make up his mind, President Willard died. Inasmuch as one of the Fellows, Dr. Simeon Howard, had died in August, there were now two vacancies. A meeting of the Board of Overseers was immediately called to authorize the filling of these vacancies. The Overseers advised an election to replace Howard, but they recommended that the professorship be filled before the presidency. Dr. John Eliot, minister of the New North Church in Boston, was promptly elected to the Corporation, and on October 30, 1804, the Overseers unanimously concurred. Since the presidency remained unfilled, Professor Pearson, as senior member of the Faculty, assumed the responsibilities of that office in the "immediate government" of the College, and he also presided in meetings of the Corporation, of which he had been a member since 1800.

There were now six members of the Corporation, whose opinions, prejudices, and quirks of character were to determine the direction and control of the University for the next century at least. Oldest both in years and in service to the College was Ebenezer Storer. A Boston merchant and man of affairs, he had been the Treasurer of the College since 1777 and had filled the post with notable success despite the uncertainties of war and a fluctuating currency. He had held a number of town offices at the time of the Revolution, and at a later date was a founder of the American Academy of Arts and Sciences. He was a prominent member of the Brattle Street Church, of which he had at one time been a deacon, and the presumption is that he participated in the gradual drift of the church in the direction of liberalism. At the very time that the controversy in Cambridge was heating up, the Brattle Street Church was calling and ordaining Joseph Stevens Buckminster, who clearly belonged in the liberal camp. It is recorded that Storer's disposition was notably "tolerant and pacific," and that he had a "naturally mild and social temper."[8] He was much attached to President Willard, though at the same time

4

he was emphatically in favor of the election of Ware; and he was one who pressed for action when the orthodox members of the Corporation were resorting to tactical delays.

Next in order of seniority was Dr. John Lathrop, minister of the Second Church, whose election as a Fellow dated from 1778. A native of Connecticut, he was a graduate of Princeton and had been a Calvinist in his younger years. His theological development was typical of that of many of his contemporaries who gradually moved in an Arminian and Unitarian direction without there being any occasion for a sharp break with the old Calvinism. His church moved with him, and on his death in 1816 it called Henry Ware, Jr., to be his successor.[9]

Judge Oliver Wendell was named to the Corporation in 1788. Like Storer he grew up in the Brattle Street Church. His daughter Sarah, however, was the second wife of the Reverend Abiel Holmes of Cambridge, whose orthodoxy eventually led to controversy and schism in the Cambridge church; and Holmes was a Yale classmate of Dr. Jedidiah Morse of Charlestown, who led the opposition to Ware's election in the Board of Overseers. Furthermore, Wendell had been one of the trustees of Phillips Academy in Andover when Pearson was Preceptor there. He was therefore closely connected by personal and kinship ties with the orthodox group. In the controversy he sought to play a mediating role, but when his attempts at compromise failed, he finally voted for the Calvinist candidate.[10]

Professor Eliphalet Pearson had been elected to the Corporation in 1800; he continued nevertheless to serve as Hancock Professor. Earlier he had been the first Preceptor of Phillips Academy, where he was long remembered without affection for the strictness of his discipline. At Harvard he was widely unpopular with the students; and those who disliked him accused him of being partial, "having favorites, for whom nothing was too good, & butts, whom he delighted to torment."[11] A man of dominating physical presence, he was as overbearing when presiding at meetings of the Corporation as he was in the classroom. Ambitious to become president, he was chiefly successful in antagonizing those on whose good opinion he was dependent. In the controversy, the inflexibility with which he adhered to the Calvinist cause came as a surprise; and Dr. Eliot, at least, reached the conclusion that ambition much more than genuine conviction was the explanation. Recollecting the events at a much later date, John Pierce went so far as to categorize Pearson as "ultra-liberal" in theology until the death of Willard. "He then suddenly claimed to be orthodox; & the change was so sudden & thorough, without the appearance of better motives, that a large proportion of his old friends considered him as merely acting a part."[12]

In 1806, when the Corporation was on the point of choosing Professor Samuel Webber to fill the post that Pearson felt was properly his, Pearson resigned both his professorship and his seat in the Corporation, complaining that developments in the University compelled him to take such a view of its "radical and constitutional maladies" as to exclude any hope of useful service. A committee of the Board of Overseers consulted with him and reported that its members did not share his gloomy fears about the future of the College, but finally recommended that the resignation be accepted.[13] Pearson returned to Andover, where he interested himself in the affairs of Andover Theological Seminary, only to discover that he was no happier there than he had been in Cambridge. By the time of his death in 1826, he had slipped into relative obscurity.[14]

Judge John Davis began a long stint of service to the University in 1803. He was successively Fellow (1803–1810), Treasurer (1810–1827), and Overseer (1827–1837). A native of Plymouth, he had moved to Boston in 1796, when appointed United States Attorney. In 1801, John Adams named him Judge of the United States District Court, where he served with distinction for forty years; his contemporaries regarded his work in the field of admiralty law as especially important. He was a member of the Federal Street Church, of which he was a deacon for many years. He was interested in matters scientific and literary, and was President of the Massachusetts Historical Society from 1818 to 1835. Memoirs of him after his death are uniformly eulogistic and make a point of stressing his unruffled and judicial temper. In the controversy of 1805, so far as the evidence shows, he did not play an especially aggressive role.[15]

Finally, there was Dr. John Eliot, elected just in time to be thrust into the midst of conflict. A graduate of the College in the class of 1772, a year before Pearson, he had succeeded his father as minister of the New North Church in 1779. He was one of the founders of the Massachusetts Historical Society and very active in its affairs. Like many of the liberals of that generation, he was deeply averse to theological controversy, and the extent to which he had departed from the orthodoxy of the creeds is indicated not so much by what he said as by the studied way in which he restricted himself to the language of Scripture whenever he touched on disputed topics. His reaction to the controversy over the Hollis Professorship is quite apparent in his diary. It is clear that Professor Pearson's personal jibes at him, as though he were another schoolboy in the classroom, helped to sour the atmosphere in which the discussions were carried on.[16]

The first meeting of the Corporation after Eliot joined it was on December 3, 1804. During the preceding month there had been renewed criticism in the Boston newspapers of the delay in filling the vacant professorship. It was even asserted that the income from the Hollis endowment had been misapplied to other uses because the lottery to raise funds for the erection of Stoughton Hall had yielded less than expected. A spokesperson for the orthodox group—who may well have been Dr. Jedidiah Morse, though proof is lacking—had warned of the danger that the governing boards might choose "professed Unitarians" for the professorship and the presidency. Prodded by public opinion from without and by the insistence of the Treasurer from within, the Corporation began its discussion of the question at that meeting. Professor Pearson was obviously dismayed by the demands for action, preferring to have no professor at all rather than run the risk of the election of a liberal.

At the next meeting on December 7, the Professor came prepared with a carefully wrought-out argument.[17] "He made a most solemn speech," Eliot recorded, "in which he told us how much he had prayed & thought upon this matter—that we were under a necessity of Electing a Calvinist—from the Records of the *College*, the public mind, the character of former professors &c." His performance at this meeting lost him the sympathy of Eliot, who thereafter referred to him in his diary as "Megalonyx."[18] Not only did Pearson subject Eliot to personal abuse, but he gave the impression that his defense of orthodoxy was motivated by calculations of personal as well as party advantage. In the afternoon, according to Eliot, "a great secret was communicated," which he expected would soon become a matter for public discussion. It is a plausible surmise that Pearson had let slip the fact that he hoped to be elected president himself.

At a meeting on December 15 at the home of Judge Davis, the only tangible accomplishment was a definition of the duties of the professorship. It is probable that individual names were discussed on this occasion. Either at this meeting or at the next one, at Judge Wendell's on December 26, each Fellow of the Corporation jotted down two names of candidates worthy of consideration. Since Pearson carefully saved the original slips of paper and the handwriting can be identified, there is solid evidence as to the preferences of each of the Fellows.[19] Contrary to what historians have generally supposed, the names offered for consideration did not follow a rigid pattern of ecclesiastical parties or factions. Pearson and Wendell both named two orthodox ministers, to be sure: Jesse Appleton of Hampton, New Hampshire, and Joshua Bates of Dedham. Judge Davis and Dr. Eliot both suggested Henry Ware of Hingham and John Pierce of Brookline, who were liberals. But Lathrop named Ware and Bates, while his willingness to consider Appleton is revealed by the fact that in November he had sought information on the latter's qualifications from his cousin, Dr. Joseph Lathrop of West Springfield. Storer's choices likewise included both a liberal and an orthodox candidate: "Mr. Ware" and "Mr. Payson." Presumably Payson was the Reverend Seth Payson, a country parson in Rindge, New Hampshire, who not long since had written a book supporting Jedidiah Morse's charge that a secret organization, the Order of the Illuminati, was conspiring to overthrow the governments of Europe and America and introduce anti-Christian principles. Payson's older brother, recently deceased, had been well known in Boston, since he had been for many years the minister of that part of Chelsea now known as Revere. It is recorded of Payson that in early life he had had some leanings toward Arminianism, but that he "settled down into a decided Calvinist."[20]

In short, the Corporation was made up of two men clearly on the orthodox side and four liberals, two of whom were ready to consider either a liberal or a Calvinist for the professorship. As the discussion proceeded, however, a stalemate developed, with three men supporting Henry Ware while three backed an orthodox man—presumably Jesse Appleton, though the nomination slips by themselves do not rule out the possibility of three votes for Pearson's preferred candidate, Joshua Bates.

Henry Ware, the candidate favored by the liberals, was then forty years of age. A graduate of the College of the class of 1785, he had been minister in Hingham for seventeen years. His liberal sympathies were indicated by the wording of a catechism he had prepared in collaboration with his neighbor, the Reverend Daniel Shute of the Second Parish in Hingham, which was Arian rather than Athanasian. A man of spotless reputation and a certain sweetness or gentleness of character, he afforded no opening for attack on personal grounds.[21]

The Reverend Jesse Appleton was also an attractive candidate, well liked by both liberals and orthodox. Only thirty-three years old, he was a graduate of Dartmouth College and had been minister in Hampton, New Hampshire, since 1797. Dr. Joseph Lathrop, who had directed his theological studies, gave him a warm recommendation in response to Dr. John Lathrop's inquiry, previously mentioned:

He is an accomplished scholar, an able divine, an accurate reasoner, an elegant writer, an agreeable speaker; easy in his manners, pleasant in conversation; evangelical, but liberal in his sentiments; and he appears to possess a serious & pious mind. . . . Probably the choice of a Professor is already made. If it is, I hope it has fallen on as good a man as Mr. Appleton; I much doubt, whether it has fallen on a better.[22]

But the Faculty and tutors at Harvard were not favorably disposed, Pearson himself preferring Joshua Bates of Dedham to Appleton. It may well be that they were influenced, as was Dr. Eliot, by the fact that he had a "dissonant & unpleasant" voice—an obvious disqualification for a man who was expected to conduct public worship for the College. Though passed over for the Harvard post, Appleton's abilities were recognized in 1807, when he was named President of Bowdoin.[23]

In view of Ebenezer Storer's emphatic preference at a later date for Ware over all other candidates, it is plausible to assume that he joined Davis and Eliot in supporting him on December 26. This would mean that Lathrop voted for an orthodox candidate and was the one who shifted to Ware a month later. Meanwhile, because of the stalemate, the suggestion was made that the advice of the Overseers be sought. Pearson was immediately aroused, fearing that this move would play into the hands of his opponents. The Board of Overseers was then made up of the Governor, Lieutenant Governor, Governor's Council, Senate of the Commonwealth, and the ministers of the congregational churches of the "six towns"—that is to say, the original towns first settled by the Massachusetts Bay Puritans. This body was accustomed to assemble in full session only in February and June, when the General Court was meeting. Between times, necessary business was transacted by thinly attended meetings made up predominantly of the clerical members, who were overwhelmingly liberal in sentiment. Pearson could readily anticipate what kind of advice such a rump session would give. Yielding to his protests, the Corporation did not formally vote to seek the advice of the Overseers, but it did request a meeting to deal with other business, knowing full well that the matter of the professorship would surely be raised by some one of those present. After all, three members of the Corporation were also on the Board of Overseers, inasmuch as Lathrop and Eliot were Boston ministers and Judge Wendell was a member of the Governor's Council.

Fifteen Overseers attended the meeting on January 3, 1805. It was one of the liberals, no doubt, who urged that the tie could be broken if the vacant presidency were filled. Those maneuvering for delay replied that this was so serious a matter that it should be referred to a full meeting of the Overseers, and they pointed to the requirement in the College Charter for "a general meeting of all the Overseers and Society, in great and difficult cases, and in cases of non-agreement." A motion to refer the matter to the whole board was voted down, however, and the Corporation was duly advised "to proceed to the choice of a president of the college . . . with all convenient speed, and present him to the overseers for their approbation." The orthodox were much exercised by these votes, since Lathrop and Eliot did not disqualify themselves as Overseers from giving advice to themselves in their other capacity as members of the Corporation. Had they done so, a tie would have resulted, and the motion that actually passed would not have prevailed.[24]

By the time the Corporation next met on February 1, 1805, Judge Wendell was advocating a compromise.[25] Why not elect Ware as president, he suggested, and Appleton as professor. Appleton was surely the kind of moderate Calvinist whom many liberals could happily accept, and such a compromise was a plausible way out of the impasse. But Pearson saw his chance of becoming president evaporating, and he violently opposed Wendell's suggestion. Storer felt that Ware was better fitted to be professor than president, while Eliot still worried about Appleton's dissonant and unpleasant voice.

Although several of the Fellows thought it premature to elect a president, it was agreed to take a straw vote to see how Wendell's proposal would fare. Five of the six trial ballots have survived, and they reveal that the compromise failed by the narrowest of margins. Ware received four votes for president, those of Lathrop, Wendell, Davis, and Eliot; but Appleton lost Eliot's vote for the professorship. To his lasting regret, Eliot cast his ballot for John Pierce of Brookline. Storer's ballot is missing, but by a process of elimination it becomes clear that he insisted on voting for Ware for the professorship, and gave his vote for the presidency to John T. Kirkland. Pearson would accept neither half of the compromise. For professor he named Joshua Bates, the minister in Dedham, while for president he supported "Dr. Smith," who may very well have been Samuel Stanhope Smith, the President of Princeton, a Presbyterian minister and an acquaintance of Jedidiah Morse.[26] Since Appleton did not receive a majority on the trial ballot, the compromise failed, and a formal ballot was taken for the professorship only. Ware got four votes, now including that of Lathrop, while Appleton, too late, received Pearson's as well as Wendell's.

Regardless of how one assesses the blame for the failure of the compromise, it is clear that nontheological and nonecclesiastical factors played a large part in the outcome. The final vote on February 1, 1805, was actually the only time when the Corporation divided along strictly factional lines. Although Pearson clearly felt that theological considerations outweighed all else, the other members of the Corporation were reluctant to see the vote rest on such grounds. Indeed, months later, when nominations for the presidency were called for, Pearson was the only one who would suggest none but men of his own theological persuasion for the post. Judge Davis and Dr. Lathrop as well as Judge Wendell were even willing to consider Pearson himself, despite all that had happened.

The public at large could hardly have been aware of such nontheological factors affecting the Corporation's decision as the problem of Appleton's speaking voice, the clash of personalities between Pearson and Eliot, and Pearson's presidential ambitions. When the nomination went to the Overseers for concurrence, therefore, the only issue that was open to discussion was the interpretation of the terms of the Hollis gift and the propriety of electing a liberal to the chair. The situation was ready-made for those who, like Dr. Morse, disapproved of friendly cooperation between the liberals and the orthodox and were eager to widen the cleavage between them. Morse played a role in the Board of Overseers equivalent to the one Pearson had played in the Corporation; he seems to have been, even more than Pearson, the one who shaped the strategy of the orthodox party and sought to exploit the issue for partisan ends.[27] If he could not prevent the election of Ware, he could at least try to convict the liberals of a breach of trust, and thereby discredit them in the eyes of the general public.

Interest was sufficiently aroused so that the attendance at the meeting of the Overseers on February 14, 1805, was unusually full. Ordinarily fewer than thirty of the lay members would turn out for such a meeting. This time forty-five of forty-seven were present and were joined by twelve of the seventeen clerical members. Senator Enoch Titcomb of Newburyport, a member of the "Old South" or Presbyterian church there, who had been carefully briefed in advance by either Morse or Pearson, inquired into the terms of the professorship as laid down by the donor, and asked what procedure the Corporation had followed to satisfy itself that Ware's doctrinal views were in accordance with the terms of the Hollis gift.[28] The main burden of attack, however, was assumed by Morse. The crux of the debate was the requirement that the electors should "prefer a man of solid learning in divinity, of sound and orthodox principles."[29] For Morse and the other Calvinists, the term "orthodox" could mean only one thing, the orthodoxy of the Westminster Confession. Thomas Hollis was not an Arminian or a Unitarian, they insisted, and would never have countenanced the election of a man who so far departed from sound doctrine. It was surely culpable negligence that the Corporation had not made formal inquiry into Ware's doctrinal views, as had been done on earlier occasions, most notably when the first Professor Wigglesworth had been named in 1722.

Of those who replied to Morse, only Samuel Dexter, Jr. can be positively identified. According to John Pierce, "by an appeal to Hollis's statutes, and a convincing address to the reason and understanding of the Board, he turned the counsels of this busy heresiarch into foolishness."[30] The position taken by the liberals was that Hollis, as a Baptist, had himself departed from Westminster standards, and was distinguished by nothing so much as his generous regard for, and willingness to work with, men with whom he was not in entire doctrinal agreement. His own minister had refused to make the Westminster Confession the test of orthodoxy and insisted on the Bible as the only standard. Hollis's concern that his endowment should be administered in accordance with his prescribed rules and orders derived from his fear that they would be given a narrower construction than he intended, and that groups like the Baptists might find themselves excluded. Most important of all, he had deliberately set aside creedal definitions of "sound and orthodox principles" when he prescribed that the only article of belief to be required of his professor would be "that the Bible is the only and most perfect rule of faith and practice," and that it is to be interpreted "according to the best light that God shall give him."[31] In short, the election of a man like Henry Ware was no breach of trust, since he qualified by the only standard of orthodoxy that Hollis himself had attached to his foundation.

It is a curious fact that we know more about what went on in the closed meetings of the Corporation than we do about the semi-public meetings of the Board of Overseers, attended by fifty-seven men. The arguments advanced by the orthodox may be found in Morse's pamphlet, published within a matter of weeks, entitled *The True Reasons on Which the Election of a Hollis Professor of Divinity in Harvard College Was Opposed at the Board of Overseers.* The liberal position was stated in a reply to Morse by William Wells in the *Monthly Anthology* for March 1805.[32] But no listing of the yeas and nays was recorded to tell us how each man voted, nor did anyone save the ballots; hence there seems to be no way to determine the extent to which the voting reflected theological loyalties, or what to make of Wells's assertion that "political considerations . . . were the cause of opposition with the majority."[33] What we have is the official minute, recorded in Dr. Lathrop's hand: "After a long and patient discussion, the question for concurrence was called and the votes being taken by ballot, it appeared that the Election of the Revd Henry Ware, Hollis Professor of Divinity, by the Corporation, was concurred by the overseers."[34] And we have scattered bits of information in Morse's pamphlet, most important of which is a report of the number of votes, 33 for concurrence, 23 opposed.[35]

After consulting with his church and receiving a dismissal by vote of an ecclesiastical council, Ware accepted his election. He carefully complied with the requirements of the founder by formally declaring, in the presence of the two governing boards, his belief "that the Scriptures of the old and new Testament are the only perfect rule of faith and manners," and promised to explain them to his pupils "with integrity and faithfulness, according to the best light, that God shall give me."[36]

At an elaborate ceremony on May 14, Dr. Pearson had the unhappy duty of presiding over Ware's induction into office. His unhappiness turned to bitterness when the fact was doubly underscored that the other members of the Corporation were not going to elect him president. In December 1805 they chose Fisher Ames, who declined on account of ill health; and in February 1806 the discussion clearly indicated that Professor Samuel Webber would be the next choice. It was then that Pearson abruptly resigned both as Fellow of the Corporation and as Hancock Professor. By that time he would not even accept an invitation to dine with the other Fellows.[37]

As Jedidiah Morse saw it, a revolution had taken place in the affairs of the College. For the first time in its history, the presidency and the professorship of divinity were held by men who could not be counted among the ranks of the Calvinists. Harvard had been faithless to the tradition by which it had been guided for more than a century and a half. An intensely partisan man, Morse interpreted these events in terms of party rivalries. He thereby intensified the sectarian conflict that was already latent in the community.

For the liberals, however, it was another Harvard tradition that was at stake. For a century, ever since the days of President Leverett, the perspectives of the College had been widening as the community it served became more heterogeneous. In the community at large, Calvinism no longer held a monopoly; and in the College, even under Calvinists like Leverett and Holyoke, a "free and catholic" tradition had developed, which declared that Calvinist and Arminian, and even Trinitarian and Arian, could cooperate for the common good. The liberals felt that this tradition was now threatened by a narrower sectarianism than had prevailed for many decades. William Wells spoke their mind in the *Monthly Anthology*, in February 1805:

> Feeling, as I do, most seriously interested in the prosperity of our Alma Mater, I shall lament, as deeply injurious to her usefulness and reputation, that hour, when her present liberal principles shall be exchanged for subscriptions to Articles of Faith: or, what is the same thing, when the belief of a certain speculative system shall be esteemed necessary in him, who aspires to the honourable station of instructor of her sons.[38]

The supporters of Henry Ware were successful, and we have been accustomed to define their success in terms of the election of a liberal to the Hollis Professorship. But one might argue that more important than the election of Ware, and even more fateful for both the College and the community, was the rebuff to Eliphalet Pearson and the defeat of Jedidiah Morse.

Piety, Morality, and the Commonwealth

The customary approach to problems of church and state is legalistic and deductive. It begins with a principle of separation of church and state, sometimes referred to as a "wall of separation," which is made to rest on Article I of the Bill of Rights of the Constitution; and it attempts to move from this general principle to specific applications of rules to guide us in particular cases, such as public aid to parochial schools, released time, flag salutes, prayer and Bible readings, and the like. Because we have a written constitution with a Supreme Court to interpret it, the basic question we ask about a given proposition involving church–state relations is not, Is it wise or prudent? but, Is it constitutional? Or perhaps we should say, all questions about the appropriateness or wisdom of a given policy must somehow be translated into the form of a constitutional issue; and not until that is done, are we satisfied with the answers to them.

It is almost impossible for us to discuss current problems in church-state relations without adopting this conventional legal and constitutional approach. If we are, for a time at least, to escape these conventions, it might be helpful to look at these problems as they arise in a society in which there is no complicating factor of constitutional interpretation. But it is not necessary for this purpose to move to some far-off corner of the world, where all the circumstances are unfamiliar. We need only to move back in time to look at the situation in Massachusetts before the constitutional prohibition in the Bill of Rights, barring an establishment of religion, was interpreted to be a restriction on the states as well as the federal government. We shall then be dealing with a world that is not wholly unfamiliar to us, but which is, at the same time, just enough different to help us achieve a degree of perspective.

In Massachusetts in the colonial period, a close relationship between church and state was taken for granted.[1] In particular, it was customary for the towns to tax their inhabitants for the support of public worship. The salary of the minister and the expense of keeping the meetinghouse in repair were met from public funds. These ecclesiastical arrangements—commonly referred to as the "Standing Order" of the churches in Massachusetts—actually outlasted the colonial period and were not finally abandoned until 1833, which was long after the First Amendment to the Constitution of the United States forbade the federal government to pass any law respecting an establishment of religion.

Because the system of tax support of public worship dates back to the first generation of Puritans in Massachusetts, it is frequently assumed that a religious "establishment" of this kind was an inherent aspect of the Puritan theory of the relation of church and state. The record, however, suggests that practical considerations rather than Puritan theory lay behind these arrangements. The Puritans insisted that the ministers were entitled to a "necessary & sufficient maintenance," which was an obligation resting on the people and not something they might grant or withhold as they pleased. But it is evident from the writings of the Puritans that maintenance of the clergy by voluntary gifts, arising from an inward sense of obligation of the people, was considered to be the most desirable arrangement. The coercive power of the state in this matter was to be resorted to only if voluntary methods failed. "In case that Congregations are defective in their contributions," states the Cambridge Platform of 1648, "the Deacons are to call upon them to doe their duty: if their call sufficeth not, the church by her own power is to require it of their members & where church-powr through the corruption of men, doth not, or cannot attaine the end, the Magistrate is to see [that the] ministry be duely provided for. . . ."[2]

Piety, Morality, and the Commonwealth

Whether a town should lay an assessment for the support of the ministry was, therefore, from the Puritan point of view, not a matter of principle, but rather of expediency, in the face of the tendency of selfish people to evade their proper responsibilities. It must be acknowledged that once the General Court had authorized the towns to lay rates for the support of the ministry it did not take long for the practise to become almost universal. Yet in Boston, the voluntary system was always followed, and taxes were never levied to augment ministerial salaries; and instances can be found of country towns that followed the system of taxation for a period of years, then relied on voluntary support for a time, only to return to parish rates when the response to voluntary methods of raising money proved insufficient.

Voluntary support of religious worship seems so axiomatic to us, and is defended by us so explicitly on grounds of principle, that it is hard for us to realize that the question was originally one of expediency and not of principle at all. Our immediate assumption is that where the voluntary system is not accepted, tyranny over the mind and conscience must prevail. Why should one be required to support religious worship of which one disapproves, or promote religious doctrines with which one disagrees? These are admittedly the questions that would be posed by a system of tax-supported churches today. It must be stressed, therefore, that this was not the issue in Puritan times, at any rate, not until the colony was close to a half a century old. Such questions are not really relevant in an exclusive society, relatively homogeneous in character. When the Puritans resorted to taxation, because voluntary methods had failed, the problem was not the reluctance to contribute of people who conscientiously preferred another way of worship. The problem was the slackness of selfish people, who were only too willing to let others carry the load that was recognized as a common obligation. Arrangements that we immediately condemn as unjust and tyrannical in a pluralistic society seemed no more than an attempt to achieve fairness and equity in an essentially homogeneous society in which common religious ideals prevailed.

Of course the exclusiveness and homogeneity of the original Puritan settlement could not be maintained indefinitely. From the earliest years, there were individuals and even small groups of persons who, for one reason or another, represented discordant elements. Some Quakers intruded in the 1650s, and some Baptists gave trouble in the 1660s; but it was actually not until the original charter was vacated in 1684, and a royal governor appeared in the person of Sir Edmund Andros, that Puritan Massachusetts Bay was forced to reckon with the fact that it would have to accept the presence of minority religious groups. Sir Edmund insisted on Anglican worship in Boston, and before long King's Chapel and the prayerbook were permanent fixtures. The rule of Andros was short-lived, and a new charter, obtained in 1691, restored at least part of the home rule that had been taken away in 1684. The old patterns had been disrupted, however, so that in a very real sense 1691 marks the end of the old Puritan theocracy.

The new charter eliminated the vestiges of a religious qualification for the franchise, but it did not abolish the system of tax support of public worship. In 1692, the General Court passed a law requiring the inhabitants of each town to provide "an able, learned orthodox minister or ministers, of good conversation, to dispense the Word of God to them; which minister or ministers shall be suitably encouraged and sufficiently supported and maintained by the inhabitants of such town." The law went on to provide that if a town failed in its duty of making proper provision for the maintenance of the minister, or allowed the post to remain vacant, complaint might be made to the court of quarter session, which would have the power to levy the necessary assessments.[3]

Unfortunately, there does not seem to be any contemporary account of this legislation, giving us the rationale for it; and so we have to proceed to interpret it on the basis of what seem to be its necessary implications. I say "its necessary implications," but what seem to me to be certain implications lead to conclusions quite different from those drawn by most historians. I must warn you, therefore, that we are entering on decidedly debatable ground, and the interpretation I propose to give is highly unconventional.

For my part, I attach considerable significance to two aspects of the law of 1692. One of them involves that part of it which states that the minister who is entitled to public support is to be chosen "by the major part of the inhabitants . . . at a town meeting duly warned for that purpose" and that he is to be regarded as "the minister of such town." The other aspect of the law to which I wish especially to draw your attention is its title: "An Act for the Settlement and Support of Ministers and School Masters." The final section of the bill makes provision for the maintenance of schoolmasters in a way roughly parallel to the earlier sections dealing with the ministers.[4]

It seems a bit odd—does it not?—that legislation providing for the support of ministers should place them in the same category as schoolmasters and should make no reference to the churches. The implication is that they are performing a public function, akin to the teaching of school, which is distinguishable from their relationship to the select body of worshipers in full communion that make up the church. The state is concerned to have this public function performed, may designate ministers to perform it, and therefore has an obligation to see that its chosen agents are properly recompensed. One might draw a parallel with our own day, when civil government relies largely on ministers, priests, and rabbis to solemnize marriages. The participants in a wedding may think of it as a religious ceremony, the couples making their vows in the presence of God. But from the point of view of the state—which is concerned about such mundane matters as the title to property, the right of children to inherit, and the responsibility of parents for the support of their children—the minister or priest is the representative of society in a matter of concern to society and has the responsibility of seeing that the established procedures are followed with respect to licenses, the recording of the marriage in the city clerk's office, and so on. The spiritual leader of a religious group is the designated agent of the civil government in a matter in which society at large, for its own protection, takes an interest.

Similarly, it may be argued that the law of 1692 implies that there are certain public functions performed by ministers of the gospel, which may be thought of apart from the role of the minister within the church itself. The nature of these functions is not spelled out by the law of 1692, but is certainly suggested by the fact that the minister is coupled with the schoolmaster. As the eighteenth century progressed, however, the gradual secularization of society itself brought out into sharper relief the nonecclesiastical functions of the minister, so that by the time the Constitution of the Commonwealth was framed in 1780, the ministers are described, not as ministers, but as "public Protestant teachers of piety, religion, and morality."[5] In other words, they are supported by public funds in order that they may expound the principles of behavior and good order that citizens must accept if society itself is to survive and free political institutions are to flourish. The minister, to be sure, also has a special responsibility for his own flock, made up of believers in accordance with the peculiarities of some Christian sect. But although this ecclesiastical role is related to the role of public teacher, it is not the same thing. Not every minister of a religious group would qualify as a *public* teacher of piety, religion, and morality; and, for that matter, the ministers of some groups, specifically the Universalists, found it hard to persuade society at large that they were teachers of morality.

A corollary to Parkinson's Law states that when an organization (e.g., the League of Nations) finally succeeds in getting adequate physical accommodations, it is on the point of collapse. In a somewhat similar way, it often happens that it is not until a human institution is on the point of becoming obsolete that its rationale is clearly set forth. So it was with the Massachusetts Standing Order. One searches in vain for an explanation in 1692, when the law we have been discussing was passed. The argument is found at best in fragmentary form in 1780, when the system was implanted in the Constitution of the Commonwealth. Thus, John Tucker of Newbury declared in 1774 that the province "has the same right to provide for the support of a public ministry, as it has for the support of schools, or to enact any thing which it judges beneficial to a civil society;"[6] and Enos Hitchcock asserted in 1795 that all groups in the community should assent to public encouragement of religion, because all benefit from "the air of respectability which elegant churches give a town."[7] Such fragments indicate well enough the direction of the argument, but they certainly fall short of being a full statement of it.

But the classic defense of the system, perhaps we may say, was made by Chief Justice Theophilus Parsons in a famous court decision in 1807, at a time when the Standing Order was increasingly under attack. "The object of a free civil government," he declared, "is the promotion and security of the happiness of the citizens. These effects cannot be produced, but by the knowledge and practice of our moral duties, which comprehend all the social and civil obligations of man to man." Civil laws, he went on to suggest, may serve to restrain vice and crime, but they cannot make men positively virtuous. "This most manifest truth has been felt by legislators in all ages; and as man is born, not a social, but a religious being, so in the pagan world false and absurd systems of religion were adopted and patronized by the magistrate, to remedy the defects necessarily existing in a government merely civil." Fortunately, the Chief Justice pointed out, in Massachusetts it was not necessary to choose a false and defective religious system, since Christianity had long been promulgated, its excellencies were well known, and its divine authority admitted. And so this religion, "as understood by protestants, tending by its effects to make every man submitting to its influence, a better husband, parent, child, neighbor, citizen, and magistrate, was by the people established as a fundamental part of their constitution."

Some might well argue that they should not be taxed for the support of public worship if they never attend it. This objection, Mr. Justice Parsons declared, is founded wholly in error:

The object of public religious instruction is to teach, and to enforce by suitable arguments, the practice of a system of correct morals among the people, and to form and cultivate reasonable and just habits and manners; by which every man's person and property are protected from outrage, and his personal and social enjoyments promoted and multiplied. From these effects every man derives the most important benefits, and whether he be, or be not an auditor of any public teacher, he receives more solid and permanent advantages from this public instruction, than the administration of justice in courts of law can give him. The like objection may be made by any man to the support of public schools, if he have no family who attend; and any man, who has no lawsuit may object to the support of judges and jurors on the same ground; when if there were no courts of Law, he would unfortunately find that causes for lawsuits would sufficiently abound.[8]

I have a notion that many of us find this rationale for the public support of the ministry less than wholly persuasive. It is all very well to argue that in taxing the people to pay the salary of the minister, the town was not concerned to advance the peculiarities of any particular denomination of Christians, but was simply promoting civic virtue and diffusing those nonsectarian principles of morality by which the foundations of a free commonwealth are secured. But is it not fallacious to suppose that the minister would be able to keep separate his public role as teacher of piety and morality and his ecclesiastical role as the minister of a congregational church? If he is a firm believer in the theology of John Calvin, isn't it inevitable that he will assume that Calvinism alone is compatible with orderly civil government? And if a large proportion of the people in a town find themselves in disagreement with the minister's doctrinal views, are they going to respect what he has to say when he presumes to stand on more neutral ground as a teacher of civil morals? Doesn't the Baptist or Universalist supporter of Thomas Jefferson have legitimate grounds of complaint if he is taxed in order to make it possible for a Calvinist minister to spout Federalist party doctrine at him from the pulpit? Isn't it fallacious to suppose that any minister could perform this public function acceptably in a society that was becoming increasingly pluralistic, in which the tensions between religious groups

24

made them increasingly conscious of their other role as expounders of controverted theological dogmas?

The defenders of the Standing Order in the eighteenth century were sensitive to these challenges, and they met them in several ways. For one thing, they pointed out that although the General Court was authorized to provide for the support of the ministry, because of the benefits to civil society that would accrue, the legislature was never authorized, and never presumed, to settle articles of faith or impose particular modes of worship. For that matter, the Massachusetts Province laws did not even prescribe that the town minister had to be a congregationalist, and in some cases he was not. "If most of the inhabitants in a Plantation, are *Episcopalians*," Cotton Mather pointed out in 1726, "they will have a *Minister* of their own Perswasion."[9] Jonathan Mayhew reiterated this point in 1763: "if any particular town in the Province should legally chuse, settle, and support a protestant minister of *any* denomination, whether episcopalian, presbyterian, congregational, baptist, or lutheran, this would be looked upon as satisfying the said law."[10] It is therefore technically not correct to assert, as historians have so often done, that the Standing Order in Massachusetts was an establishment of the congregationalist churches. What was "established" was the institution of public worship.

But the congregational churches represented the dominant group in most towns, and so, from the point of view of the Quakers, Episcopalians, and Baptists, the law of 1692 did not go far enough in recognizing the rights of minorities. The Quakers provided the first effective opposition. They did not believe in a hireling ministry anyway, and so would have nothing to do with proposals for a town minister supported by public funds. In Dartmouth and Tiverton, where they were in a majority, they simply refused to comply with the law. Various steps were then taken by the Province authorities, which we need not review in detail, to secure compliance. The General Court finally went so far as to provide that a minister might be sent to a reluctant town, whose salary would be paid from the Province treasury, which would in turn be reimbursed by an assessment on the town. On this basis, Dartmouth was assessed £100 and Tiverton £72 11/-. The selectmen refused to make the necessary levy on the freeholders, so the local assessors were imprisoned. Thereupon, instead of showing repentance for their flagrant disregard of the law, the towns voted indemnification to the law-breaking assessors and appealed to the Crown, which in 1724 ordered release of the prisoners and remission of the tax.[11]

There followed a period of acceptance, if sometimes grudging acceptance, of the principle that even necessary and wholesome laws may create hardship for particular groups in society, so that minorities may sometimes be entitled to special relief from the general operation of a law. Such relief was granted in 1727 to the Episcopalians, and the following year to the Quakers and Baptists. The various laws providing relief differed in detail and were subject to modification from time to time, but the underlying principle was that the members of a minority religious group should be allowed to have their money go to the support of their own worship. As the Constitution of 1780 put it: "all moneys paid by the subjects to the support of public worship, and of the public teachers aforesaid, shall, if he require it, be uniformly applied to the support of the public teacher or teachers of his own religious sect or denomination, provided there be any on whose instruction he attends . . . ."

The Standing Order in Massachusetts, the principles and practises of which we have been reviewing, is commonly described by historians as an "establishment" of religion, and the congregational churches are customarily spoken of as "established churches." Yet in the eighteenth century, we find men like Charles Chauncy, Jonathan Mayhew, and John Tucker—all of them conspicuous advocates of freedom of conscience—proclaiming their utter abhorrence of all establishments of religion, at the same time that they strongly supported the Standing Order. "We are, in principle, against all civil establishments in religion," Charles Chauncy declared, "and as we do not desire any such establishment in support of our own religious sentiments or

26

practice, we cannot reasonably be blamed, if we are not disposed to encourage one in favor of the Episcopal Colonists . . . we desire not, and suppose we have no right to desire, the interposition of the state to establish our sentiments in religion, or the manner in which we would express them. . . . It does not indeed appear to us, that God has entrusted the state with a right to make religious establishments."[12]

The usual present-day reaction to statements like the one just quoted from Chauncy is to accuse the defenders of the Standing Order of inconsistency, if not hypocrisy. How was it possible, we ask, for the authors of Article III of the Declaration of Rights of the Constitution of 1780 to say "no subordination of any one sect or denomination to another shall ever be established by law," while at the same time they were authorizing the legislature to require the towns "to make suitable provision, at their own expense, for the institution of the public worship of GOD . . ."? How was it possible for presumably intelligent men to be so inconsistent as to declare that the state has no right to make religious establishments, and then provide for one in the Constitution itself?

I submit that these are the wrong questions to ask. The right question is this: From what perspective must we view the Standing Order, if we are to understand why its defenders regarded it neither as representing an establishment of religion, nor as an infringement on freedom of conscience—which in the eighteenth century they cherished as sincerely as we do. The answer is that as soon as one realizes that the ministers were thought of as performing an essential civil or public function, which may be distinguished from their ecclesiastical function, the whole confused business suddenly begins to make sense. As soon as one realizes that a public teacher of piety, religion, and morality was not the same thing as a minister of a church, even though the same person was designated to serve in both capacities, it becomes clear why the Puritans, and their descendants down into the nineteenth century, cherished the principle of separation of church and state, yet thought tax support of public teachers of religion to be no violation of it.

We may not agree with them as to how to draw the line between church and state and whether a particular practice violates the principle of separation, but we must not immediately assume they were fools or hypocrites. If it comes to that, we are far from agreement among ourselves as to whether it is a violation of the principle of separation of church and state for towns to provide bus transportation for children in parochial schools, for "nonsectarian" prayers to be said at opening exercises, for the federal government to lend money for the construction of buildings for Catholic colleges, or even for it to put "In God We Trust" on the dollar bill. Who knows, perhaps our grandchildren will call us fools or hypocrites for declaring that the wall of separation between church and state must not be breached, at the same time that churches and meetinghouses are exempt from taxation on the grounds that the activities that go on in them serve to elevate the moral tone of the community.

Two quotations may serve to summarize the basic rationale of the ancient Standing Order of Massachusetts, and to them I invite your particular attention:

> The diffusion of religious knowledge is . . . essential to the well being of the State. And it cannot be effected but by the settlement and support of teachers in towns, parishes, and societies incorporated for religious purposes.[13]

> A set of common beliefs is essential for the health and vigor of a free society. And it is through [religious training] that these beliefs are developed in the young and carried forward into later life. . . . The . . . tax-supported [parishes] are the sinews of our society; they are . . . a concrete manifestation of our unique ideals, and the vehicle by which [they] may be transmitted to our future citizens.

Clearly these two quotations say virtually the same thing, in slightly different language. Perhaps I should identify the authors as a matter of curiosity. The first of the two quotations is from the writings of Chief Justice Parsons—not from the court decision in the Barnes case quoted earlier, but from a charge to the grand jury prepared at about the same time, in 1806 to be exact. As for the second quotation, I must acknowledge that it has been somewhat edited, and so I suppose it is only fair that I give you the original version as well:

> A set of common beliefs is essential for the health and vigor of a free society. And it is through education that these beliefs are developed in the young and carried forward into later life. . . . The free tax-supported schools are the sinews of our society; they are . . . a concrete manifestation of our unique ideals and the vehicle by which the American concept of democracy may be transmitted to our future citizens.[14]

Now it should be no surprise to you to learn that the quotation is from a book published as recently as 1949, entitled *Education in a Divided World*, by a distinguished American educator, James Bryant Conant.

Is it too much to say that we accept without question, when applied to the public schools, a principle that we reject automatically when we find an earlier generation applying it to the public teaching of religion? For what the apologists for the Massachusetts Standing Order were saying, two centuries ago, was that for human society to endure, certain moral values must be held in common by the people, and that their preservation must not be left to chance. Rather, society must support those who make the transmission and elevation of the moral or ethical values of society itself one of their chief concerns. Chief Justice Parsons would have had little difficulty in understanding what Mr. Justice Frankfurter was saying, in 1940, in one of the flag salute cases.

> The ultimate foundation of a free society is the binding tie of cohesive sentiment. Such a sentiment is fostered by all those agencies of the mind and spirit which may serve to gather up the traditions of a people, transmit them from generation to

generation and thereby create that continuity of a treasured common life which constitutes a civilization. . . . The precise issue, then, for us to decide is whether the legislatures of the various states . . . are barred from determining the appropriateness of various means to evoke that unifying sentiment without which there can ultimately be no liberties, civil or religious.[15]

What happened, of course, between the time that Parsons gave the decision of the Court in the case of *Barnes* v. *The First Parish in Falmouth* and Frankfurter prepared his opinion in the Gobitis case, was that society found it increasingly difficult to use the ministers as the instrumentalities by which common moral values could be perpetuated, and so turned to the schools to perform this function. The past century and a half has seen the school supplant the church as the chief instrument (apart from the family) by which social norms are transmitted to the new generation. As the church declined in importance, society relinquished concern for it, a process we call "the triumph of the principle of separation of church and state." At the same time, the school gained in importance, and society both universalized and subdued it, a process we call "the triumph of the principle of free public education." Furthermore, we think nothing of taxing the whole community for support of the public schools, even though various minority groups are profoundly out of sympathy with the kind of intellectual and moral training that the schools may afford. We do not even grant tax exemptions to dissenters, as the Constitution of 1780 did to religious minorities. One can almost hear our ancestors chiding us for our illiberality, for our undemocratic disregard for the rights of minorities, which they were ever so much more generous in recognizing.

The transfer of function, which we have just mentioned, from the churches to the public schools, took place in the first part of the nineteenth century. The key figure in the process was Horace Mann, who served as Secretary of the Massachusetts Board of Education from 1837 to 1848.[16] What the experience of those years demonstrated, however, was that to make the schools rather than churches the agents of society for the transmission of moral values did not resolve any of the basic issues. It simply changed the arena in which the struggle was to be fought among competing groups in a pluralistic society.

The collapse of the Standing Order had been inevitable because the ministers could no longer be generally accepted as public teachers of piety and morality, in view of the fact that they also spoke for particular denominations of Christians. But it was still thought possible to distinguish certain nonsectarian principles of piety, justice, and love of country, which all religious groups cherish as the basis of good citizenship and which might therefore be taught in the schools without offense to any of them. This policy was laid down by the General Court in 1827, when a law was enacted that began by enjoining instruction in "the principles of piety, justice, and sacred regard to the truth" as "the basis on which the Republican Constitution is founded" and ended by forbidding schools to use books "which are calculated to favor any particular religious sect or tenet."[17]

Horace Mann wholeheartedly endorsed this policy, even though a survey soon convinced him that unobjectionable textbooks would not be easy to find. A passage in the Third Report of the Board of Education, in 1840, states the accepted policy in these terms:

> Although it may not be easy theoretically, to draw the line between those views of religious truth and of christian faith, which are common to all, and may, therefore, with propriety be inculcated in school, and those which, being peculiar to individual sects, are therefore by law excluded; still it is believed that no practical difficulty occurs in the conduct of our schools in this respect.[18]

Yet scarcely had Mann taken up his duties when he found himself embroiled in controversy with Frederick A. Packard, the Secretary of the American Sunday School Union, who sought to introduce books of an evangelical nature into school libraries. Packard spoke for a very considerable body of people, for whom moral instruction as the basis for citizenship necessarily implied evangelical Protestantism, of a broadly nondenominational or nonsectarian kind. Mann, a Unitarian, responded to such pressures by advocating the reading of the Bible, without commentary. Although different sects might draw different doctrinal conclusions from the Bible, the sacred text, at any rate, was common to all. The only trouble was that Mann's solution to the problem was a characteristically Unitarian one, which seemed to the orthodox to be as sectarian in spirit as their proposals did to him. And if this complaint from the orthodox Calvinists were not enough, before long the Catholics were complaining that the reading of the Bible without commentary was a typically Protestant way of attacking their faith, since the version prescribed was the King James translation, and the avoidance of commentary was an expression of the Protestant dogma of the right of private judgment. In short, Mann's experience suggests to us, even if it did not persuade him, that there was no way to draw the line between the nonsectarian values that undergird civil society and the sectarian concerns of particular groups, which would not plausibly seem to be in itself a sectarian act by one group or another.

Now that we have reviewed the history of church and state in a single, limited area over a period of a century and a half, are there any conclusions that we can draw that have relevance to our own situation?

Here we have examined a specific practise, namely the tax support of public worship, that our generation immediately rejects as a violation of the principle of separation of church and state, but that our ancestors advocated and explicitly denied was a violation of that principle. If the resolution of these issues is to be sought in the conventional way by starting with the principle and deducing from it by logic certain applications to be made to concrete situations, then we are right and our ancestors were wrong, or vice versa.

But if we assume that we are right on this matter of tax support of public worship, and the Puritans were wrong, we find ourselves in an unexpected logical predicament. In that case, something must be wrong with the argument by which they justified tax support of the public teaching of piety, religion, and morality, as essential to the preservation of civil society itself. But if that is so, why isn't there something equally wrong with the same argument when we use it to justify tax support of the public schools as the vehicle through which democratic values are inculcated and sustained? Logic is logic, as the Deacon once said; and if consistency is a virtue, maybe our ancestors have the better of us after all.

On the other hand, perhaps the lesson to be drawn is not that we must be more logical in our deductions from abstract principles, but that we should be more sensitive to differences in the situations in which the principles are being applied. And there are, after all, significant differences between colonial Massachusetts and the present day. They revolve around the basic difference between what is appropriate in a relatively homogeneous society on the one hand, and in a pluralistic one on the other. The nature of the consensus that is possible in these situations is markedly different; what is axiomatic in one case may be intolerable in another. Perhaps we might say that the changing attitudes toward the relationship between church and state in Massachusetts seem to be functions of the process by which the society became increasingly pluralistic, rather than the expression of the unfolding of logic in history. We draw the line between church and state in a different way than the founding fathers did, not because we are wiser or more virtuous than they, but because we are confronted with a different social situation.

Every social group develops attitudes and values, which have to be understood as norms of the group, and which are not identical with the attitudes and values of the individuals who originally composed it. The survival of the group depends on the development of such norms and their transmission to newcomers. By this we mean both the indoctrination of converts and the training of the rising generation. Someone has said—and parents will certainly know what is meant—that each new generation represents a fresh incursion of barbarians.

The existence of group norms, which the group attempts to make prevail among its members, is not necessarily felt as an infringement of personal liberty by the individuals concerned, since the norms come to be internalized, and hence a part of the personality structure of the members of the group. In a small group, if it is stable over a considerable period of time, the group norms can cover a wide range of human experience. Consider, if you will, how despite the existence of differences in temperament and status among members of your own family, there are nonetheless prevailing attitudes toward food, religion, education, sex, morality, finances, hobbies, and the like, that differentiate you from other American families, perhaps even the one next door. A larger group cannot achieve such inclusiveness, partly because of the tendency for large groups to break up into smaller subgroups, all of which have their own norms on particular aspects of human experience. Thus we are all Americans, and that fact says something about values that we share. But we are also New Englanders, men or women, as the case may be, of varying immigrant stocks, of different religions, graduates of different colleges, members of different voluntary associations. Hence the consensus that makes us Americans cannot be as inclusive as the consensus that makes us members of our own families.

In small, homogeneous groups, the protection of the rights of the minority is not a problem. In a larger social organism, made up of many subgroups, this problem quickly arises, because the tendency of dominant groups always is to attempt to enlarge the area of consensus by promotion of their own norms, at the expense of competing norms of minority groups. And they are likely to suppose that the very survival of civilized society depends on their success in achieving greater uniformity of attitudes and values—on their own terms, of course. Dominant majorities, we must admit, are usually most insensitive as to where a particular minority will feel its rights to be infringed.

Dominant groups in society will use whatever instrumentalities are available to them for the alteration of the attitudes of others, in order to achieve their goal. In an earlier day, the institutions of religion were among the chief of such instrumentalities. Since the time of Horace Mann, the institutions of public education have become even more important. More important, because in the field of religion, we have come to accept a principle of toleration and give over the institutions of religion to subgroups in a pluralistic society, at the same time that we assert that it is the function of the schools to create the citizens of democracy by shaping their attitudes and values appropriately. We should not be surprised to find, therefore, that the debate over the control of religious institutions, which was finally neutralized by the discontinuance of tax support of public worship, should be renewed as a battle to control tax-supported education. For although not so important as formerly, the institutions of religion still represent significant groups in our pluralistic society, which continue to seek to make their attitudes prevail more widely. Hence the issue of separation of church and state is now being fought out in the field of education.

In this conflict, the role of the Supreme Court is important but, one suspects, largely misunderstood. It is to blunt the crude confrontation of rival groups by giving to each successive temporary accommodation between them the appearance of a logical deduction from eternal verities. It is to give plausible, or acceptable, constitutional justification for conclusions that depend ultimately on the balance between power groups in society.

Today we are moving rapidly into a period when the relative strength of the various groups interested in the processes of education in this country is shifting rapidly. What this may portend for church–state relationships is far from clear. But the observer who seeks a clue to the direction in which we are moving should pay less attention to the Supreme Court and legal logic than to the strength and self-conscious purpose of the interested groups in American society. In the last analysis it is the balance among these forces that counts, and the courts can be relied on to find ways to legitimize the outcome.

35

Ministers, Churches, and the Boston Elite
1791–1815

It is commonly asserted that when the churches of the Standing Order in Massachusetts divided into two bodies in the course of the Unitarian controversy, the liberals claimed a disproportionate share of the prominent merchants, lawyers, and men of affairs of their communities. Thus Winthrop Hudson called Unitarianism "the faith of well-to-do, urban New Englanders," while Merle Curti spoke of the rationalistic faith of early Unitarians as satisfying "the upper classes who were its principle but by no means only adherents." James Truslow Adams wrote that Unitarianism "became the religion of all the higher social circles of Massachusetts, and Calvinism occupied the lower social position of dissent."[1]

The basis for such generalizations about the relationship between liberal religion and social structure has usually been impressionistic comments by contemporary observers. Most familiar is doubtless Harriet Beecher Stowe's characterization of Boston in the 1820s, when her father went there to turn back the Unitarian tide. "All the literary men of Massachusetts were Unitarians," she wrote. "All the trustees and professors of Harvard College were Unitarians. All the elite of wealth and fashion crowded Unitarian churches." But Lyman Beecher was not the only one to complain that his opponents had monopolized the key positions of decision-making. As far back as 1814, Jedidiah Morse described his liberal opponents as "a formidable host . . . combining wealth talents and influence." In 1833, William Ellery

37

Channing was sensitive to the accusation by the orthodox that Unitarian views of Christianity "are suited to the educated, rich, fashionable, and not to the wants of the great mass of human beings."[2]

These generalizations are plausible enough, but how well-grounded are they? To what extent can they be supported by hard evidence? And what method of analysis is appropriate to deal with this problem? This essay addresses these questions with specific reference to Boston in the years 1791 to 1815, and it suggests that the construction of a "living model" is an especially fruitful way of approaching them.

Two ways to explore the relationship between religious affiliation and social structure immediately suggest themselves. One is to start with an examination of the religious group in question in an attempt to determine its social class composition. The other is to begin with the members of a particular social group— such as sedentary merchants or sea captains—and trace their church connections.

If we begin with the congregation of a particular church, or the congregations of a group of related churches, we need lists of members or adherents, together with information as to their occupations, wealth, and family connections. Yet such information is often ambiguous and invariably incomplete. Lists of admission to full communion may be compiled if the record books have survived, and sometimes it is possible to identify proprietors of pews (in Boston) or those assessed for the support of public worship (in outlying communities). But the category of members in full communion became increasingly irrelevant in liberal churches as the nineteenth century progressed, and reliance on it as a primary indicator of religious preference introduces a conservative theological bias. The lists of pew proprietors introduce a bias in favor of the well-to-do: one may identify a Boston merchant as the owner of a pew, and occasionally even find one as pew proprietor in more than one meetinghouse; but how does one discover who were sitting in the limited number of free pews, often in the gallery? It may well be possible to locate information about the wealth and occupations of pewholders, and it is plausible to argue that they were the ones who carried weight in parish affairs and gave to the church its social class identification. But the less affluent are more anonymous, and the extent to which they were part of a given congregation is difficult if not impossible to determine.

It is hard enough to construct a social-class profile of a particular church, it is even harder to generalize about a group of churches. Even churches that seem to be in accord on theological matters may have markedly different socioeconomic profiles. The element of bias enters in here, since it is the wealthier churches or societies that kept the best records, and whose records are most likely to have survived (and been printed).

The alternative approach is to begin, not with particular congregations, but with the members of an identifiable group and locate their church connections. If the wealthy merchants of Boston all crowded Unitarian churches, as Harriet Beecher Stowe asserted, while artisans and small tradesmen went elsewhere, some conclusions are permissible with respect to the social class character of the congregation—even though the most fashionable of churches may have had some members in modest circumstances, or for that matter, objects of charity.

The most extensive use of this second method of analysis seems to have been undertaken by Robert S. Rich in his dissertation, "Politics and Pedigrees: The Wealthy Men of Boston, 1798–1852" (UCLA, 1975). Chapter Six is entitled "Religion and the Elite." The author worked with two lists of wealthy men, one consisting of 255 men as of the year 1798, identified from the Federal Direct Tax list, the other 714, listed in popular pamphlets published in 1846 and 1852 as checked against tax lists. Of the list of 255 in 1798, the church connection of 149 was determined. "Unitarians" were found to be 69.8 percent of these, Episcopalians 15.4 percent, orthodox congregationalists 14.1 percent, and Catholics 0.9 percent.[3]

There are problems here, both with respect to the assumptions on which the analysis rests and with the presentation of the results. It is assumed that wealth is a sufficient indicator of social class. That it can be a useful if crude indicator need not be questioned. But there are times and places where occupation is more important, or family connections, or ethnic identity, or educational background, or cultural preferences, or religious affiliation, or location of domicile, or informal associational ties, or the presence of particular communications networks. Factors such as these also pattern social relationships, and the method of analysis needs to be sensitive to them and to be able to account for them.

A further difficulty of this dissertation is that it does not provide, even in an appendix, the names and church connections of the men on the lists. One cannot determine, without replicating the entire research program, whether the correct assignment to particular churches has been made. Nor can one determine whether there are significant differences between the social standing, shall we say, of the Brattle Street Church and the Hollis Street church.[4]

Such problems may be avoided by the construction of what the late Robert K. Lamb would have called a "living model," in which social structure is revealed by the patterned interaction of identifiable individuals, rather than represented in terms of formal categories defined by statistical aggregates.[5] A community, such as Boston in the 1790s, may be conceptualized as involving an intricate network of such relationships among its inhabitants. Within the community, a social class may be understood as a dynamic grouping, more extensive than a family or kinship group, of persons who interact—or are so situated as to be likely to interact—more frequently and over a wider range of activities with one another than they do with persons of a different class. When the group is made up of persons in a position to make the major decisions shaping the community at large, it may be identified as a "decision-making elite." Such a grouping is often assumed to be "upper class," but this may or may not be the case. Politicians and entrepreneurs may both make crucial decisions affecting an entire community, but they may well be drawn from different social classes. Whether the local elite is unified, or whether there are discrete loci of decision-making, is important for an understanding of the social dynamics of a given community.

It would be impossible to represent the entire web of interactions of a decision-making elite, let alone of an entire community. The alternative is to construct a living model based on identified individuals, selected in such a way as to be representative of the whole. For Boston in the period from 1791 to 1815, this means identifying a limited number of persons occupying key positions of decision-making in such fields as finance, commerce, entrepreneurship, politics, and education. The interactions among them, and between them and other individuals, such as artisans and small tradesmen, will reveal much about the social structure of the community.

Whether the Boston clergy, or some part of them, are to be included in the elite group is one of the points to be determined. To the extent that merchants and men of affairs attended particular churches, there was interaction with their ministers. But that is not enough. The larger question is whether the ministers, or certain ones among them, interacted with merchants and men of affairs beyond the boundaries of their own flocks. Fortunately, useful evidence is at hand in the membership lists of the various voluntary associations organized in the 1780s and 1790s to promote, not just the self-interest of particular groups within the community, but the cultural and humanitarian well-being of the whole.

Admittedly, to concentrate on participation in a limited number of cultural and philanthropic societies is to be concerned with only one very specific sphere of interactions. A more fully realized living model would include family connections,[6] location of domicile, college friendships, literary or social cliques (such as the Anthology Society or the Wednesday Evening Club), and the like. But much can be discovered even by a sharply limited investigation.

When the Reverend John Lathrop of the Second Church addressed the Charitable Fire Society in 1796, he commented on a recent development, the organization of societies "to cultivate

41

useful knowledge, and to encourage the efforts of human ingenuity." He listed twelve of them:

> Besides the University in Cambridge, established by the patriarchs of America, and which may be considered as the parent of all the literary institutions in our country—The Marine Society; The American Academy of Arts and Sciences; The Society for Propagating the Gospel; The Humane Society; The Massachusetts Congregational Charitable Society; The Episcopal Charitable Society; The Massachusetts Charitable Society; The Medical Society; The Agricultural Society; The Historical Society; The Massachusetts Charitable Fire Society; and the Society for the information of strangers, have received charters of incorporation, and some of these are possessed of considerable funds.[7]

Of these, the ones in which the clergy were conspicuously active were those having as their objective the shaping and elevation of society at large by the encouragement of humane letters, the arts, and the sciences, and also those having a philanthropic purpose not restricted to their own membership.[8] The Reverend Jeremy Belknap founded the Historical Society (1791) because he felt the collection and preservation of historical materials to be "of public utility"; the American Academy (1780) was incorporated "to cultivate every Art and Science which may tend to advance the Interest, Honor, Dignity and happiness of a free, independent and virtuous People."[9] Comparable statements may be found in the acts of incorporation of the other societies in which the ministers were active: the Massachusetts Humane Society (1786), the Massachusetts Congregational Charitable Society (1786), the Society for Propagating the Gospel Among the Indians and Others (1787), the Massachusetts Charitable Fire Society (1794), and the Massachusetts Society for the Aid of Immigrants (1794). To these seven newly organized societies may be added, for present purposes, the Harvard Corporation, likewise involved in shaping the intellectual culture and moral values of the region.

To what extent were the Boston ministers ready, as Jeremy Belknap was, to participate in the labors of these cultural and beneficent societies? How many of them similarly assumed responsibility in this way for the intellectual life and moral values of the larger society beyond their own congregations? Which ones are listed among the officers and members of the eight organizations chosen here for examination? Are there patterns to be discerned arising from social expectations, or was participation simply a matter of idiosyncratic interest and personal choice?

Forty-three men served Boston churches in the period from 1791 to 1815. Twenty-two occupied the desks of the ten congregational churches—twenty-four of eleven churches if King's Chapel is included. There were eight Baptist ministers in three churches, three Universalists, three Roman Catholics, three Episcopalians, and two Methodists.[10]

All but the congregationalists may quickly be eliminated from consideration. Of the nineteen ministers of the other religious groups, only eight were members of any of the societies, only two (both Baptists) were trustees or directors, and only one (an Episcopalian) was an officer. Memberships were concentrated in the two societies, the Humane Society and the Fire Society, that had no restrictions on the number of members and were open to anyone to join. Other societies, such as the American Academy, the Historical Society, the Indian Society, and of course the Harvard Corporation, were limited in membership, and Baptists, Episcopalians, Methodists, Catholics, and Universalists were never elected.[11] The two non-congregationalists who served at different times as trustees of the Fire Society were Samuel Stillman of the First Baptist Church and Thomas Baldwin of the Second. By the time they were chosen, both had achieved a respected standing in the community by long ministries. Samuel Parker of Trinity was the one who served as an officer: recording secretary, corresponding secretary, and finally treasurer of the Humane Society from 1786 until his death in 1804. Though his church was not then one of the influential ones, at least he was a Harvard graduate. But ten of the ministers of the non-congregational churches were not college or seminary trained, and the group as a whole was made up of outsiders, so far as the local power structure was involved.

When the twenty-four congregationalists are listed by the year of birth, a significant pattern emerges. Instead of a gradual progression by which one generation succeeds another, two distinct clusters are evident. The first comprises six men born in the 1750s; the second is made up of nine born in the 1780s. The youngest of the first cluster is James Freeman, born in 1759; the eldest of the second is William Ellery Channing, born more than twenty years later, in 1780. Between these two clusters there are only four men, who form a sort of mini-cluster with birth dates in 1769, 1770, and 1771. If we add four older men to the first cluster and add the mini-cluster to the second group, the difference between the median ages of the two groups is thirty years.

The two groups are alike in many respects, to be sure. No significant difference appears either with respect to place of birth or college attended. In most cases, the place of birth was Boston or some town not very remote, and Harvard was the college attended. In both cases the theological stance was predominantly Arminian—that is to say, proto-Unitarian—though the later group had a somewhat more explicitly liberal cast, and by way of contrast there was at least one aggressively orthodox minister. What does differ is the degree of participation in the several cultural and beneficent societies under consideration. In Table One, a rough measure of involvement is achieved by scoring each minister in accordance with the number of societies in which he served as an officer (score 3), as a trustee or incorporator (score 2), or as an ordinary member (score 1).[12]

Members of the older generation were evidently much more likely to belong to several societies. John Eliot belonged to all eight; Jeremy Belknap and Peter Thacher belonged to seven, and John Lathrop to six. Simply to be a member, however, may well have represented very passive involvement. As striking and more significant is the record of participation as officers. John Lathrop was an officer of four of them; John Eliot was an officer of four and a member of the council of three others. But ministers born in

Table One
Participation of Boston Congregational Ministers
in Eight Societies, 1791–1815

Born		Officer	Trustee	Member	Weighted Score
1733	Simeon Howard, HC '58	3	1	2	13
1738	Samuel West, HC '61	0	1	3	5
1740	John Lathrop, Coll. NJ, '63	4	0	2	14
1744	Jeremy Belknap, HC '62	1	1	5	9
1751	Joseph Eckley, Coll. NJ, '72	2	1	2	10
1752	Oliver Everett, HC '79	0	0	2	2
1752	Peter Thacher, HC '69	1	3	3	12
1754	John Eliot, HC '72	4	3	1	19
1755	John Clarke, HC '74	1	2	2	9
1759	James Freeman, HC '77	3	0	1	10
1769	William Emerson, HC '89	1	2	1	8
1770	Edward D. Griffin, Yale '90	0	0	0	0
1770	John T. Kirkland, HC '89	3	0	5	14
1771	John Snelling Popkin, HC '92	0	0	2	2
1780	William Ellery Channing, HC '98	1	0	4	7
1781	Horace Holley, Yale '03	0	0	2	2
1782	Charles Lowell, HC '00	0	1	3	5
1783	John L. Abbot, HC '05	0	0	0	0
1784	Joseph Stevens Buckminster, HC '00	1	1	2	7
1785	Samuel Cary, HC '04	0	0	2	2
1785	Samuel Cooper Thacher, HC '04	0	0	2	2
1786	Joshua Huntington, Yale '04	0	0	2	2
1788	Francis Parkman, HC '07	0	1	1	3
1794	Edward Everett, HC '11	0	0	0	0

1780 or later became members of fewer of the societies and seldom served as councillor of more than one.

Part of the explanation is that a large proportion of the younger men on the list left the ministry or died before they could compile a record of leadership in any of the societies. Popkin and Everett departed almost at once to teach at Harvard; Buckminster, Abbot,

Cary, and Samuel Cooper Thacher died before the age of thirty-two. Channing, Lowell, and Parkman did serve as officers in certain of the societies. Even so, their record both before 1815 and later in life is very different from that of Howard, Lathrop, Eliot, and Freeman, who seem to have taken it for granted that it was their obligation to devote time and energy to activities concerned with elevating the intellectual tone and philanthropic concern of the entire community.

The participation by the older generation required of the ministers an enlarged understanding of the proper role of the ministry in the life of the community. Ministers of the Standing Order had of course long assumed responsibility for shaping and elevating the moral tone of the communities they served. In addition to their strictly ecclesiastical role within the convenanted body of communicants known as the church, they were called upon to perform a civic function for all the inhabitants, whether church members or not, as "public Protestant teachers of piety, religion, and morality."[13] Traditionally, this civic responsibility had been exercised chiefly through preaching and public worship. But an urban society was in the making in Boston.[14] Its social structure was becoming more complex; differentiated economic activity was producing a variety of occupational groups; theological diversity was creating tensions; cosmopolitan influences were felt; the size of the population was beginning to increase. Though Protestant Christianity still largely shaped the value system of society, the traditional role of the minister was too limited to encompass the whole community and its increasingly secular interests. If the ministers were to maintain positions of moral authority in society at large, they could not retreat to the care of their particular flocks, but had to acknowledge a responsibility for humane letters as well as theological discourse, and to share in the leadership of the new instrumentalities being organized for larger cultural and philanthropic ends.

The ministers were not alone in this larger enterprise. Who participated with them in organizing and running the several societies? Specifically, to what extent were these societies an undertaking of the local decision-making elite? The starting point is to identify key positions of decision-making in education, finance, entrepreneurship, and politics. The Harvard Corporation may be taken as the chief locus of decision-making in education. The Boston ministers who served on the board were Howard, Lathrop, Eliot, Kirkland, and Channing; the lay members living in Boston were Ebenezer Storer, Oliver Wendell, John Lowell, James Bowdoin, and John Davis.[15] Financial leadership may be represented by the presidents of the Massachusetts Bank: William Phillips, Sr., Samuel Eliot, Benjamin Greene, William Phillips, Jr., and Jonathan Mason, Sr.[16] Entrepreneurial activity is represented by the directors of the Middlesex Canal Company in 1805: Joseph Coolidge, Aaron Dexter, Christopher Gore, John Coffin Jones, Benjamin Joy, Mungo Mackay, Ebenezer Oliver, William Payne, and James Sullivan.[17] The Massachusetts Medical Society was an early incorporated professional society with power to grant credentials to qualified physicians; the officers and directors of longest tenure were John Warren, Aaron Dexter, Thomas Kast, John Collins Warren, and William Spooner.[18] A sample of the political leadership is found in the senators from Suffolk County in the General Court in three sessions (1795–1796, 1799–1800, 1804–1805): Oliver Wendell, Thomas Dawes, Sr., John Coffin Jones, Theophilus Cushing, Jonathan Mason, Jr., William Tudor, Jr., and David Tilden.[19] Since there is some duplication, there are twenty-eight names in all. This particular cast of the net does not catch all the big fish in the Boston pond—there are no Lees, or Higginsons, or Jacksons. But these specimens will surely be recognized as persons of consequence. Indeed, nine of them— almost a third—are included in the *Dictionary of American Biography*.[20]

Of this group, eighteen served as an officer or director of at least one of the eight societies; James Sullivan, indeed, served as president of four of them. Additionally, seven of the twenty-eight, though not officers or directors, were members of at least one society. The Humane Society enrolled twenty-two of the twenty-eight. How deeply involved these men were in the activities of the societies doubtless differed greatly. But although these listings do not reveal the degree or quality of involvement, they do reveal in a general way who went around with whom. That is to say, they help to define the segment or segments of society from which community leadership was recruited.

It should be noted that almost all of the twenty-eight men were born earlier than 1765. This makes them contemporaries of the earlier generation of ministers previously identified. Their degree of involvement was somewhat less than that of the ministers, but was enough to indicate a shared concern to advance the moral and cultural condition of the community through the organization of beneficent societies. Using the admittedly crude measure of participation in the societies previously adopted for ministers, the results are shown in Table Two.[21]

The construction of a living model may be carried a step further by a comparison between the men of affairs and the organizers of the Massachusetts Charitable Mechanic Association. The historian of that society compiled a list of those who participated in its organization, eighty-three in number. The Association was limited to mechanics and manufacturers. If a mechanic, the member had to be a master workman; if a manufacturer, he had to be the proprietor of a manufactory. Inasmuch as this was before the introduction of power machinery and the factory system as established by the Boston Associates in 1813, the members were operating what would be by later standards rather small establishments. Still, they included men of consequence, like Paul Revere, goldsmith; Benjamin Russell, proprietor of the *Columbian Centinel*; and Edmund Hartt, shipwright and builder of the frigate *Constitution*. Some of the members accumulated a good deal of wealth; one of them, it is reported, "belonged to a set very hospitable, whose side-boards were loaded with plate, and who brought up their families in expensive style."[22]

Yet the participation of members of the Mechanic Association in the eight societies was limited. Of the eighty-three original members, twenty-two joined the Humane Society or the Fire Society, or in eight cases both. None was elected to office there,

Table Two
Participation of Boston Men of Affairs
in Eight Societies, 1791–1815

Born		Officer	Trustee	Member	Weighted Score
1722	William Phillips, Sr., merchant	0	1	1	3
1725	Jonathan Mason, Sr., merchant	2	0	1	7
1730	Ebenezer Storer, HC '47, merchant	3	0	1	10
1731	Thomas Dawes, Sr., merchant	0	0	4	4
1733	Oliver Wendell, HC '53, jurist	2	0	3	9
1738	Benjamin Greene, merchant	0	0	0	0
1739	Samuel Eliot, merchant	1	0	3	6
1740	Mungo Mackay, merchant	0	1	1	3
1743	John Lowell, HC '60, jurist	1	2	1	8
1744	James Sullivan, attorney	3	1	1	12
1744	David Tilden, merchant	0	0	2	2
1747	Joseph Coolidge, merchant	0	1	1	3
1750	Aaron Dexter, HC '76, physician	1	2	2	9
1750	John Coffin Jones, HC '68, merchant	0	0	1	1
1750	Thomas Kast, HC '69, physician	0	0	1	1
1750	William Phillips, Jr., merchant	1	2	0	7
1752	James Bowdoin, HC '71, merchant	1	1	2	7
1752	Ebenezer Oliver	0	0	1	1
1753	John Warren, HC '71, physician	1	1	1	6
1756	Jonathan Mason, Jr., Coll. NJ '74, attorney	0	0	1	1
1757	Benjamin Joy, merchant	0	0	1	1
1758	Christopher Gore, HC '76, public service	2	0	1	7
1760	William Spooner, HC '78, physician	2	0	1	7
1761	John Davis, HC '71, jurist	2	1	3	11
1764	William Payne	0	0	1	1
1778	John C. Warren, HC '97, physician	1	0	1	4
1779	William Tudor, Jr., HC '96, merchant	0	0	1	1
?	Theophilus Cushing	0	0	0	0

though Benjamin Russell was a trustee of the Fire Society (1805–1813) and Nathaniel Balch of the Humane Society (1786–1806). But the coopers, hatters, tailors, housewrights, bricklayers, bakers, and the like who made up the major part of the original membership represented a different segment of society than the ministers and men of affairs. None was a graduate of Harvard College. They doubtless took pride in their contribution to the community through honest and productive labor, which they considered to be of equal moral worth to that of other segments of society. But that they were conscious of a difference in status and influence between themselves and "the mercantile part of the community" is suggested by the fact that when the Association was organized in 1795, it turned to "twenty of the principal merchants of Boston" for assistance in securing a charter of incorporation from the General Court. That privilege was granted only after a long delay.[23]

It is not at all surprising that the men of affairs whom the ministers encountered in the management of the several societies were to be found in their churches as well. A merchant is sometimes on record as a pewholder or as a member of a Standing Committee. Notations may be found of admission to full communion, or more frequently the presentation of a child for baptism. A death may be recorded, or a funeral sermon preached in which the minister praises the deceased for his loyalty to the church of which he was a longtime communicant. The evidence must be constructed from fragments, and it is sometimes puzzlingly inconsistent, since some movement from one church to another took place, and individuals may even be found as pewholders of one meetinghouse but active elsewhere.[24] Furthermore, the records vary in consistency and quality, and for some churches are not readily available. Table Three is a compilation of such evidence as has thus far been located.[25]

The concentration of these men in three churches—Brattle Street, King's Chapel, Old South—is striking. Almost as striking is the absence of affiliations at the Second Church, the New North, and the New South. The ministers of these churches—

Table Three
Church Connections of Boston Men of Affairs

	Clergy	Laymen (verified dates of participation)
First Church 1630	John Clarke (1778–1798) William Emerson (1799–1811) John L. Abbot (1813–1814)	David Tilden (1789–1814) Benjamin Joy (1808, 1811)
Second Church 1650	John Lathrop (1768–1816)	
Old South 1669	Joseph Eckley (1779–1811) Joshua Huntington (1808–1809)	William Phillips, Sr. (1756–1804) Jonathan Mason, Sr. (1780–1798) Thomas Dawes, Sr. (1749–1809) William Phillips, Jr. (1772–1827) Jonathan Mason, Jr. (1782)
King's Chapel 1689	James Freeman (1782–1835) Samuel Cary (1809-1815)	Joseph Coolidge (1747–1820) Aaron Dexter (1776-1829) John Coffin Jones (1785, 1789) Ebenezer Oliver (1785–1826) Christopher Gore (1776–1827) William Tudor, Jr.
Brattle Street 1699	Peter Thacher (1785–1802) Joseph S. Buckminster (1805–1812) Edward Everett (1814–1815) James Sullivan (1786–1808)	Ebenezer Storer (1730–1807) Oliver Wendell (1733–1804) John Lowell (1783, 1786) John Coffin Jones (1788, 1796, 1829) James Bowdoin (1752) John Warren (1784–1815) William Spooner (1760–1836) John C. Warren (1816, 1818)
New North 1714	John Eliot (1779–1813) Francis Parkman (1813–1849)	
New South 1719	Oliver Everett (1782–1792) John T. Kirkland (1794–1810) Samuel C. Thacher (1811–1818)	
Federal Street 1727	Jeremy Belknap (1787–1798) John S. Popkin (1799-1802) William Ellery Channing (1803-1842)	John Davis (1814, 1847)
Hollis Street 1732	Samuel West (1789–1808) Horace Holley (1809–1818)	
West Church 1737	Simeon Howard (1767–1804) Charles Lowell (1806–1861)	Samuel Eliot Mungo Mackay
Park Street 1809	Edward D. Griffin (1811–1815)	
Christ Church 1722	William Walter (1792–1800)	Thomas Kast
Trinity 1734	Samuel Parker (1794–1804) J.S.J Gardiner (1792–1829)	Benjamin Greene (1776–1806)
Unknown		Theophilus Cushing William Payne

Lathrop, Eliot, Kirkland—were conspicuously active in the several societies, their point scores being the highest of all. One would expect that they would have recruited members of their own congregations to join them, at least in the Humane Society and the Fire Society. Evidently, their congregations included fewer of the elite, and their prestige socially was doubtless affected in consequence.

One might have thought that Jeremy Belknap's enthusiasm for the Historical Society would have resulted in some representation from Federal Street during his tenure there. (John Davis's connection with that church was of later date.) But Federal Street, as also appears from other evidence, did not emerge into prominence until Channing's ministry. Channing, we are told, was approached to become the minister at Brattle Street in 1803, but because of impaired health chose what he assumed would be a less demanding pulpit.[26] The choice is understandable when one considers the array of prominent jurists, doctors, and merchants who would have greeted him at Brattle Street.

When the split finally came between the Trinitarian congregationalists and the Unitarian congregationalists, Old South remained orthodox, while the two other leading churches were found in the liberal camp. But the intermingling of ministers and laymen from these churches is a reminder that their theological differences were not regarded as of major consequence. A comment on the Boston ministers by Ashbel Green, a distinguished Presbyterian from Philadelphia, can be generalized to apply to the whole body of men of affairs in their churches. "Some are Calvinists, some Universalists, some Arminians, some Arians, and at least one is a Socinian," he wrote in 1791. He thought it absurd for men of "such jarring opinions" to meet together, and thought that "the parties should divide, and that those who are agreed should walk by themselves." Yet that plan, he acknowledged, would be condemned as bigotry and narrowmindedness; "and so they will meet, and shake hands, and talk of politics and science, and laugh, and eat raisins and almonds, and apples and cakes, and drink wine and tea, and then go about their business when they please."[27]

This is enough to make it clear that the insistence of Jedidiah Morse beginning in 1805 that orthodox Calvinists should not maintain fellowship with liberal Christians was not a limited theological matter. It threatened the established social structure of the community, not just relationships among the churches. Hence resistance to it was found at the Old South under Eckley as well as Federal Street under Channing. Of Eckley, Charles Lowell wrote: "His relations were certainly more intimate with the 'liberal party' as they were termed, than with the Calvinistic party."[28] The Old South refused to participate in 1809 with the formation of the Park Street Church, with its avowed policy of exclusion. It continued to send ministers and delegates to ordinations and installations at the liberal churches until finally, as late as 1819, it succumbed to evangelical pressures and voted not to join in the ordination of John Pierpont at Hollis Street.[29]

In the 1790s, the power structure of Boston was dominated by an elite that was remarkably unified. The leadership—political, commercial, intellectual, religious—was drawn from one segment of society. It was predominantly Federalist in politics, commercial in its economic base, Arminian or very moderate Calvinist in theology, and united by many family connections. Those addicted to Gramscian analysis may find here a classic case of cultural hegemony exercised by a ruling class. Nevertheless, a sense of responsibility for the community as a whole served to temper the temptation to be guided purely by narrow class interest.

This degree of coherence could not last. One of the factors making for unity among the factions of Federalists was a common perception that the French Revolution, with its reign of terror, was a threat to social order; when New England got over that fear, one of the reinforcements of unity dissolved. The Democratic Republicans elected a governor of the Commonwealth in 1807; he was James Sullivan, member of the Brattle Street Church, president of the Canal Company, first president of the Historical Society. As for the mercantile interests, they were soon to lose their position of dominance in economic decision-making when a new group of entrepreneurs known as the Boston Associates built textile mills first in Waltham and later in Lowell.

For the ministers and the churches, the first significant break in the prevailing comity came in 1805 with Jedidiah Morse's protest over the election of Henry Ware as Hollis Professor of Divinity at Harvard. Morse had been called to the Charlestown pulpit in 1789, largely on the recommendation of Jeremy Belknap, who seems to have assumed that a man of geographical and historical interests would be a welcome addition to the local ministerial circle. Morse was enrolled in due course in the American Academy, the Historical Society, the Congregational Charitable Society, the Humane Society, the Society for the Aid of Immigrants, and the Indian Society. Somehow he skipped the Fire Society. As a Yale graduate he could not expect to become a member of the Harvard Corporation, but even there he had a point of contact as a member of the Board of Overseers. Among his colleagues of the Boston Association of Ministers, however, he proved to be a discordant element because of his rigidly orthodox theological views and his preference for confrontation over consensus.[30] Coming from Connecticut, where the alignment of theological factions was very different, he was dismayed by the friendly intercourse between moderate Calvinists and Arminians. He bided his time as long as infidelity spreading from the French Revolution seemed to all parties to be a serious threat, but his purpose was to split the two groups apart whenever the time should be ripe.

Morse accomplished this end, not by theological argument but by constructing institutions in which Calvinists of various stripes would be brought into closer interaction with one another, while intercourse among Calvinists and Arminians (Liberal Christians) would be discouraged. He exploited networks of ministers and laity based in outlying towns, with limited connection to the Boston elite. One of them, moderate Calvinist in theology, might be termed the Andover connection. Its institutional focus was Phillips Academy (1778), the principal founder of which was Samuel Phillips, sometime president of the Massachusetts Senate and lieutenant governor. His grandfather, the Reverend Samuel

Phillips (1690–1771), was the first minister of the south parish of Andover, and members of the family identified strongly with the town, even when—like William Phillips, Sr.—they moved to Boston and were successful merchants there. Three generations of the Phillips family, both the Andover and the Boston branches, were benefactors of the Academy and members of its Board of Trustees. The first preceptor of the Academy, and a member of its board, was Eliphalet Pearson, who left Andover in 1786 to become Hancock Professor at Harvard and in due course a member of the Harvard Corporation. Here he worked closely with Jedidiah Morse, already a member of the Andover board, in a vain effort to prevent the election of Henry Ware as Hollis Professor. Defeated in that skirmish, and frustrated in his ambition to become president of Harvard, Pearson resigned his professorship and position on the Corporation, and returned to Andover.[31]

Morse was likewise in touch with a second and quite distinct group of Calvinist ministers, which might be termed the Yale connection. Its members were predominantly "New Divinity" men, or "Hopkinsians." As Yale graduates as well as "consistent Calvinists," they found themselves somewhat isolated from most of the congregationalist ministers in eastern Massachusetts, who were moderate Calvinists or Arminians, educated at Harvard. In 1799 this group organized the Massachusetts Missionary Society, which sponsored the *Massachusetts Missionary Magazine*. Jedidiah Morse promptly joined the society, as did his Yale classmate, the Reverend Abiel Holmes of Cambridge. Only the Reverend William Emerson of the Boston ministers is listed as a member, and none of our twenty-eight men of affairs joined.[32]

The election of Henry Ware in 1805 was a signal to Morse that the Boston elite was in firm control of Harvard College. Since the theological orientation of the college was now unmistakably liberal, evangelicals could no longer consider it a fit place for the education of young men preparing for the ministry. Two proposals for orthodox theological seminaries were promptly made, one by leading members of the Andover connection to be grafted onto Andover Academy, the other by members of the Yale connection centered in Newburyport. Jedidiah Morse made effective use of his contacts with both factions, and he more than anyone else was responsible for bringing them together to found the Andover Theological Seminary in 1808.[33] Clearly, he was a key decision maker, though for a very different constituency, or segment of society, than that of the Boston elite, which had once welcomed but now rejected him.

The institutionalization of the split between liberals and orthodox proceeded rapidly in the decade from 1805 to 1815. When Morse founded the *Panoplist* (1805), the liberals turned to the *Monthly Anthology* in which to respond. When the Calvinists organized the Society for Promoting Christian Knowledge (1803), of which Morse was the secretary and Eliphalet Pearson the president, the liberals answered with the Society for Promoting Christian Knowledge, Piety, and Charity (1806). In order to meet the challenge of Andover Theological Seminary, the liberals decided it was necessary to improve the resources in Cambridge for training for the ministry, and the Harvard Divinity School (1811, 1816) was the result.[34]

This activity did not completely end all cooperation between orthodox ministers and their liberal colleagues. When the Massachusetts Bible Society was organized in 1809, its founders included Griffin, Eckley, and Huntington from Park Street and the Old South, as well as Lathrop, Freeman, Kirkland, Buckminster, Emerson, Holley, Eliot, and Lowell from the liberal side. Yet one cannot resist the surmise that the ministers were increasingly preoccupied with developing sectarian organizations, and that this was an important reason why they did not participate as actively as their forebears had in the older societies with their community-wide orientation.

Morse was particularly insistent that orthodox ministers should not acknowledge Christian fellowship with liberals by engaging in pulpit exchanges. This issue became a source of friction between many of the orthodox ministers and their congregations in towns outside Boston. Much more than theological differences, it was what separated the liberals and the orthodox in the first decade (1805–1815) of the Unitarian controversy. It produced a bitter dispute in the Second Parish in Dorchester (1810–1812); it was an ingredient in the events leading up to the split in Dedham that occasioned the litigation in *Baker* v. *Fales* (1818–1820); it was still central in the controversy in the First Parish in Cambridge (1827-1829).[35] None of the Boston churches split over this issue, no doubt because it was possible for individuals to move from one church to another in search of more congenial preaching.[36] The division of the community of Boston churches came rather through the organization of new evangelical churches to challenge the increasingly explicit liberalism of all the older churches except the Old South. By 1815, the comity among the Boston ministers, so much prized in the 1790s, was gone.

The local power structure was gradually being transformed, as industrial entrepreneurs were assuming the leadership roles once occupied by sedentary merchants. But the ministers played a diminished role. Harvard College had a layman as its president from 1829 to 1849; only one minister was chosen to be a Fellow of the Corporation between 1818 and 1853, and he had already forsaken the parish for an academic appointment. The officers of the Athenaeum from its founding in 1807 were all laymen, and the three ministers on the initial roster of trustees were not replaced. The first three presidents of the Boston Dispensary (1796) were ministers; from 1811 to 1849 the presidents were all lay. The Massachusetts General Hospital (1814) was run entirely by men of affairs, without a single minister among them.[37]

After 1815, the liberal ministers of Boston gave up their efforts to hold the religious community together. Jedidiah Morse published the pamphlet *American Unitarianism* that year as an attempt to expose the liberals as deceitfully concealing their true heresy. William Ellery Channing responded, but it was all too evident that the breach had become too wide for unity to be restored. Thereafter, new faces and new institutions would produce a new configuration of the local power elite, in which the ministers would play a smaller part.

But the identification of the Boston decision-making elite with religious liberalism had by this time been well established. Morse's opponents were indeed "a formidable host . . . combining wealth, talents and influence."

The Controversial Career of Jedidiah Morse

Jedidiah Morse (1761–1826), minister of the First Church of Charlestown, was without any question the most active and effective opponent of the liberal Christians who dominated Boston pulpits in 1805. Not greatly interested in the discussion of theological issues for their own sake, he was a shrewd ecclesiastical strategist, concerned to control the institutional structures of religion and to influence popular opinion. There seems to be no reason to question the assertion of his first biographer that he "early formed the purpose of doing his utmost to effect an important change in the ecclesiastical condition of Massachusetts—first, by separating the Unitarians from the Orthodox, and then, by drawing the Orthodox of different shades into more intimate relations." Nor is there any reason to dispute the judgment that these objects were effected, "more, probably, through the influence of Dr. Morse than that of any other man."[1] A vigorous partisan, who more than once overreached himself and finally destroyed himself, he nevertheless influenced events at every turn from 1804 to 1815.

It is of some importance, therefore, to try to understand what kind of man Morse was. Yet the problem is not simple, for he was not only frequently embroiled in controversy, but was a controversial figure, who presented two irreconcilable images to the public. The orthodox saw him not merely as a stalwart defender of the faith once delivered to the saints, but also as a Christian gentleman of exemplary piety, the victim of venomous persecution by his political and religious adversaries. In their eyes, he was

59

a faithful minister whose kindnesses to members of his flock were legion; a preacher of distinction possessing a soft, but well-modulated and effective, pulpit voice; a philanthropist always active for the promotion of the welfare of his fellow men; and a geographer whose industry and achievement reflected credit on his country as well as himself.

The liberals, on the other hand, came by degrees to think of him as one who was persistently engaged in controversy, often of a very petty and personal kind, in which he repeatedly displayed a conspiratorial temper; the possessor of a waspish tongue, who was altogether too quick to make accusations without evidence and to impute dishonesty to his opponents, and especially given to saying one thing in public and another in private; a geographer whose work was marred by political, sectional, and religious prejudices; and a man of letters intent on financial gain, who was alert to protect his own literary rights but ruthless when the rights of others were concerned. This image of Morse developed gradually, and before the outbreak of the Unitarian controversy in 1805, it was held by only a few of the liberals. By 1815, however, it was generally accepted among them.

It is tempting to assert that these contrasting images of Morse were created by bitter partisanship on both sides, and that the truth lies somewhere in between. It is probably more accurate to say that both images, however incompatible they may seem, are equally true. The integrity of some persons in public life is such that partisan thrusts never injure their reputations. Others, however, make it easy for people, whether unjustly or not, to believe the worst about them. Morse was one of the latter sort. It did no good for his friends to protest with all sincerity that he was an honorable man, shamefully traduced by his ecclesiastical and political opponents. He was unfortunately the kind of man who repeatedly behaved in such a way as to make exaggerated and even malicious accusations about him seem plausible. If the liberals succeeded in destroying his standing in the community, he was the one who made it easy for them to do so.

Morse repeatedly attributed the hostility of the liberals to his action in opposing the election of Henry Ware as Hollis Professor in 1805; and in particular he insisted that had there been no revolution in the affairs of the College, there would have been no controversy with Miss Hannah Adams. From 1793 to 1804, he pointed out, the liberals made no complaint as to his character or opinions; and indeed, they maintained "constant and intimate intercourse" with him. To judge by the behavior of his adversaries, he remarked, "there must have suddenly taken place an almost total change in my disposition and habits of life, *just at that time, when my opposition commenced* to their favourite project of [taking] possession of the College. . . ."[2] The very bitter, and even spiteful, personal attacks that he encountered in the decade that followed convinced him of both the lack of integrity of many of the liberals and the justice of the orthodox cause for which he was the most prominent champion.

Without question a change in the treatment of Morse by the liberals occurred after 1805, and his opposition to Henry Ware's election certainly played a part in it. Yet the decline of Morse's reputation was not quite so sudden as he would have one believe. The liberals knew well enough the kind of man Morse was. One could work with him congenially so long as the project at hand was one of common concern. But he was the sort of man who could never stand in friendly opposition to anyone. A basic difference of opinion would quickly produce enmity on one side and cries of martyrdom on the other. If this pattern had been peculiar to the relationship between Morse and the liberals, one might be inclined to agree with him that he was ill used. Yet the fact of the matter is that—even apart from his recurrent lawsuits over the publication of his books—he came into conflict not only with the liberals, but with his own associates; and every time, he alienated men with whom he had previously been friendly. In 1814, for example, he was simultaneously involved in a lawsuit occasioned by the failure of a New York publisher, in controversy with the liberals over his alleged mistreatment of Miss Hannah Adams, and in conflict with Elijah Parish, his one-time literary collaborator, over the copyright they held jointly on a history of New England. Given the personality of Morse, it is not surprising that there should be a change in the attitude of the liberals toward him just as soon as an important difference of policy came between them.

I

Morse had originally been called to the Charlestown pulpit very largely on the recommendation of Jeremy Belknap, one of the liberals. A native of Connecticut and a graduate of Yale, he would hardly have been thought of for a church in Harvard territory had not Belknap come to know of him because of his geographical writings. In 1784, Morse had published *Geography Made Easy*; and in January 1788, while at work on a much more ambitious universal geography, he sent a draft of his account of New Hampshire to Belknap for comment and criticism.[3]

Early in 1788, Belknap sought information on Morse's qualifications as a minister from his friend, Ebenezer Hazard of Philadelphia. Hazard, whose niece Morse was soon to marry, spoke of him in the highest terms, and Belknap prepared the way for him to candidate in Charlestown. Two days after Morse's installation, in April 1789, Belknap wrote to Hazard that Morse had "the character of an agreeable and a growing man," and expressed delight that he was settled "where he can have so many literary advantages as at Charlestown." Accordingly, Morse was soon elected to the Historical Society, and as a matter of course he took his place as a member of the Boston Association of Ministers and the Board of Overseers of Harvard College.[4]

That Morse's theology was Calvinistic and his temper evangelical was well known to Belknap and the other liberals. But the Boston Association included men of many shades of opinion, who took satisfaction in the good will and harmony that prevailed among them. Ashbel Green, a distinguished Presbyterian from Philadelphia, visited Boston in 1791 and went with Morse to a meeting of the Association. "Some are Calvinists, some Universalists, some Arminians, some Arians, and one at least is a Socinian," he reported. Such a situation struck him as absurd; it seemed obvious that "the parties should divide, and that those who are agreed should walk by themselves." Yet he acknowledged that such a plan "would be esteemed by them as the effect of bigotry and narrowness of mind."[5]

What the liberals did not know, at least for a long time, was that Morse agreed with those who felt that friendly intercourse between liberals and orthodox was absurd and that he was ready to push for a separation whenever the time should be ripe. Morse kept his own counsel in the matter, avowing his real sentiments to orthodox friends only. In 1792, in a letter to Green, he declared that nothing was likely to come of a plan for closer relationships between Massachusetts congregationalists and the Presbyterian General Assembly because too many would throw cold water on any proposal. But if the plan were frustrated, Morse declared, "the aggrieved party" would be tempted to form a separate body and frame an ecclesiastical constitution for itself. "But this is *sub rosa* for the present," he warned. "I have hinted the matter to Dr. Rogers, and have conversed with Mr. Miller and Mr. Eckley upon it."[6]

The liberals soon discovered that Morse's inclination was to turn points of difference into points of controversy. Doctrinal issues that they would not broach, at least in public, lest disharmony result, he embraced without hesitation. In 1790, he began a course of sermons in defense of the Trinity at the Thursday lectures. "The Clergy fear the controversy should be opened & yet the Orthodox will be meddling with it," William Bentley wrote in his diary.[7] Morse had been led—or provoked—to this step by a letter that had come to him, signed simply "A Layman," asking his comment on the proofs of the divine unity to be found in Thomas Emlyn's *Humble Inquiry*.[8] Inasmuch as a reprint of the book was published in Boston that same year, without any indication as to the sponsor, Morse seems to have reached the conclusion that a subtle but well-planned attack on evangelical doctrine was being masked by a conspiracy of silence.

In the fall of 1790, Morse chanced to discover at a Boston bookseller's an edition of Isaac Watts's *Divine and Moral Songs for*

Children. Thumbing through it, he found a number of revisions of the text, the effect of which was to eliminate references to the Trinity and original sin, and to tone down the imagery of Satan and the fires of Hell. He promptly sought to expose what seemed to him to be another indirect attack on orthodox doctrine, by sending a communication to the *Columbian Centinel,* signed "A Friend to Honesty." The letter, which appeared under the heading "Beware of Counterfeits," closed as follows: "For if this should pass upon the publick unnoticed, from altering children's books, more important one's might be undertaken, until, grown bold in the business, even the sacred truths of the HOLY BIBLE may be in danger."[9]

Isaiah Thomas was the printer, and he was much annoyed by the accusation that he had deceived the public. After all, the title page specifically declared that the text had been "revised and altered," and a prefatory note indicated quite clearly the nature and purpose of the changes. Furthermore, as Thomas stated in a letter to the *Centinel,* the alterations had not been made by him, since the edition had been reprinted verbatim from an English version, at the request of the Reverend James Freeman and several other Boston gentlemen. Thomas himself had always carried in stock both the original and the altered versions to accommodate differing tastes, and he had even printed two editions of the former. Since he was struggling to put out a new quarto Bible, Morse's implication that the text of it would be suspect seemed to him dishonorable.[10] Although Morse hastened to absolve the printer of blame, he never acknowledged that he himself had been in the least at fault; and as late as 1814, he still spoke of his "exposure" of a "mutilated edition" of Watts.[11]

This episode was enough to sour any friendly relationships that might have developed between Morse and Freeman. Freeman resented Morse's accusation of dishonesty; and Morse was not happy to learn, soon afterwards, that his anonymous correspondent on the subject of the Trinity had been John Amory, one of Freeman's parishioners.[12] Freeman got his revenge, three years later, when he published a review of Morse's *American Universal*

Geography, enumerating many errors of fact as well as pointing to instances of gross prejudice.[13] But this bickering between Morse and Freeman did not necessarily involve the other liberals at all. The Stone Chapel, with its Episcopalian antecedents, was not regarded as properly congregationalist, and its minister was not then a member of the Boston Association. Besides, Freeman's Socinianism was quite unacceptable to the other liberals. Morse's first encounter, then, was with one segment only of Boston liberalism.

II

From 1793 to 1804, as Morse himself freely acknowledged, he remained on friendly terms with the other members of the Boston Association. They were Federalists, virtually to a man; and the political events of those years, "connected as they were with the alarming spread of infidelity in our country," were matters of common concern.[14] But Morse's political activity soon aroused the antagonism of William Bentley, minister of the East Church in Salem, who was one of the very few Jeffersonians among the liberals. As a classmate and intimate friend of Freeman, he was doubtless all the more inclined to find fault. Bentley was less devious than Morse, but no less partisan; and once he had taken a dislike to a man—like Morse—or to a group—like the Hopkinsian Calvinists—he could be as prejudiced and intolerant as Morse himself, as the entries in his diary abundantly reveal.

That Morse almost instinctively equated political opposition with conspiracy, and eagerly made accusations based on flimsy evidence, was the conclusion Bentley and the other liberals drew from Morse's unhappy excursion into party politics in 1798. As had happened before (in 1790) and was to happen again (in 1815), Morse discovered a book that convinced him that a conspiracy was the cause of all the ills of the day. This time the book was John Robison's *Proofs of a Conspiracy Against All the Religions and Governments of Europe, Carried on in the Secret Meetings of the Free Masons, Illuminati, and Reading Societies.* Published in Edinburgh in 1797, it was reprinted several times, both abroad and in this country. For Morse, this book cast a flood of light on "the causes which have brought the world into its present state"; and in particular he found in it proof that it was to the infernal work of a secret organization known as the Society of the Illuminati that were to be ascribed such apparently unrelated phenomena as the French Revolution, the dissemination of Paine's *Age of Reason*, and the rise of democratic societies in America. All this Morse hastened to proclaim at length in a Fast Day sermon in May 1798. The charges were echoed by other ministers of Federalist sympathies, while Republicans ridiculed the theory of a conspiracy and asked for evidence.[15]

Morse had not attacked the Masonic order directly, but his endorsement of Robison at the very least implied that some lodges might have been infiltrated by the Illuminati. An active Mason as well as a Democratic-Republican, Bentley was annoyed by Morse's vague and insubstantial charges, and he made a casual disparaging reference to them in a Charge to the Worcester Lodge the following month.[16] Morse, predictably, rushed into print to defend himself; whereupon Bentley retorted that "the notice taken of the American Geographer in a late Charge, was on account of his zeal, in his public character, to give authority to a wicked and mischievous Book."[17]

Meanwhile some theological aspects of the dispute were exposed by William Wells, Jr., a young protégé of James Freeman, and hence well known to Bentley. Wells wrote a long letter to the *Massachusetts Mercury* condemning Robison for the scurrilous personal attack he had made on Dr. Joseph Priestley, Dr. Richard Price, and other English liberals. "Let us not terrify our fellow citizens with groundless alarms," Wells wrote, "nor become the dupes of every foolish tale, which the prejudices or ignorance of Europeans may fabricate."[18] Morse was already busy filling the pages of the *Mercury* with excerpts culled from Robison to corroborate the charges he had made in his Fast Day sermon; but he took time to dismiss Wells's comments as merely reflecting his loyalty to Priestley, his one-time preceptor. "One can hardly avoid smiling," Morse wrote, "to hear a young man of *four and twenty*, accuse a gentleman of Professor R's age and distinguished literary acquirements of 'extreme ignorance.'" As for Bentley, Morse insinuated "that he has himself been *illuminated*" and recognizes the founder of the Illuminati as "a brother."[19]

The newspaper communications, replies, and counter-replies occasioned by Morse's Fast Day sermon continued throughout the year 1798. They were renewed the following year when he stood in his pulpit to declare that he had "an official, authenticated list of the names, ages, places of nativity, professions, &c. of the officers and members of a Society of *Illuminati* . . . consisting of *one hundred* members, instituted in Virginia. . . ."[20] The reference was to the Wisdom Lodge of Masons in Portsmouth, Virginia. How much Bentley was directly involved in the controversy that ensued, it would be hard to say. We do know that in 1799, Christopher Ebeling, the German geographer, wrote letters to both Bentley and Morse, giving similar information discrediting Robison; that Morse represented the letter he received as supporting his charges with respect to the Illuminati, but refused to make the text public; and that parts of the letter to Bentley appeared in print under circumstances that led people to suppose it was the letter to Morse. In due course, after much recrimination, that confusion was clarified. But the net result was to reveal Morse as one who was ready to suppress evidence unfavorable to his position and to distort facts to partisan ends.[21] Morse himself finally gave up when he wrote to Josiah Parker, a member of Congress from Virginia, to find out more about Wisdom Lodge, only to be told on the basis of first-hand knowledge that it was what it appeared to be: a lodge of honest, industrious men, of good reputation in the community.[22]

Next, Morse was involved in the controversy over the election of a successor to David Tappan as Hollis Professor of Divinity at Harvard. He was certain that a concerted attempt was quietly being made to elect a liberal to the chair, thereby accomplishing a "revolution" in the University. When the Harvard Corporation finally voted, four to two, to appoint the Reverend Henry Ware, the matter came before the Board of Overseers, of which Morse was a member. He led the opposition, but the appointment was confirmed. Promptly carrying the dispute to the public, he defended his position in a pamphlet entitled *The True Reasons on Which the Election of a Hollis Professor of Divinity in Harvard College Was Opposed at the Board of Overseers.*[23] A dozen years later, he recalled that it "was then, and *has ever since been,* considered, by one class of people, as my *unpardonable offence,* and by another class, as *the best thing I ever did.*"[24]

The terms of the Hollis chair as established by the donor stipulated the appointment of "a man of solid Learning in Divinity, of sound or orthodox Principles."[25] Morse argued that the adjective "orthodox" necessarily meant "Calvinist." The liberals replied that if Hollis had wanted to specify the Calvinism of the Westminster Confession or some other creed he could have done so; but that he had set aside creedal definitions of orthodoxy when he prescribed that the only article of belief to be required of the professor would be "that the Bible is the only and most perfect rule of faith and practice," to be interpreted "according to the best light that God shall give him."[26]

Morse lost the fight in the Board of Overseers, but he gained points just as important to him. He made an internal decision in the affairs of the College a matter of public dispute; and he succeeded in defining the issue as a theological one, as a conflict between rival theological parties. The liberals on the Corporation who finally voted for Henry Ware did not see it that way. Indeed, at one point two of them actually voted for Jesse Appleton, the leading orthodox candidate. A compromise advanced by Judge Oliver Wendell of the orthodox faction would have made Ware the President and Appleton the Hollis Professor; but only three of the six members of the Corporation went along with both halves of it. The three who did not were Ebenezer Storer, the Reverend John Eliot, and Professor Eliphalet Pearson. Storer, a liberal, thought Ware would make a good professor but not a good president. Eliot, likewise a liberal, felt that Appleton was not the best choice for professor, because his "dissonant & unpleasant voice" was a disqualification for a position involving the conduct of public worship. To his lasting regret he allowed this consideration to decide his vote. Professor Eliphalet Pearson, Morse's ally on the Corporation, who could have carried the day for Appleton, would have nothing to do with either half of the compromise, because he wanted the position of president for himself. But considerations such as these could hardly be broached in the Board of Overseers, so only the theological issue was left for public discussion.[27]

The result was to increase greatly the antagonism between the liberals and the orthodox, and to subject Morse to bitter criticism for his part in promoting it. Previously, only Freeman and Bentley of the liberals had actively opposed him. Most of the liberal clergy deplored religious controversy, and, themselves Federalists, they did not openly criticize his extravagant fears of Illuminism. But the Arminianism and incipient antitrinitarianism of the liberals alarmed Morse as much as Illuminism had, and he was the more upset because the liberals avoided preaching on disputed points of doctrine. When the editors of the *Monthly Anthology* published a critical review by William Wells of Morse's *True Reasons*, he could identify that little clique of liberals as unfriendly to him personally. But the liberals generally, he was convinced, were maintaining a conspiracy of silence while all the time they were as eagerly seeking partisan advantage as he himself was doing.

Morse did not accept his defeat in the Board of Overseers as final. At one time he toyed with the notion of recapturing the College by legislative action. If the evangelical forces could be concentrated, he suggested, "we might yet bring about a *counter revolution* in our University, by an alteration of Charter, and a new Board of Overseers." Then he added, characteristically: "Keep this idea in your own bosom."[28]

There were more plausible ways of countering liberal Christianity, however, and soon Morse was marshaling his forces for simultaneous moves along three lines of attack: an attempt to organize the congregational churches into a more closely structured body; the establishment of a magazine to rally the forces of evangelical religion; and the founding of a theological seminary, since Harvard could no longer be considered a fit place for the education of properly orthodox ministers. He failed in his attempt to presbyterianize Massachusetts congregationalism, but was successful with the magazine and the theological seminary. His success depended on bringing into cooperation two factions of the orthodox: those who were content with the familiar formulations of the Westminster Confession, often called "Moderate Calvinists," and those who had been strongly influenced by the New Divinity of the followers of Jonathan Edwards. The latter were sometimes called "consistent Calvinists," or "Hopkinsians," after Samuel Hopkins of Newport, Rhode Island. In Connecticut, where Morse came from, the gradation between Moderate Calvinist and Hopkinsian was even and unbroken, while those of Arminian tendencies had to find refuge in the Episcopal church, quite distinct from the congregational churches of the Standing Order. But in eastern Massachusetts, Morse found to his dismay that the factional lines were drawn in the wrong place, and the wrong people got along well together. The Arminians and the Moderate Calvinists submerged their differences and engaged in friendly intercourse, both socially and professionally, whereas it was the Hopkinsians—typically Yale graduates in Harvard territory—who were isolated. By painstaking negotiations over the course of two years, Morse encouraged the Hopkinsians, who were hoping to establish a theological seminary in Newbury, to join forces with Moderate Calvinists in Andover. Only someone with Morse's tenacity of purpose would have persevered, and the accomplishments of Andover Theological Seminary in its early years are to be credited to Morse's negotiating skill and his single-minded insistence that all factions of Calvinists had to work together in opposition to liberal Christianity.

III

In 1808, Jedidiah Morse was at the peak of his power and influence. His several projects for uniting "the friends of truth" against the common enemy were moving forward, and the opening of the Andover Theological Seminary in September of that year was very much a triumph of persistent and tactful persuasion on his part.

But as in a Greek tragedy, it was at this time of triumph that a flaw in Morse's character opened the way for his eventual personal humiliation. While he was working harmoniously and effectively with his orthodox colleagues, he was engaged in a running controversy of a personal kind with certain of the liberals. This time the issue was the alleged injustice he had done to a deserving but penniless author by the publication of a history of New England. This was the pettiest of controversies and would have had no bearing on the theological disputes of the day had not Morse proclaimed that the liberals were using it disingenuously in retaliation for his principled opposition to them. Just as Morse had insisted that the election of a Hollis Professor was not simply an internal College affair, so now he insisted that a private dispute over rival publications was a matter of the public to judge between him and his theological adversaries. Indeed, the two issues were related, inasmuch as Morse argued that it was because he had opposed the election of Henry Ware that certain liberals had underhandedly begun to spread malicious reports about his personal character.

If the dispute was not enmeshed in ecclesiastical maneuverings at the outset, Morse soon made it so. The result was to afford additional grounds for criticism of Morse and additional evidence of his readiness to regard criticism of himself as an attack on the religion of Jesus Christ. As Morse saw it, he was surrounded by enemies secretly conspiring to destroy the faith once delivered to the saints. Every enemy thrust had to be answered; secret plans had to be exposed; counterattacks had to be quietly prepared. Some awareness of the extent to which Morse's fear of the liberals verged on paranoia is needed if his involvement in the events of 1805 to 1815 is to be understood; and it is in the controversy with Hannah Adams that his prickly personality and conspiratorial temper are most clearly revealed.

In September 1804, at the close of the Thursday Lecture in Boston, Morse was approached by a middle-aged maiden lady who was obviously very much troubled and upset. She was Hannah Adams, the author of a *Summary History of New England* (1799), which she was occupied in rewriting and abridging for school use. In collaboration with the Reverend Elijah Parish of Byfield, Morse had just published a *Compendious History of New England.* What would be the consequence for Miss Adams's labors if Morse, with his great reputation as a geographer, should likewise turn out a shorter version for school use? Since she was struggling to support herself by her pen and the profits from a book for school use were critical to her—though much less so to him—she sought to find out what his intentions were. She was an extremely timid person, and perhaps she did not make clear what was bothering her. She asked Morse if he was willing that she publish such a book, to which he replied he had not the slightest objection. She took this to mean that she had a clear field.[29]

What was her shock, therefore, to receive a letter from Morse shortly after in which reference was made to the conversation. "I have since mentioned the subject of our conversation to my partner, Rev. Mr. Parish," he wrote, "who appears not altogether pleased with the idea, *as it will look too much like rivalship, and might provoke* to an abridgment of ours." It would *"hardly be proper,"* Morse's letter continued, "for you to publish another of the same kind, at a less price. *The public would say, that either the one or the other was unnecessary."*[30]

This letter seemed "cruel and menacing" to Miss Adams, and she read it as intended to discourage her from proceeding with her abridgment. She wrote to Parish and received assurances that he had misunderstood the situation, supposing that her proposed abridgment had been provoked by the publication of the *Compendious History.* So Miss Adams continued her labors, and her school text appeared in July 1805. But when she called at a bookstore in Salem to ask that copies be taken for sale, she was refused and was told to her dismay that the authors of the *Compendious History* were about to print a cheap edition on a reduced scale.[31]

What might have been dismissed as common rivalry between competing authors now took on the appearance of trickery and deceit. Miss Adams had told her troubles to her friends, among them William Smith Shaw of the Anthology Society, the Reverend James Freeman of the Stone Chapel, and the Boston merchant, Stephen Higginson, Jr. Knowing Morse as they did from earlier encounters, they were most sympathetic with Miss Adams's predicament and undertook to collect a fund for her support. But stories began to circulate that Morse had taken advantage of a defenseless female. She had engaged in months of laborious research in old manuscripts at risk of her eyesight to prepare her *Summary History*, only to have the results of her labors exploited by others in a way that would deprive her of her legitimate and expected financial reward. It was even noised about—though the report was not true and was promptly denied by Miss Adams herself—that Morse had borrowed her manuscript and plagiarized from it. It can be argued that a misunderstanding was at the bottom of it all, since there is no evidence that Morse had set out deliberately to injure Miss Adams, whom he had known and indeed had assisted on occasion. But the inescapable fact is that such accusations, circulated as rumors, were believed because they were believable.[32]

In 1808, Morse and Parish finally decided to bring out the second edition of their *Compendious History*. Before long, Morse discovered that the result was to set tongues wagging again and that his alleged mistreatment of Miss Adams had not been forgotten. On December 7, 1808, he wrote to Stephen Higginson, Jr., one of Miss Adams's most loyal benefactors, calling for an end to whispering campaigns and innuendoes, and asking that if there were any real charges they be brought out into the open and cleared up once and for all. "This sort of dark and indefinite attack on my character," he wrote, "so pertinaciously and industriously persisted in, after every honourable and Christian mode of preventing it, proffered on my part, is altogether insufferable, and I must have assurances from you, that it shall be immediately discontinued, and Christian reparation made for past injuries, or I shall expose your conduct to the public."[33]

Higginson not only sympathized with Miss Adams, but had a quarrel of his own with Morse. The published documents refer obscurely to an accusation by Higginson that Morse had made an attempt "to make mercenary matches, and for his own interest and benefit."[34] The substance of the accusation was that Morse had lent money to a certain Dr. Putnam, secured by a mortgage, and he had also endorsed Putnam's note for a bank loan. Unfortunately, Putnam became overextended, and Morse was quietly informed that his friend was virtually insolvent. So Morse helped him secure a loan from a Mr. Fairweather, by which the bank loan, for which he himself might become answerable, was paid off. Next he thought to encourage Putnam's marriage to a woman with money. The first attempt at matchmaking came to nothing, so he tried the same tactics on Miss Fairweather, without intimating that he himself was financially involved with Putnam and would suffer loss if Putnam were declared bankrupt. He even sent some of Miss Fairweather's friends to plead for Putnam. One of them reported "that Dr. M. had told her every thing favorable of Dr. P. and that Dr. M. was waiting at her house till her return!" All of this came to Higginson's knowledge, since one of the ladies in question was related to him; and he spread the word among members of the family that Morse was duplicitous. Morse, to be sure, stoutly maintained that the charges were malicious and false.[35]

Before long it was decided to present the issues between Morse and Miss Adams to three disinterested referees. Morse suggested the names of eight prominent citizens, and Higginson chose three of them. They were Thomas Dawes, John Davis, and Samuel Dexter. Dawes was judge of probate and had earlier been a justice of the Superior Court. John Davis was judge of the Federal District Court, where he served forty years. Samuel Dexter had been United States Senator, Secretary of War, and Secretary of the Treasury.[36] That up to this time Morse was still thinking of the quarrel as a personal one, not as a phase of the ecclesiastical struggle, is suggested by the fact that all three referees chosen on his nomination were liberals. Dawes and Davis were parishioners of William Ellery Channing at Federal Street, while Dexter attended the Brattle Street Church.

Thus far, in the absence of evidence of malice on Morse's part, one would not be inclined to criticize him severely for his treatment of Miss Adams. He argued plausibly enough that no one had a right to preempt the field of New England history and that it was for the public to choose between alternative school texts offered for sale. But to his shock, the referees ruled against him in one important particular. They acknowledged that Parish and he had not *"violated any right, which any Judicatory, legal or equitable is competent to enforce"*—that is, Miss Adams had no grounds for a lawsuit against them. But they also declared that "by her pre-occupation of the subject, and her assiduous and useful labours in the management of it," and especially in view of "the peculiar circumstances of that Lady," she should have been treated with "particular tenderness and attention, in any procedure which might tend to diminish the profits of her literary labours." In sum, Morse's behavior fell short of what one would expect of a compassionate Christian minister. It followed that "some amicable overtures were due to Miss Adams, for satisfying her undefined claims, before a publication should be made so similar to her performance, and so likely to interfere with her reasonable expectations." As for Higginson, the referees declared that they had seen nothing to justify the harshness of his censures, and they suggested that his actions might have impeded a satisfactory settlement.[37]

That the referees intended some financial settlement, not as a legal but as a moral obligation, seemed clear to Miss Adams's friends. But the referees had felt it inappropriate to try to state what that settlement should be, or whether it should be in money, or assignment of copyright, or some other way, leaving it to Morse, as a Christian gentleman, to make an appropriate offer. Their hesitation on this point resulted in wording sufficiently ambiguous that Morse could not believe that he was actually expected to yield a part of his profits. He turned at once to his friends to ask what they thought the award meant, and reached the conclusion that what was expected was for him to sit down with Miss Adams and agree "as to the course to be pursued in regard to the present and future editions of our respective works" so that they would not interfere with one another. He suggested a conference to that end, at the same time making it very clear through an intermediary that he did not "consider any pecuniary compensation recommended." Miss Adams saw no reason for a conference if the main recommendation of the referees were to be excluded from discussion, and paid no attention to his overtures.[38]

Morse's attempt to straighten out matters and clear his reputation by reference to a disinterested tribunal had only made matters worse. To his original, ill-defined fault in interfering with Miss Adams's expectation of profits from her publication, he had added the very specific fault of proposing a reference, nominating the referees himself, and then refusing to accept their judgment. In addition, with his usual sensitivity on matters involving his own dignity and honor, he took the mild criticism by the referees of Higginson's behavior to mean that as part of the settlement, Higginson should apologize to him, and that was to be done "before 'offers of compromise' be made" on his part.[39] The liberals now more than ever were convinced that Morse was guilty of bad faith.

IV

There the matter rested for a time. After a final fruitless exchange of letters, neither Miss Adams nor her friends made any further attempt to secure compliance with the award. But the last act of the drama was yet to be played. In October 1812, Morse got wind of the fact that seven years earlier, in 1805, when Miss Adams's friends were solicited for donations for her support, William Smith Shaw had shown them an autobiographical letter from her, explaining how she had been attempting despite great difficulties to support herself by literary work.[40] Morse immediately reached the conclusion that this secret letter, surreptitiously passed from hand to hand, had been the source of all his troubles and had been the basis for malicious accusations against him. He demanded to see it. Once again the petty dispute was on people's tongues, and once again the liberals were reminded that Morse had submitted his case to disinterested referees of his own choosing, who had advised him to reach a financial settlement, and that he had failed to respect the decision he himself had solicited.

Since the interpretation of the judgment of the referees was once more in question, an obvious solution was sought. Why not ask the three distinguished gentlemen to resolve the ambiguities in their decision of four years earlier and to explain whether they really meant that Morse was expected to reach a financial settlement. So Morse wrote to them and received the following response:

> You seem to intimate some doubt as to the *meaning* of our Award. We cannot perceive that it is difficult to be understood, but if it is so, it arose from our desire to express our opinion in a manner that could not wound the feelings of you and your friend Dr. Parish. We have made one attempt to explain it, and will now make another effort to render it as incapable of being misunderstood, as the nature of language permits. We did mean to say, that Doctors Morse and Parish equitably owed to Miss Adams a substantial and valuable recompense for their interference with her work. We did not estimate the amount, because we did not know how much she had suffered. We did not say it should be money, because we thought it possible that an arrangement as to the sale of the books, and the disposition of the proceeds, might be agreed upon by the parties, more satisfactory and beneficial. The form of compensation, as well as the amount, we left for the parties to adjust.[41]

Anyone but Morse would have then said, in effect: If that's what was intended, I guess I am stuck with it, even though I still see things differently. But nothing so gracious as even a grudging concession came from him. Instead he wrote back a long letter full of protests and quibbles, arguing that he and his friends could not see how the original award could be interpreted as the referees themselves now interpreted it. His conclusion amounted to an accusation of double-dealing on the part of the referees: "Your last communication, therefore," he wrote, "is, in my view, a *new Award*."[42]

It was now August 1813. Nine years had passed since the initial conversation at the Thursday Lecture that had begun the controversy. Morse was surely correct in believing that his reputation was still under a cloud, perhaps more so than ever. One more direct approach to Miss Adams came to nothing, since Morse tried to reopen all the issues in contention as if the award of the referees had never been made. Morse then made the most amazing suggestion yet: that there be a new reference to a new panel of judges to determine whether his interpretation of the award was correct, rather than the interpretation of it by those who wrote it. He continued to deny "that any *pecuniary* compensation" was due Miss Adams "within the fair construction of the Award," and offered "to have the correctness of his opinions tested by three competent men, appointed in the manner he had proposed to Miss A."[43]

By this time, there was nothing Morse could do to retrieve his credibility in the community at large, though he continued to have friends who assured him that he was being persecuted for righteousness' sake. One would have supposed that there was little he could do to make things worse. But Morse, who had moved unerringly from blunder to blunder, discovered a way to make the worst blunder of all. He decided to lay the matter before the public by publishing the documents in the case. The result was a book—a two-hundred-page book—in which were printed all the letters that had passed between Morse and Miss Adams and her representatives, and the decisions of the referees, and the explanations of the referees, and reassuring letters from Morse's friends, together with running comment, explanations, interpretations, and protests by Morse himself.[44] The result was hardly what Morse intended; for when he distributed copies to his friends, some of them told him, in effect, that he should have paid up and shut up long ago. To be sure, not all of the orthodox reacted thus. But what could he say to a letter of reproach from Dr. David Osgood of Medford, one of his oldest associates, who had given him the Right Hand of Fellowship at his installation a quarter of a century earlier and had been a faithful adviser in connection with the founding of Andover Seminary? Osgood's letter is dated July 8, 1814:

> ... whether the judgment of the referees in your controversy with Miss Adams were correct or not, you were bound in honor and conscience to abide by it though it should have lessened your profits. That *judgment* to my apprehension evidently implied that you owed Miss Adams some pecuniary compensation. All your attempts to evade this meaning appear to me & to every one else whom I have heard mentioning it, unworthy of your character. I have heard mercantile men repeatedly say, that were one of them to have recourse to similar evasions, his reputation would be forfeited.
>
> It was to remarks such as these that I referred when I said to you yesterday "that I would not be in your situation for all the profits ever made by books." You greatly erred when you charged me with judging a cause without hearing it. I judge nothing but the effects of the dispute. For this am I not sufficiently informed? As I have no other interest or concern, in the subject, it appears to me on the whole that my time will not be well spent in reading any more of its publications.
>
> For this reason I beg leave to return your book unopened.

Then, after commenting on other differences of opinion between him and Morse, Dr. Osgood concluded:

> But in telling you of this, as well as your other mistakes, I shall be sorry to break friendship.
>
> The articles of my faith, are perhaps substantially the same with your's, tho' I differ with respect to the best method of supporting & advancing them. The method adopted by you, for some time past, appears to me, to be ill judged and in

its consequences greatly prejudicial to the causes which you wish to promote. I very much regret that you have not continued to progress in the same candid & catholic course in which your ministry commenced. In that way, I verily believe, you would have been far more useful as well as more happy.[45]

Miss Adams responded at once with *A Narrative of the Controversy Between the Rev. Jedidiah Morse, D.D. and the Author*, which added little to the dispute. Appended to her narrative were two statements, a brief one by Stephen Higginson, Jr., and a longer one by John Lowell, a member of the Harvard Corporation, denying that the controversy had been whipped up by the liberals because of resentment over Morse's opposition to the election of Henry Ware. In turn, Sidney Morse defended his father in a pamphlet entitled *Remarks on the Controversy Between Dr. Morse and Miss Adams*. By this time, the arguments had descended to the level of personal vilification. Lowell derided Morse for "the vast number of worldly affairs, in which he is engaged, his profitable publications, his printing speculations, his notes at the bank, his mortgages, and his various disputes and lawsuits and references thereout arising."[46] Sidney Morse responded that Lowell was "a *true Jacobin*, according to the strict definition of the term, and we may add too, that the *Unitarianism* which he advocates is the genuine *Jacobinism* of Christianity." Of Higginson he remarked that "he is a noisy man, not supposed by any one to be overstocked with sense or wisdom, but he is just fit to preach Socinianism in coffee-houses and stage coaches."[47]

V

Morse was now beset by troubles on many sides. The members of his Charlestown congregation were restive. They had earlier complained that he was spending too much time on his literary ventures and neglecting his flock, and he had had recurrent disputes with the parish over the amount of his salary.[48] Two years later, a large part of them pulled out and organized the Second

Congregational Society in order to hear liberal preaching.[49] His old friend and ally, Dr. Joseph Lyman of Hatfield, found it prudent not to exchange pulpits with him because of the current "unpleasant feelings among some in most of our congregations, relating to yourself."[50] He was embroiled in a lawsuit and threatened with a second; the details are obscure, but in one case judgment for $600 was entered against him, which he paid with characteristic reluctance. He had lost money on an investment in some turnpike stock and seemed to think that the person who sold it to him should reimburse him for his loss.[51] Dr. Elijah Parish, his former collaborator on the *Compendious History*, was disputing over $800 that Morse owed him. "Do you mean to intimidate & frighten me to make a sacrifice from an idea of your *insolvency?*" Parish wrote. "I also have lost $5000 but I pay my debts without whining. . . ."[52]

It was doubtless a relief to Morse to be able to turn his attention to more congenial concerns. In the spring of 1815, his son Samuel, then in England studying painting under Washington Allston, ran across Thomas Belsham's *Life of Theophilus Lindsey*, published three years earlier. Belsham was a leading Unitarian of the Priestley school; Lindsey had been a presbyter of the Church of England who had sought in vain to promote liberal, and indeed specifically antitrinitarian, doctrine within the established church. One of the chapters of the book was based largely on letters to Lindsey from James Freeman, telling of the progress of liberal religion in New England. Freeman, it will be recalled, was the minister of the Stone Chapel, with its Anglican liturgy and tradition; and his antitrinitarianism was of the Priestley variety. That is to say, his was a Socinian Christology, conceiving of Jesus as a man like other men, though one specially chosen of God to be the channel of divine revelation. The liberals in the churches of the Standing Order, on the other hand, generally held to an Arian Christology, regarding Jesus as a superangelic being, created before the world and through whom the world was made, though not one person of a triune God. The letters from Freeman to Lindsey dealt particularly with a few scattered instances of Socinian preaching; but they also spoke of the general atmosphere in Boston of toleration and accommodation, in which divisive theological issues were avoided in the pulpit.

Once again, as on two memorable previous occasions, Morse had found a book that gave him evidence that a conspiracy was afoot. He had long suspected that the refusal of the liberals to preach on the points of doctrine regarded as critical by the Calvinists was not because they sought peace, but because they were masking their designs against the Gospel by a conspiracy of silence. Now he was sure that he had documentary proof—just as earlier he had had proof that the Bavarian Illuminati had infiltrated a Masonic lodge in Portsmouth, Virginia. He arranged for a reprint of the chapter as a pamphlet; and lest anyone overlook its significance, the pamphlet was reviewed in the *Panoplist* by Jeremiah Evarts, who once again accused the liberals of dishonest concealment and called upon all good evangelical Christians to deny them Christian fellowship.[53]

How William Ellery Channing responded to these publications, how the liberals vainly protested that they were not Unitarians of the English or Socinian type, and how the Unitarian controversy widened in the years that followed are matters beyond the scope of this essay. But it has to be acknowledged that despite his troubles, Jedidiah Morse was successful in what he sought most eagerly: cooperation between the Hopkinsians and the Moderate Calvinists, and isolation of the liberal Christians. So in a curious inverted way, Jedidiah Morse was the founder of American Unitarianism as a distinct religious denomination.

But by 1819, even his own church in Charlestown had had enough and dismissed him.

Institutional Reconstruction
in the Unitarian Controversy

The Unitarian controversy began in 1805 with the election of Henry Ware as Hollis Professor of Divinity at Harvard. It lasted for about thirty years, until in 1835 the younger Henry Ware regretfully acknowledged that the Unitarians were a community by themselves.

These thirty years divide neatly into three phases, each a decade in length, each with a characteristic prevailing concern. From 1805 to 1815, while Jedidiah Morse was the dominating figure, the dispute centered on what Channing was later to call "the system of exclusion and denunciation in religion." This phase ended with Morse's publication of the pamphlet *American Unitarianism*, Jeremiah Evarts's review of it in the *Panoplist*, and the interchange between Channing and Samuel Worcester that followed. The middle decade, from 1815 to 1825, was dominated by theological discussion, the most important single event being Channing's Baltimore sermon in 1819. Pamphlet debates followed between Andrews Norton and Moses Stuart over the doctrine of the Trinity, and between Leonard Woods and Henry Ware over the doctrine of human nature. The final phase began in 1825 with the organization of the American Unitarian Association. This was a crucial step in the development of Unitarianism as a separate denomination, sponsoring its own institutions for missionary activity, the publication of tracts and periodicals, Sunday school work, and organized charity.

The attention of historians has been especially drawn to the middle decade, with its high drama of the conflict of ideas. The critical reviews, sermons, and pamphlets of this period have provided rich material for intellectual historians and historians of doctrine. But the very abundance of this material and its relative accessibility tend to distort our understanding of the larger controversy by overemphasizing the doctrinal aspect of it. Despite the vigor of the theological debate, this was not a time of theological innovation or fresh religious insights. It was rather the final stage of a confrontation between Arminian and Calvinist, Arian and Trinitarian, that had been developing for two generations.[1]

The Unitarian controversy added nothing significant to familiar theological arguments except for the introduction of new methods of biblical interpretation, which the liberals assumed would bolster their long-held position.[2] The liberals were groping for a more appropriate vocabulary in which to express their unevangelical doctrine and were developing a more literary preaching style, innovations that have been of interest to literary scholars.[3] But the doctrine itself, even in Channing's Baltimore sermon, did not represent a break with the tradition of Chauncy, Mayhew, Gay, Belknap, and Bancroft. Two generations of Arminians had achieved a creative theological adjustment to Enlightenment currents of thought and had amassed the intellectual capital on which the liberal Christians drew in the time of controversy.

If thirty years of conflict produced little in the way of fresh theological insights—at least until transcendental stirrings began to be felt at the very end of the period—nevertheless they radically transformed the ecclesiastical institutions of New England. Yet this is the part of the story that historians have treated least adequately. They have generally been content with a simple narrative of events, with minimal analysis of the process by which a rapid reshaping of institutional structures was taking place. The Standing Order was abolished, its demise hastened in Massachusetts by the split between liberals and orthodox. The territorial parish disappeared, and new ways of financing public worship had to be devised. The long-established practice of pulpit exchanges was subverted. Ecclesiastical councils as instruments to moderate conflicts lost credibility and soon became vestigial. Theological seminaries replaced apprenticeship training for the ministry. Religious journals and magazines emerged as important instruments for the shaping of opinion; they depended on business organization for their success. Voluntary societies were created for the promotion of missionary activity and the publication of tracts; they introduced bureaucratic methods and values into ecclesiastical affairs. These are aspects of an institutional restructuring far more radical than anything taking place in the realm of doctrine.

The conflict between liberals and orthodox within the churches of the Standing Order was not the only reason for such changes. Forces widely operative in the larger society had much to do with them, and other groups and other parts of the country were likewise affected. Religious pluralism was rendering the Standing Order obsolete. The territorial parish, appropriate for a rural society, could not accommodate the mill village. Improved transportation had its effect on ministerial exchanges and ecclesiastical councils. Technological change in the printing trades had a bearing on the increased output of books, tracts, and magazines. Population growth and migration westward gave impetus to the development of voluntary associations for benevolent causes. But the disruption of the Standing Order meant that such social forces operated with special intensity in Massachusetts and produced change the more rapidly.

Many of these changes had their inception in the first decade of the Unitarian controversy, from 1805 to 1815, and so that period is deserving of more attention than it has received. Jedidiah Morse founded the *Panoplist* in 1805. The Andover Theological Seminary was established in 1808, and the first steps leading to the establishment of the Harvard Divinity School were taken three years later. The Park Street Church was gathered in 1809. The American Board of Commissioners for Foreign Missions was organized in 1810. A General Association of Ministers on an evangelical basis, formed in 1802, finally began to attract wide support from the orthodox after 1810. The *Christian Disciple*, forerunner of the *Christian Examiner*, dates from 1811.

In short, the institutionalization of the split between the two parties was well advanced before the period of liveliest theological debate. This process went on for a generation, producing the *Christian Register* and the Berry Street Conference in 1820 and the American Unitarian Association in 1825. Some divisions in local parishes occurred even after that date. But by 1835, it was clear that no more major victories for either side were possible. Some sniping continued, but other issues were emerging. The liberals now had to decide what to make of Transcendentalism within their midst, while the orthodox became concerned about the way the Plan of Union seemed to be operating to their disadvantage.

The institutionalization of the division between the liberals and the orthodox proceeded mainly by small events and local actions, no one of which by itself seems of great consequence. But there was one dramatic episode that deserves recognition—more recognition than it has received—as a major representative event of the entire period of controversy. It was the dispute in the Second Parish in Dorchester from 1810 to 1812, which resulted in the withdrawal of the liberal faction to organize the Third Religious Society.[4] The Dorchester controversy produced no memorable theological statements for later historians to analyze. But what happened in Dorchester was widely noted elsewhere and became an object lesson to other parishes, which soon found themselves grappling with the same social forces and disputing over the same issues. Pulpit exchanges, the limits of Christian fellowship, the role of ecclesiastical councils in moderating conflict, the relationship of church to parish—all these problems, which surfaced in Dorchester, had ramifications in the larger society that call for exploration.

But first, the story of some parochial events of the years 1810 to 1812 must be told. There at the parish level—which is, after all, where congregationalism insists the church exists—Dorchester is the Unitarian controversy in miniature.

The Second Church in Dorchester was gathered on January 1, 1808, by twenty-seven men and thirty-seven women recently dismissed from the First Church. No doctrinal dispute occasioned the separation; rather, the growth of population made a division of the town for ecclesiastical purposes unavoidable. But unlike many such towns, Dorchester was not divided geographically. Instead the Second Parish was a poll parish, made up of those persons who found the location of the new meeting house more convenient and chose to be assessed for the support of public worship there. First a meeting house was constructed, in 1805 and 1806; next, the Second Parish was incorporated by the General Court in 1807; and finally, the Second Church was gathered within it.[5]

The new parish, like the old First Parish, included both liberals and orthodox. They had been accustomed to the preaching of Thaddeus Mason Harris, which was mildly liberal without being notably offensive to the orthodox. Harris deplored sectarianism and shunned party labels. But prior to his ordination in 1793 he had served briefly as librarian of Harvard College, and he was a member of the Historical Society and a fellow of the American Academy. He was, in short, one of those ministers whose culti-vated urban ways and liberal associations, quite as much as their half-acknowledged Arminianism or Arianism, seemed to the more doctrinally minded of the orthodox to be subversive of the gospel.[6]

Harris had been reluctant to see his flock divided, but he participated in the service when the church was gathered in the new Second Parish. The other ministers who participated on that occasion were likewise liberals. Dr. Eliphalet Porter of Roxbury, who gave the Right Hand of Fellowship, spoke of the "harmony and friendly intercourse" that had long prevailed among the churches and ministers of the neighborhood, and expressed confidence that with the new church peace and friendship would "continue and abound."[7]

In September of that year, the Church voted unanimously to invite John Codman to be its minister; and the Parish, with only four dissenting voices, agreed to his settlement and voted him an annual salary of a thousand dollars.[8] Codman, the son of a prosperous Boston merchant, had graduated from Harvard College in 1802. He began to read law under his kinsman John Lowell; but the untimely death of his father seems to have turned him toward the ministry. For a while he studied theology under Henry Ware, then minister in Hingham, who had earlier prepared him for college. After about a year, he moved to Cambridge, where Joseph Stevens Buckminster and William Ellery Channing were close friends. Like them, Codman was moved by an intense, essentially evangelical piety; unlike them, his theological views were developing in an orthodox direction. His biographers attribute much to his reading of William Cooper's *Doctrine of Predestination Unto Life*, then just reprinted, which he was asked to review for the *Monthly Anthology*. The result was too orthodox for the editors of that magazine, and the review appeared in the *Panoplist* instead.[9] His orthodox tendencies were strongly reinforced thereafter when he traveled abroad for almost three years, spending a considerable part of that time reading theology in Edinburgh.

Codman had only recently returned, and he had actually preached in Dorchester only twice when he was invited to settle there. He was aware of the mixed character of the parish, and before he accepted he took pains to avoid all misunderstanding as to his doctrinal position. Lest there be doubt in the mind of anyone, he wrote to the parish committee, "I think it my duty in the presence of a heart searching God, and of this Church, to declare my firm, unshaken faith in those doctrines, that are sometimes called the doctrines of the reformation, the doctrines of the cross, the peculiar doctrines of the Gospel." He went on to reject specifically "*Arian* and *Socinian* errors." He also affirmed his adherence to the congregationalism of the Cambridge Platform, thereby dissociating himself from Jedidiah Morse's attempts to presbyterianize congregational polity.[10]

Both church and parish responded promptly and favorably to Codman's letter. The reply of the parish committee made no issue of his orthodoxy but expressed confidence that all would be well, given "a spirit of condescension, patience, and toleration." "We have no doubt," the committee stated, "but you will use your endeavors to promote peace and friendship among the people of your charge, and to continue and confirm it among our sister churches and their pastors, and the university, of which you will be an overseer." To this Codman replied that it would be his earnest endeavor *"as far as consistent with the faithful discharge of ministerial duty"* so to promote peace and friendship. An ecclesiastical council was assembled, made up of both liberals and orthodox; Codman presented to it an unambiguously orthodox confession of faith; and he was ordained on December 7, 1808. He received the Right Hand of Fellowship, symbolic of the communion of the churches, from Thaddeus M. Harris. The sermon, by William Ellery Channing, was warmly applauded by both liberals and orthodox. Its success perhaps lay in the skillful way it communicated an evangelical spirit at the same time that it avoided what the orthodox termed "the peculiar doctrines of the Gospel."[11]

Though the seeds of dissension had already been sown, Codman's first year in Dorchester went smoothly enough. He had been frank about his Calvinism, and there was no criticism on that score. But he had not made it clear that he favored the exclusive policy of nonintercourse between liberals and orthodox that men like Jedidiah Morse were beginning to advocate with increasing urgency. Indeed, at least three members of the parish had conversed with him on the matter previous to his settlement and had received what they thought were assurances that he expected to join the Boston Association, with which he meant to be "upon the most intimate terms of friendship," and that "he did not see any difficulty respecting exchanges."[12] The liberals, knowing of Codman's early associations and family connections, took it for granted that under him the Second Parish, like the First from which it had sprung, would encompass diverse opinions. In this they were disappointed, and they came to feel that he had misled them.[13]

In November 1809, forty members of the parish addressed a respectful letter to Codman expressing concern over rising uneasiness in the congregation. They took pains to make it clear that they had no desire "to prescribe what doctrines would be most congenial" to hear from him, but they indicated disappointment over his failure to exchange generally with the other members of the Boston Association—many of whom, after all, had joined in the occasion of his settlement. "This we did expect," they wrote, "and this we think we have a just claim to expect from your own observations, previous to your being settled as our Minister." But Codman replied: "you must give me leave to say, that I never can nor never shall PLEDGE myself to exchange pulpits with any man or body of men whatever; and that I never did, from any observation previous to my being settled as your minister, give you any just claim to expect it."[14]

Relationships between Codman and the disaffected members of his parish deteriorated steadily in the months following. At a parish meeting on April 19, 1810, a motion requesting Codman to alter his policy with respect to exchanges was defeated; but on October 22, a similar vote went the other way, forty to thirty-five. Unless Codman altered his position, the parish declared, his connection with it ought to "become extinct." A committee was instructed to write to the orthodox ministers with whom Codman had been exchanging, asking them not to do so for the time being lest they further "convulse a parish already shaken to its centre." Joshua Bates of Dedham and Jedidiah Morse of Charlestown responded with letters of righteous indignation at the suggestion. Codman's supporters rallied behind him; one statement commending him was signed by seventy-three gentlemen, and another by 181 ladies. Attempts were evidently made to alter the balance within the parish meeting by recruiting new members from the First Parish and from Roxbury. In August, some thirty-eight pews in the meeting house had been offered for sale; and again in December, an advertisement appeared in the *Centinel* offering sixty-nine pews for sale "together with all the right, title, and interest the proprietors of the above pews have in the Rev. Mr. Codman." Friends of the minister seized upon this demeaning reference to him as illustrating the indecent level to which his opponents had stooped.[15]

Various extraneous issues readily crept into the dispute. It was recalled that on the evening of Codman's ordination, some of his parishioners planned an "ordination ball" and courteously invited him to join them for "innocent amusement." He declined in an abrupt note, which gave great offence; but his friend Joshua Bates was convinced that the ball had been planned "to try and perplex" him, in view of the evangelical attitude toward "polite amusements." Again, while the tenor of Codman's preaching was never made a matter of formal complaint, there is no doubt that it was pungent and plainspoken. It was the firm conviction of Codman's supporters that the issue of exchanges was a manufactured subterfuge on the part of the opponents, who, as might have been expected, were artfully concealing their real objection, which was to the truths of the Gospel that Codman was so faithful in maintaining. Next, Codman was accused of trying to persuade members of his congregation not to attend the funeral of the son of one of his opponents because he had not been asked to officiate. His explanation was that all he had said was that he hoped the funeral would not interfere with the attendance at his lectures. Finally, he was accused of trying to arouse opposition to Dr. Harris of the First Parish by circulating a card warning against the adoption there of Watts's catechism in place of the Assembly's. Some, at least, of these complaints were trivial, and there were those among the liberals who protested as much. But they were symptomatic of a situation in the parish that was unhealthy and growing worse.[16]

In June 1811, the Parish voted to recommend to Codman that he resign; but should he decline, he was requested to join in calling an ecclesiastical council "to hear and determine on all matters of controversy between him and said society." Should he refuse to join in a mutual council, the Parish was prepared to call an *ex parte* council to advise it as to a proper course of action. Prolonged negotiation followed, with many letters back and forth, until the parties finally agreed on a definition of the scope of the articles of complaint and the makeup of the council. Finally, on October 4, 1811, letters missive went out to twelve churches, inviting each to send the minister and a lay delegate. Half were nominated by each party. Meanwhile, seven of the aggrieved persons had preferred similar charges against Codman in church meeting but found themselves very much in the minority there.[17]

The council assembled on Wednesday, October 30, 1811. Advocates for the parish were Benjamin Parsons, Esq., and the Honorable Samuel Dexter. Dexter had been United States senator, secretary of war, and secretary of the treasury; he had the reputation of being an especially accomplished advocate. Representing the interests of the church, even though it was not directly a party to the dispute, was Daniel Davis, Esq., solicitor general of the Commonwealth; and representing Codman was his neighbor, the Reverend Joshua Bates of Dedham. It is a measure of the importance of the dispute that such distinguished advocates were enlisted; it is a measure of the seriousness with which the issues were regarded that the council was in session for eight days. The presentation of evidence and the arguments of counsel occupied the time from Wednesday through Saturday; Dexter's three-hour speech on Saturday was long remembered, even by the orthodox, as dazzling in its eloquence. From Monday until the following Thursday, the members of the council debated among themselves. They easily dismissed the trivial extraneous charges. But on the central issue, whether the aggrieved brethren had "just cause of complaint" against Codman for his practice with respect to exchanges, the council split down the middle. The six ministers with their lay delegates nominated by Codman voted to vindicate him; the six ministers and their lay delegates nominated by the parish voted to condemn. The most that could be achieved was a recommendation to the pastor, church, and congregation to preserve "a condescending, mild, peaceable, and charitable disposition."[18]

Matters had clearly gone too far for mild admonitions to have any effect. On November 28, 1811, the Parish voted, fifty-seven to thirty-six, to request an ecclesiastical council to consider whether Codman should be dismissed, or at least asked to resign. The first council had been requested to pass judgment on Codman's behavior with respect to exchanges; the new council would be asked to pass judgment on the troubled state of the parish and advise whether Codman's withdrawal would be in the interests of peace and reconciliation. His supporters took the position that he had been sufficiently vindicated by the failure of the first council to condemn him and argued that his dismissal would simply open the way to more dissension. The church nevertheless agreed to join Codman in accepting the proposal of the parish for a second mutual council.[19]

Once again the selection of members of the council was a long, drawn-out process. This time, each party chose four churches, each to be represented by its minister and a lay delegate; and by mutual agreement, the Reverend Joseph Lathrop of West Springfield was prevailed upon, despite some reluctance, to be the impartial moderator. The council met on May 12, 1812, this time for three days only. As before, the ministers and delegates split along party lines, and so the burden of casting the deciding vote fell on Lathrop.[20] He then voted against dismissal, but he appended to the Result of the council the notation that his vote had been taken "on a full belief and strong persuasion" that Codman would now "open a more free and liberal intercourse with his ministerial brethren." Should he fail to do so, and should the question come before him again, Lathrop declared, he would "have no hesitancy" in voting for Codman's dismissal.[21]

Two months later, Codman received a letter from the parish committee, sounding him out as to his intentions with respect to the more free and liberal intercourse enjoined by Lathrop. Perhaps injudiciously they included a list of twelve ministers of the Boston Association, to which Codman belonged, and asked specifically whether he intended to exchange with them. Codman seized on this as an invitation to repeat that he would not pledge to exchange with any particular individual, though he would attempt to consult the feelings and wishes of his people in general. Two more months passed, and Codman had exchanged with only two of the twelve. The discontented members of the parish became impatient and addressed to him two long letters of complaint. Finally, on November 24, 1812, the parish voted fifty-five to forty-five to dismiss him. This vote, to be sure, was directed to his relationship to the parish, as its "public teacher of piety, religion and morality"—to use the language of the constitution of the Commonwealth. His salary, paid by the parish, would be discontinued; and the meetinghouse, title to which vested in the parish, not the church, would be denied him. Strictly speaking, he could be dismissed as minister of the church only by vote of the church, following an ecclesiastical council. But so closely related were these two distinct bodies that it inevitably seemed to the majority of the church that a majority of the parish was wrongfully depriving their minister of his proper standing.[22]

Codman had been planning an exchange for the following Sunday, but the other minister withdrew on representation by a delegation from the parish that his presence might create difficulties. The parish committee arranged for a substitute preacher, the Reverend Warren Pierce, formerly minister in New Salem, but not then regularly settled, who lived nearby in Milton. Rather earlier than usual on the Sabbath, Codman and his friends went to the meetinghouse, only to find that eight men were posted on the pulpit stairs to deny him access. He therefore began to conduct the service from the floor, in front of the pulpit. During the first prayer, Pierce arrived and was admitted to the pulpit, where he remained quietly until Codman and his faction had concluded their worship; then he in turn conducted worship for the rival faction. During the noon hour Pierce prudently remained in the pulpit, where refreshment was brought to him, and then he conducted the afternoon service. Finally, Codman returned with his supporters and conducted their second service. The orthodox party remarked triumphantly that there had been 220 worshipers on the lower floor of the meetinghouse at their afternoon service, but only 48 at the service of the liberal party.[23]

Some weeks earlier, the suggestion had been made that the friends of Mr. Codman should purchase the pews of the disaffected members of the parish at the same price that had been paid for them. Now at last a solution of the dispute along such lines was seriously explored. The opposers sold their pews, resigned their parish offices, received exemption from future parish taxes, received a proportionate share of the ministerial fund, and were set off as a separate religious society. They were incorporated as the Third Religious Society and gathered the Third Church; with the blessing of the Boston Association they dedicated the "New South Meeting House in Dorchester" on October 6, 1813; and in due course they installed Edward Richmond as their minister.[24]

Codman could be unyielding when it seemed to him necessary, as in the matter of exchanges, to take a stand for principle; but he was not, like Jedidiah Morse, of a contentious or conspiratorial disposition. For their part, the liberals were ready to acknowledge that in such disputes "many things would be said and done, by individuals, on both sides, which they, in their more cool and tranquil moments, would condemn, and which the deliberate judgment of no one could approve." Hence both parties welcomed the settlement as permitting the return of civility and harmony to the town.[25]

But there were to be lasting consequences for the larger community. The issues had been made known through the publication by the church of a pamphlet of more than a hundred pages, containing the proceedings of church and parish, and much of the correspondence between Codman and his critics. The liberals stated their position in an appeal to public opinion published as they were preparing to dedicate their new meetinghouse. But at the same time that Codman was contending with his critics in Dorchester, Jedidiah Morse was engaging his enemies on many sides, and in his view the Dorchester controversy was another skirmish in the larger struggle. Morse himself was a member of the first ecclesiastical council, as was his parishioner Jeremiah Evarts; and Samuel Dexter, counsel for the parish, had been one of the referees whose decision, in the dispute between Morse and Hannah Adams, Morse was doing his best to evade. Little wonder, then, that the *Panoplist* printed a long review by Evarts of the pamphlets in the case in which Codman's troubles were laid at the door of the liberal party in Boston, "a party always vigilant to extend its influence, and active to bear down those who stand in its way,—

a party, which under the guise of charity and candor, is aiming to establish a strong and lasting domination,"—a party, in short of the most illiberal sort, which all the time proclaims its own "strength, and wisdom, and learning, and liberality."[26] If the people of Dorchester were ready to accept some tolerable accommodation that could be honorably adopted, the Jedidiah Morses were eager to use the episode to multiply antagonisms and widen the breach in the churches of the Standing Order. Increasingly thereafter, a refusal to exchange with any but evangelical ministers became the fixed practise of the orthodox.

In the Dorchester controversy, several of the recurrent issues of the larger Unitarian controversy were already vigorously disputed. Most immediate was the question of pulpit exchanges: Was this a matter for the minister alone to determine, or were there legitimate expectations of the congregation to be respected? This question was part of a larger issue, namely, the limits of Christian fellowship: How much diversity were the churches willing to encompass? Who is to be excluded and on what basis? The problem of the adequacy of ecclesiastical councils for the resolution of disputes was also posed, as was the appropriateness of the traditional relationship of church and parish within the Massachusetts Standing Order. These several aspects of the controversy invite particular examination.

Pulpit Exchanges. Of the various forms of intercommunion among the churches of the Standing Order, the most important in the latter part of the eighteenth century were ecclesiastical councils and pulpit exchanges. Although councils may be regarded as in keeping with the second way of communion authorized by the Cambridge Platform (1648), ministerial exchanges were essentially an eighteenth-century development. By the end of the century, both councils and exchanges were familiar and accepted institutional practices, a part of the custom of the country.

How regularly and frequently ministers were accustomed to exchange no doubt depended on a variety of circumstances: their personal preferences, their reputations as preachers, the degree of collegiality among members of a given ministerial association, the accessibility or inaccessibility of their locations, the time of year. Hence there was doubtless considerable variation in the practise. In Salem, from March 1785 through the end of 1786, William Bentley exchanged twenty-seven times, on many occasions for half a day, with Thomas Barnard of the North Church. In Northborough, Joseph Allen was in his own pulpit about half the time in the early years of his ministry, 1816 and 1817. In the six months following his ordination at Charlestown in March 1817, Thomas Prentiss preached fifty times, exactly half of them away from home. From October 1822 through April 1823, John Brazer of the North Church in Salem preached to his own congregation twenty-eight times out of fifty-three; eleven different ministers preached for him when he was away. It is clear that at this time exchanges were an important part of the life of the churches.[27]

From the point of view of the minister, the great advantage was that he was relieved of the burden of preparing two sermons every Sunday for his own congregation. That burden had undoubtedly increased as sermons became less exegetical and more literary in character. The minister could carry with him on exchange the manuscript of one of his more successful sermons; and this was the more readily possible since most preaching was on moral or doctrinal themes, with no necessary reference to topics of the day of immediate and transient concern that would require fresh preparation.

From the point of view of the congregation, the advantage was that over a period of time it might hear different voices expressing a variety of points of view. At a time when long pastorates were common and lifetime pastorates not unusual, and when transportation was difficult, people in rural communities could not easily escape if they found it hard to tolerate the preaching of their own minister. So long as the system of exchanges prevailed, their misery was alleviated to the extent that they could hear a different accent of the spirit from time to time. A liberal in West Cambridge might hear Dr. Stearns of Lincoln once in awhile; a Calvinist in Lincoln might get a chance to listen to Dr. Osgood of Medford. In a time of increasing doctrinal diversity within churches of the Standing Order, pulpit exchanges served as a necessary safety valve. To restrict them, as the orthodox ministers increasingly sought to do, was inevitably to produce an explosion.

The disputes that resulted were the more rancorous because each party could claim to be adhering to long-standing tradition. The orthodox could plausibly argue that it had always been assumed that it was for the minister to determine when and with whom he would exchange, and that it had never been supposed that he was subject to instruction by the congregation in the matter. So Codman regarded it as axiomatic that he should not pledge to exchange with any man or body of men. The liberals acknowledged that the detailed arrangements necessarily were the responsibility of the minister but insisted that a party line had never been invoked, as though certain regularly ordained ministers of congregational churches, in good standing, were unworthy of Christian fellowship. Accordingly, in a given ministerial association, all members would exchange freely as occasion offered. It was within this accepted framework that the ministers themselves would make particular arrangements for a given Sunday.

The logic of the orthodox position was simple enough. Dr. Samuel Miller of New York stated it with exemplary clarity in a letter to Codman. If it is wrong to preach heterodoxy ourselves, he argued, it is wrong to be accessories to the same sin committed by others. To admit a liberal to the pulpit on exchange is to suggest that his heresies are of small consequence after all. Even if liberals avoid an explicit assertion of unsound doctrine, the effect will be to undermine evangelical truth. "They are not only betrayed by their omissions, but also, at every turn, by their phraseology and by their theological language; so that, in fact, they seldom enter our pulpits without holding out to our people false grounds of hope." Even worse, the preaching of the orthodox themselves will be corrupted. Their duty is to preach "the peculiar doctrines of the Gospel in a plain, pointed and pungent manner." If they preach to liberals on exchange, they will be tempted to temper their language—if not absolutely to omit important truths, "at least in a considerable degree to soften and polish it down, that it may be received with as little irritation as possible." But if they exchange frequently, such laxity will seem acceptable and become habitual. Twenty years of such preaching, Miller thought, would banish religion from the church.[28]

Instances may be cited earlier than the Dorchester case where ministers adopted the exclusive policy. Park Street in Boston was founded on that basis from the beginning in 1809. But the events of 1810 to 1812 forced the issue for many and resulted in increasing pressure on orthodox ministers to join the "strict party." These pressures became well-nigh irresistible in the 1820s. In Northampton in 1824, Mark Tucker was installed as minister of the First Church after the liberals had sought, and thought they had received, assurances that his policy "would satisfy the expectations of all." Once installed, Tucker made it clear that he felt no obligation to exchange and rebuffed the overtures of the liberal Reverend William B. O. Peabody of Springfield.[29] In Bedford the same year, the Reverend Samuel Stearns reversed a policy of long standing and ceased to exchange with any but evangelical preachers; the ultimate outcome was the formation of a separate Trinitarian Congregational Society.[30] In the Second Church in Waltham the first minister was the Reverend Sewall Harding, whose exclusive policy produced dissension in the parish. He was dismissed in 1825 and departed, together with a group of followers calling themselves the Trinitarian Congregational Church.[31] In Lincoln, where Charles Stearns had been minister for forty-five years, his successor in 1826 was the orthodox Elijah Demond. His exclusive practice resulted in massive desertions and the town voted to dismiss him in 1830; his supporters then organized an independent parish.[32] In Cambridge the Reverend Abiel Holmes adopted the exclusive policy in 1826, after more than thirty years of friendly intercourse with the liberals and harmony in the parish. Two years of controversy ended in his dismissal by the parish in 1829 and his departure with a majority of the members of the church.[33]

Christian Fellowship. The system of exclusion was soon extended to other acts of fellowship. When Codman was ordained in December 1808, none of the orthodox protested that both liberals and orthodox were participating in the ordaining council and the service that followed. Even Jedidiah Morse had no qualms, despite the presence, among other liberals, of Joseph Stevens Buckminster and the choice of William Ellery Channing to preach the sermon. But such comity could not last, and soon the line would be drawn on such occasions also. An early instance was the ordination in May 1809 of Ichabod Nichols as colleague of Dr. Samuel Deane at the First Church in Portland, Maine. There had been some coolness over the years between the First Church, where Deane was an Arminian, and the Second Church under Dr. Elijah Kellogg. Deacon Freeman of the First Church approached Edward Payson, Kellogg's staunchly orthodox young colleague, representing it as the wish both of the church and of Nichols that he give the Right Hand of Fellowship, "that there might be harmony between the churches." Payson replied that he could not say whether he would participate until the council had examined the candidate and it was clear "what were the sentiments he intended to inculcate." Payson, alone among the members of the council, not only refused to take part in the ordination, but publicly protested against it.[34]

Payson at least participated in the deliberations of the council, even if he refused to join in the ordination ceremony itself and to exchange with Nichols thereafter. Soon, however, some of the orthodox began to argue that merely to act in an ordaining council with a liberal is an act of fellowship, and so impermissible. This question arose in November 1813, when the church in Greenfield, seeking to ordain an orthodox minister, included the Deerfield church among those to which letters missive were sent convening an ecclesiastical council. The Deerfield church responded favorably, sending its minister, Samuel Willard, and a lay delegate.

A large minority of the council then declined to participate as long as Willard was to be one of their number. They recalled that when he had been settled in Deerfield six years earlier, the council had refused to ordain on the grounds that his views were insufficiently orthodox. Resort had then been made to a second council made up largely of liberals from the eastern part of the state. By convening a second council drawn from distant parts, the argument went, the Deerfield church had separated itself from the local body of churches, and Willard was not in regular standing with the other ministers. Is it not "subversive of the order and hazardous to the faith and purity of the Churches," the orthodox asked, to expect that such a minister "should enjoy the fellowship of those Pastors and Churches who had regularly, according to long usage and scriptural authority, determined that such candidate ought not to be ordained in a Church of their connexion?"[35]

The climax of this first phase of the Unitarian controversy came in 1815. That was when Jedidiah Morse published the pamphlet entitled *American Unitarianism*, a reprint of one chapter of Thomas Belsham's *Life of Theophilus Lindsey*, describing the spread of liberal theology in New England. Morse's purpose was to make it appear that the New England liberals were Unitarians after the manner of Belsham, who was Socinian in Christology, and that they were dishonestly concealing their true opinions. Lest anyone miss the point, the pamphlet was reviewed in the *Panoplist* by Jeremiah Evarts, who called upon the orthodox party to come out and be separate. "It is the reproach and sin of Massachusetts," he wrote, "that while all the orthodox, from Connecticut to Georgia, are unanimous in withholding communion from Unitarians, she is lagging behind, and dallying with this awful and responsible subject. It is high time for decisive action on this point."[36]

To these publications William Ellery Channing responded in his *Letter to the Rev. Samuel C. Thacher*. Samuel Worcester of the Tabernacle Church in Salem replied, and the interchange continued until 500 pages of polemics had accumulated. From these pamphlets, it appears that the most basic disagreement between the two parties was the question what the debate should be about. For the liberals it was the limits of Christian fellowship; for the orthodox it was evangelic truths as authoritatively stated in the creeds and confessions of the Church, most particularly the Westminster Confession.

From the liberal point of view, the real issue was not doctrine. The theological differences, they acknowledged, were real but of small consequence compared to the truths on which all agreed. Both liberals and orthodox believed in the unity of God, even while they differed over the doctrine of the Trinity; both regarded human beings as accountable under God's moral government, even if there was disagreement as to their natural state and their power to do the will of God; there was agreement that our hopes rest in the divine mercy, even if all were not of one mind as to the terms of salvation; all acknowledged that Jesus Christ came to deliver us from sin and its consequences, even if there was disagreement as to how this could be accomplished. The position of the liberals was that it is Christian character that makes a Christian, not subscription to creeds expressing doctrinal subtleties remote from practical living. The honor of religion, Channing declared, "can never suffer by admitting to christian fellowship men of irreproachable lives, whilst it has suffered most severely from that narrow and uncharitable spirit, which has excluded such men for imagined errours."[37]

To the orthodox, the theological differences separating the parties were not trivial. "The God whom you worship is different from ours," Samuel Worcester declared; "the Saviour whom you acknowledge is infinitely inferiour to ours; the salvation which you preach is immensely diverse from that which we preach." These differences are not merely speculative, but are "most vitally and essentially practical."[38] From this perspective, the reluctance of the liberals to preach on controverted points of doctrine, lest Christian fellowship be endangered, could only be interpreted as hypocrisy and concealment.

In the Dorchester case, when the liberals protested Codman's policy with respect to exchanges they emphasized that they had no wish "to prescribe what doctrine would be most congenial to [their] feelings to hear" but were willing to let him exercise his own opinion. But the orthodox responded: "We believe that the complaint against Mr. Codman with respect to exchanges, has been with many only *ostensible*, and, *that opposition to his religious doctrines is the radical cause of complaint and dissatisfaction.*"[39]

The first phase of the Unitarian controversy was clearly a defeat for the liberals. The hope was frustrated that—as Channing put it—the controversy would "terminate in what is infinitely more desirable than doctrinal concord, in the diffusion of a mild, candid, and charitable temper."[40] The liberals were quickly drawn into the kind of theological debate that would sharpen differences and encourage provocative language. Soon John Lowell was publishing a pamphlet entitled *Are You a Christian or a Calvinist?* In due course Channing himself would liken the orthodox view of the crucifixion to a gallows in the center of the universe, and assert that the spirit of a government "whose very acts of pardon were written in such blood, was terror, not paternal love."[41] From Dorchester to Morse's publication of *American Unitarianism* was a short step. Though some of the liberals were unwilling to admit it to their dying day, the cause of catholicity was lost and Jedidiah Morse had won.

Ecclesiastical Councils. The Cambridge Platform does not use the term *councils,* but it does contemplate a consultation of churches "if a Church be rent with divisions amongst themselves."[42] In 1695, Massachusetts law made provision for a council in case of disagreement between a church and the inhabitants of a town over the calling and settlement of a minister. In 1705, a series of proposals was submitted to the Massachusetts Ministers' Convention, recommending among other things that the "Associated Pastors, with a proper Number of Delegates from their several Churches, be formed into a standing or stated Council."[43] The proposal was never implemented in Massachusetts, though it bore fruit in Connecticut in the Saybrook Platform (1708). In Massachusetts a much less structured institution for moderating disputes developed, until by the time of the Dorchester controversy there were generally understood procedures for sending letters missive, for the appointment of delegates, for organization by the choice of a moderator and a scribe, for the presentation of testimony and the consideration of evidence, for deliberation in private, and for the preparation of the written decision, or Result. The first council meeting in Dorchester, with all its formal procedure, was the fully elaborated outcome of a long process of institutional development.

Yet both mutual councils in Dorchester failed. They neither restored harmony to a divided parish nor pointed the way to an alternative settlement that both parties would feel under obligation to accept. The final solution, by which the liberals withdrew and were compensated for their pews, was achieved by direct negotiation, not by mediation or arbitration by council.

Ecclesiastical councils could be effective only if their members were genuinely disinterested. In the beginning that could ordinarily be assured. If a minister came into conflict with his parishioners, the ministers and delegates composing the council would be concerned to restore harmony but would not have some special interest of their own to promote. As long as New England was not divided into theological factions or parties, an issue that would come before a council would be peculiar to a local situation, not a local version of a larger divisive issue.

Down to the time of the First Great Awakening, therefore, ecclesiastical councils were a plausible device for moderating conflict. As soon as New England divided into Calvinist and Arminian, it became very difficult to assemble a disinterested council in any case involving doctrinal differences. Given the improvement in transportation, it then became easy to pack a council by reaching out to secure the participation of churches likely to render a favorable verdict. The Mathers had sought to avoid such a distortion of the system by establishing stated councils, and Connecticut did so by its established system of county consociations and ministerial associations. But Massachusetts, adhering to the Cambridge Platform, was vulnerable.

As early as 1747, when the West Church in Boston sought to ordain Jonathan Mayhew, a council of representatives of nearby churches was unable to proceed when two of the local ministers boycotted the event, at least in part because of Mayhew's reputation for doctrinal irregularity. A month later, a second attempt was made. This time the Boston churches were ignored and more distant churches, carefully selected, were invited.[44] In 1785, when Aaron Bancroft was ordained in Worcester, five of the nine churches invited were from Boston, Cambridge, and Salem, and only four from Worcester County; all were predisposed in his favor.[45] In 1807, as we have seen, it took a second council to ordain Samuel Willard in Deerfield; the successful council, which endorsed him unanimously, included well-known liberals from Lancaster, Concord, Lincoln, Weston, Salem, Bridgewater, and Beverly.[46]

The resort to ecclesiastical councils to resolve disagreements was reduced to absurdity in Dorchester. When every member of both councils lined up in accordance with the expectations of those who had chosen them, the Result could hardly be accepted as disinterested advice. One consequence was that in later disputes, the failure of a mutual council was promptly followed by the convening of an *ex parte* council. Protocol prescribed that an *ex parte* council might be summoned if one of the parties unreasonably refused to join in a mutual council. Thus in Cambridge in 1829, a committee sought to arrange a mutual council to consider the grievance of the parish with respect to Dr. Abiel Holmes's exclusive policy on exchanges. The effort came to naught when the church insisted that it had to be a party to the calling of a council, while the parish responded that its dispute was only with Dr. Holmes, not with the church, hence the church had no standing in the matter. Eventually the parish summoned an *ex parte* council, which supported its position in every particular.[47] In Groton in 1826, where the question at issue was the right of the parish to provide for preaching when the minister had become incapacitated through infirmities of age, the orthodox convened a council on their own without even suggesting that the matter be referred to a mutual council.[48]

By this time, councils served only to validate actions the parties concerned were prepared to take in any event. For this limited purpose, they continued to be used both by the liberals and by the orthodox as a public recognition of ordinations. On the liberal side, one last attempt to use a council for the reconciliation of

105

differences came in 1840, when the Proprietors of the Hollis Street Church sought to dismiss the Reverend John Pierpont. A mutual council struggled conscientiously to sort out the issues and reached the conclusion that adequate grounds to require his dismissal had not been offered. But the Proprietors voted not to accept the Result and urged Pierpont "to acquiesce in the dissolution of the connexion between himself and this Society."[49] The whole proceedings were then subjected to the bitter sarcasm of Theodore Parker. After that experience, no one was tempted to go that route again.

Church and Parish. In Dorchester, a majority of the church consistently supported Codman. Almost as consistently, his opponents were in the majority at parish meetings. A comparable divergence between church and parish appeared in controversies elsewhere, the most widely discussed cases being Princeton in 1817, Dedham in 1818 to 1820, Cambridge in 1827 to 1829, and Brookfield in 1829 to 1831. This recurrent discord between churches and parishes is a clear indication of a failure of long-established institutions and suggests that the Standing Order of the churches was no longer functional. Originally, in the seventeenth century, when the franchise was restricted to members in full communion of one of the particular churches, no such discord would be likely to arise. By the end of the century, the franchise had been broadened, so that Baptists or Quakers or members of the Church of England, as well as the religiously apathetic, might be voting in town meetings on ecclesiastical affairs.

In 1692, the General Court passed a law requiring the inhabitants of each town to provide "an able, learned orthodox minister or ministers, of good conversation, to dispense the Word of God to them; which minister or ministers shall be suitably encouraged and sufficiently supported and maintained by the inhabitants of the town." The minister entitled to public support was to be chosen "by the major part of the inhabitants . . . at a town meeting duly warned for that purpose," and he was to be regarded as "the minister of such town." Similar provisions were made in the same law for the employment of schoolmasters.[50]

It may seem anomalous that a law for the settlement of ministers should make no reference to churches. The implication is that ministers, like schoolmasters, were performing a public function, distinct from their ecclesiastical role, and that it was as the minister of the town, not as the minister of the church, that he was to be supported by taxes. Within the church, he administered the ordinance of baptism and communion and participated in the discipline of church members. In the community at large, he was concerned to transmit, clarify, refine, and advance the values on which civilized existence in this life was deemed possible. All the inhabitants of a town benefited from this service—hence the appropriateness of taxing all for the support of public worship and of providing that those who were taxed should be the ones to choose the town minister.

It was taken for granted that the minister of the gathered church in the town would also be the "minister of such town." Yet congregational polity as stated in the Cambridge Platform made it clear that a gathered church chooses its own minister. So a clarifying amendment was made the following year to specify that the initiative in the choice of a minister would rest with the church, which would then refer its choice to the town for concurrence and legal settlement. But if there was no gathered church, as in a new town just settled, the town meeting would nevertheless have full authority to "choose and call an orthodox, learned and pious person to dispense the word of God unto them."[51]

These arrangements presupposed a religiously homogeneous population in which the ministers could perform acceptably two different roles: one ecclesiastical, the other civic. Adjustments had to be made when minority religious groups became large enough to protest that they were being unfairly assessed for the support of a town minister of a different persuasion. In 1727, exemption was granted to the Episcopalians, and the following year to the Quakers and Baptists. The Great Awakening complicated the situation further, as "separate" congregational churches made their appearance and conflict arose between Calvinist and Arminian within the Standing Order. It became increasingly difficult to state the binding consensus uniting the social order in traditional theological language. The Calvinists believed firmly that the social order would collapse unless evangelical religion prevailed; the liberals insisted otherwise. An increasingly pluralistic society meant that the Standing Order, which existed to promote the binding ties of cohesive sentiment, was obsolescent.

The Massachusetts Constitution of 1780 met this problem by distinguishing the civic role of the minister from the ecclesiastical role and making "civic religion" the common responsibility of the ministers of all religious groups. The importance of public worship to promote "the happiness of a people, and the good order and preservation of civil government" was restated. No mention was made of "ministers"; they were identified rather as "public teachers of piety, religion and morality," who might be of any sect or denomination. The constitution acknowledged that the support of public teachers would continue to be by towns or territorial parishes, as well as by dissenting religious societies. It followed appropriately that those who were assessed for public worship should "have the exclusive right of electing their public teachers, and of contracting with them for their support and maintenance."[52]

By logical extension, it could be argued that the town that chooses a minister to be its public teacher also has the right to dismiss him. This issue arose in 1803 in the Berkshire town of Tyringham. Joseph Avery had been settled there in 1788. In May 1803, the town meeting voted to consider him no longer the minister of Tyringham. Avery sued for his salary on the grounds that his settlement was for life; the town replied that the settlement was for no certain time and should therefore be interpreted according to the law governing civil contracts. That would mean that when no fixed period is agreed upon, "the law construes it to be a contract determinable at the will of either party, or, at the most, hiring for a year."

Chief Justice Theophilus Parsons's decision acknowledged that the settlement of ministers had always been understood to be for life. It followed that he might not be removed at the pleasure of the town, but only for cause. A minister guilty of immoral conduct or negligence in performing parochial duties would forfeit his position. The town would be justified in dismissing him; if he did not acquiesce, his recourse would be to sue for his salary, whereupon "the charges made by the town, as creating a forfeiture, are questions of fact properly to be submitted to the jury." Judgment in Avery's case was entered for him, since the town had voted to dismiss as a naked act of will, not on the basis of charges preferred. But the decision in *Avery v. Tyringham* indicated that the relationship between a public teacher of religion and the town was independent of the relationship between a minister and his church. If a town disapproved the choice of a church as the minister, and the church refused to propose another candidate,

> or the town, for any cause, shall abandon the ancient usages of the country in settling a minister, it may, without or against the consent of the church, elect a public teacher, and contract to support him. And such teacher will have a legal right to the benefit of the contract, although he cannot be considered as the settled minister of the gospel, agreeably to the usages and practice of the Congregational churches in the state.[53]

When the Second Parish in Dorchester voted to dismiss Codman and to deny him the use of the meetinghouse, which belonged to the parish and not to the church, the decision in *Avery v. Tyringham* was cited as the legal basis for the action. A list of twelve charges was prepared, and the parish was ready to defend its position on that basis if Codman brought suit against it. Instead the compromise settlement was reached, by which Codman's friends bought the pews of his opponents and they withdrew.

Although a legal basis existed for a recognition of the separate and independent existence of church and parish, each with its own rights and privileges, it was hard for many people to understand what was happening. Both liberals and orthodox within the Standing Order had been so accustomed to a connection between church and parish that they assumed it was necessary and indissoluble, and that the minister of the church must necessarily be the public teacher also. The liberals thought the way out was for the minister to be more inclusive in his preaching, avoiding divisive doctrinal issues, seeking consensus at a more basic level of agreement. The orthodox likewise sought agreement but thought to achieve it by exscinding those who held Arminian, Socinian, or deistic views, so that evangelical Christianity might prevail universally.

Neither tactic worked. Eventually it was recognized that the kind of religious unity that had once prevailed was no longer possible. *Avery* v. *Tyringham* was pointing the way out; unfortunately that path was not followed. Instead the court stumbled into *Baker* v. *Fales*, which was not only bad law based on a misreading of history, but an unrealistic solution to the problem of conflict between orthodox majorities in churches and liberal majorities in parishes. It made a difficult situation much worse. In Dorchester, at least, the contending parties were finally persuaded to compromise.

The decision of any one evangelical minister not to exchange with a liberal neighbor on a given Sunday was a trivial matter; the decision of many such ministers not to exchange at all drastically changed a familiar institution. The failure of two ecclesiastical councils to restore harmony in Dorchester did not discredit the institution in any formally recognized way; but its credibility was undercut nonetheless. The "public teacher of piety, religion and morality" found his influence in the whole community shrinking to the boundaries of his own church; the Standing Order was slowly disintegrating long before its remnants were abandoned in 1833. New enterprises were begun, such as magazines and newspapers, tract and missionary societies, theological seminaries; but it was only by a gradual process that the rival groups developed a full range of denominational organizations to take the place of the Standing Order with its lost dream of a united community serving God through an ordered society. The separation of the two denominations was a process, not an event. It was nonetheless a radical dissolution and reconstruction of social institutions, which took place over a relatively brief span of years.

The Dedham Case Revisited

In 1888, when the First Church in Dedham cel-
ebrated its 250th anniversary, the main address was a historical
survey of the relationship between church and parish in Massachusetts by the Reverend George E. Ellis. A scholar by temperament, Ellis had always been interested in historical studies, and
after retiring at the age of fifty-five as minister of the Unitarian
church in Charlestown he devoted the rest of his life to historical
and antiquarian interests. At the time of his invitation to speak at
the celebration in Dedham, he was the president of the Massachusetts Historical Society, a distinction that perhaps meant more to
him than any other that he enjoyed, more indeed than his long
ministry in Charlestown.

The invitation to Ellis came on behalf of both branches of the
Dedham church. He was reluctant to accept at first, well aware
that scars remained from the wounds of the old controversy of
seventy years earlier. One could hardly deliver a historical address
for the Dedham church—or churches—and say nothing about the
ordination of Alvan Lamson in 1818 and the legal decision in the
case of *Baker* v. *Fales* that followed. Ellis procrastinated, but after
two months he finally accepted, resolved to deal "with the subject
in a calm and impartial spirit as one of historical review and
retrospect."[1]

Even so, Ellis tiptoed very gently around the touchy issues. His
address is some thirty-seven pages long; not until page twenty-
seven did he get to the Dedham church, to which he devoted just
four pages. He accorded the case of *Baker* v. *Fales* four paragraphs,

one stating the issues being litigated, one quoting the decision, and two commenting on the reaction in the community. There was no analysis of the reasoning of Chief Justice Isaac Parker, who wrote the decision, or of the adequacy of his historical argument. Ellis acknowledged that the decision had been criticized on legal grounds when it was handed down. But those who are not lawyers, he suggested, should be "diffident about any questioning or discussing of it."[2] His language implies that he had doubts about it but that he did not want to run the risk, by acknowledging them, of reopening old sores and arousing old animosities.

It would appear that no one in the century since Ellis spoke has done, at least in print, what he conspicuously avoided doing and given the decision the scrutiny it deserved, both from a historical and a legal point of view. Professor Leonard Levy has perhaps come closest to it, in a book dealing with Lemuel Shaw, who became chief justice of the Massachusetts Supreme Judicial Court in 1830 on the death of Chief Justice Parker. Shaw wrote the decision in a later case very similar to the Dedham one and resolved in the same way. Of both cases, Professor Levy has remarked: "They do not withstand close legal scrutiny."[3] But the hesitations of Ellis have commonly prevailed, as when Dean Fenn said of the decision: "It would be presumptuous for a layman, whether Unitarian or Orthodox, to question it."[4]

The Dedham case served as precedent in the settlement of similar disputes in other towns and parishes, and so it was not of merely local concern. It exacerbated rivalries and tensions already existing between the liberals and the orthodox, and much energy was devoted to arguing the rights and wrongs of conflicting claims. Perhaps it is only fair to indicate at the outset where a fresh analysis seems to come out. The liberals had an excellent case up to a point; perhaps we might say they were half right. That of course suggests they were half wrong. The orthodox had a strong case so far as their historical analysis of the concept of the church in New England congregationalism is concerned. Where they went astray was in their refusal to acknowledge that times had changed, and that prerogatives the church once enjoyed could no longer be maintained, either legally or as a practical solution of the dispute. As for the decision of the Court, it was completely wrong and so had mischievous consequences.

For the lack of informed scrutiny, recent references to the Dedham case in accounts of the Unitarian controversy have often misunderstood the legal issues and misrepresented the decision. The commonest of these inaccuracies is that control of church property was given to the parish. One historian summarizes thus: "an orthodox majority of church members might be overruled in questions affecting church property by the 'society' or parish, in which the actual communicants might be and frequently were in the minority."[5] Another states that "church property was vested in the voters of the parish rather than in the communicants."[6] The most recent and widely used general history of American religion states that "the larger parish or religious society had the legal power to call a minister and retain control of the property, even if a majority of the communicant members of the church were opposed."[7]

That, emphatically, is not the way the decision reads. No one at the time ever questioned that church property—records, communion silver, funds held by the deacons—belonged to the church. The issue was a different one. Which of two bodies both claiming to be the First Church in Dedham was entitled to the claim? Hence, which of two groups of men both claiming to be the deacons of the First Church was the rightful custodian of the property of the church?

First we must remind ourselves of the sequence of events leading up to the court decision and become aware of some of the theological and political crosscurrents that already divided the community. In February 1818, the Reverend Joshua Bates was dismissed from his ministry in Dedham at his own request in order to accept the presidency of Middlebury College. He preached his last sermon on February 15, 1818. It was filled with expressions of warm affection for his flock and gratitude for its confidence and attachment.[8] That is the kind of sermon one expects on such an occasion and usually gets. There is no suggestion of any alienation, however slight, between him and his congregation. It would appear, however, that some members of the parish were restive. Although there had been no overt movement among the disaffected to terminate his ministry, there were those who were very glad to see him go when he decided that it was his duty to leave his dearly beloved flock and accept the challenge of new responsibilities.

Two distinct reasons for dissatisfaction with Bates had developed, one of them theological, the other political. With respect to the first of these, the problem was that over the course of a ministry of fifteen years, Bates had come to believe that evangelical Christians should not maintain fellowship with the liberal Christians of the day. At the time of his ordination, no division as yet existed along these lines in the churches of the Standing Order, even though theological differences had been developing for two generations. It was still possible for orthodox ministers to exchange pulpits with liberals and to participate in acts of fellowship, such as ordinations. The practice in the Dedham church had been inclusive under the ministry of Bates's predecessor, the Reverend Jason Haven. The church covenant of 1793 prescribed no theological test for admission to communion but was rather a commitment "to live together as a band of Christian brethren; to give and receive counsel and reproof with meekness and candor; and submit with a Christian temper to the discipline which the Gospel authorizes the church to administer; and diligently to seek after the will of God, and carefully endeavor to obey all his commands." Haven, himself, had on one occasion asserted that a disposition prevailed in the parish "to permit everyone freely to enjoy the right of his private opinion provided he doth not break in upon the rights of others."[9]

There must have been underlying uneasiness in the parish, however, for on Haven's death an attempt was made to limit his successor's term instead of making the customary settlement for life. Choleric Dr. Nathaniel Ames reported in his journal: "we wanted mutual freedom to go to worship, unhandcuffed, not to be obliged to support a preacher after he grows disgustful, unable, or too lazy or negligent to perform his duty."[10] Nevertheless, when Bates was ordained in 1803 and granted a comfortable settlement, it was generally assumed that his ministry would continue the inclusive spirit that had prevailed under Haven. Dr. Lamson, writing 1839, stated that "it was the common impression . . . that in his views of christian doctrine he belonged to what was called the moderate, or rational school, and that in his measures and general tone of preaching, he would not appear in the character of an innovator."[11] There were liberal Christians among Bates's associates with whom he was on friendly terms. Henry Ware, then minister in Hingham, had helped him prepare for college. Among his classmates were Joseph Stevens Buckminster, soon to become minister of the Brattle Street Church in Boston; Charles Lowell, whom the West Church ordained in 1806; and Lemuel Shaw, from 1830 to 1860 chief justice of the Massachusetts Supreme Court. The Reverend Jacob Flint, under whose ministrations the Cohasset church became Unitarian, preached his ordination sermon.

But Bates had studied theology with the Reverend Jonathan French, the orthodox minister in Andover, soon to be involved in the founding of the Andover Theological Seminary to counteract liberal tendencies at Harvard. When Henry Ware was elected Hollis Professor of Divinity at Harvard in 1805, the distinction between moderate Calvinists and liberal Christians widened into an open breach. Bates was then clearly identified with the orthodox party, which, at the urging of the Reverend Jedidiah Morse of Charlestown, began to insist that the liberals had so far departed from the faith once delivered to the saints that they should be excluded from Christian fellowship.[12]

This meant specifically that orthodox ministers should refuse to exchange pulpits with those who did not agree with them on adherence to the Calvinism of the Westminster Confession. Pulpit exchanges had long been a tradition, and surviving preaching records indicate that it was common for a minister to be in his own pulpit for only about half the time. Ministers were thus relieved of the burden of preparing two sermons each week, for the morning and afternoon services on Sunday, while their congregations had the opportunity to hear other voices from the pulpit. If one did not like one's own minister or disagreed with his doctrine, this system had much to commend it. At a time when travel was difficult, and lifetime pastorates were not uncommon, the system of exchanges served as a sort of safety valve for the disaffected. The misery of a liberal parishioner whose minister's sermons were persistently and pungently orthodox, or of an evangelical whose minister programmatically refused to discuss the peculiar doctrines of the Reformed theology, would be alleviated to some extent when a minister of a different persuasion occupied the pulpit.

Whatever Bates's policy on exchanges may have been at the time he was ordained, during the course of his ministry he adopted the exclusive system. He was identified with it very conspicuously during a major controversy in the Second Parish in Dorchester in 1811. That parish was a mixed one, including both liberals and orthodox. When the Reverend John Codman was installed in 1808, the liberals in the congregation thought he had given assurances that his policy would be an inclusive one. When that proved not to be the case, the liberals felt they had been misled and sought to dismiss him. Bates was one of those who came to his defense; and when the dispute came before an ecclesiastical council, Codman asked Bates to serve as his advocate. Dedham was well represented at the council, since the Honorable Samuel Dexter, a son of Dedham, was one of the advocates on the other side.[13]

Bates's identification with what was sometimes called the "strict party" did not produce a comparable controversy in Dedham, but there was a continuing undercurrent of dissatisfaction. "Certain it is," wrote Dr. Lamson, "that he gradually withdrew from ministerial intercourse and exchanges with a portion of the clergy, whom the people had been accustomed, with pleasure, to hear in this place, and who belonged to the liberal party, as it was then termed; while the young gentlemen from a Theological Seminary in a neighboring County, not always as prudent as the Pastor himself, were frequently introduced into the pulpit."[14] The refusal of evangelicals to exchange pulpits with liberals was repeatedly the precipitating factor in the disputes that led to schisms in particular churches. Historians of the Unitarian controversy have almost without exception defined it in theological terms, as the difference between Trinitarian Calvinism and Unitarian liberalism. It became that before the controversy had run its course; but in the first decade, from 1805 to 1815, it was Christian fellowship, not theology, that was the core of the debate. The problem that the Dedham parish had with Bates was far from unique; it could be matched in dozens of other congregations.

If the policy of exclusion, and the theological differences that occasioned it, were reasons for dissatisfaction with Bates, political differences made the situation worse. In the party disputes between Federalists and Republicans, Dedham was a Republican stronghold. Erastus Worthington estimated that the town was Republican by a margin of three to one.[15] But Bates was a Federalist, and at times a conspicuously aggressive one.

As long as Thomas Jefferson was president, religious issues could not be kept out of party politics. Jefferson was a very private person, so far as his own religious beliefs were concerned; and to this day it is difficult to categorize him precisely. We know that from time to time he attended the services conducted in Philadelphia by Joseph Priestley; but we also know that, unlike Priestley, in his interpretation of the life and mission of Jesus he rejected completely the miracles described in the Gospels. It is obvious that he was not an evangelical Christian; it is less clear that he should be identified with the Unitarians, even though he spoke well of them on occasion. He was repeatedly attacked for his presumed religious views, accused of being an unbeliever, an infidel, a denier of Christianity as divinely revealed truth. These were damaging accusations in the early nineteenth century. Such opinions were considered a threat to civil society, as the French Revolution had clearly demonstrated, with its attempt to establish a religion of reason supplanting Christianity, followed by the Reign of Terror.

When Federalist ministers condemned infidelity from the pulpit, their defense of Christianity easily turned into an attack on their political opponents. Bates did not resist the temptation.

According to Erastus Worthington, he "deemed it his duty to proclaim aloud his fears and apprehensions from the influence of infidelity." Hence in his mind, his predominantly Republican congregation included many who were at best doubtful Christians. "His frequent and explicit definition of a true Christian," Worthington went on to say, "when applied by his hearers to themselves, so clearly excluded them, that a large portion of the society saw that their religious instructor viewed them in no other light than that of unworthy pretenders to the christian name."[16] Supporters of Thomas Jefferson did not relish paying taxes for the privilege of hearing Federalist politics from the pulpit any more than liberal Christians enjoyed exclusion from fellowship.

Bates thus left behind a divided congregation. The orthodox faction had welcomed his evangelical preaching and doubtless approved his exclusive policy. The members of the church, as distinguished from the parish, were predominantly of this sort, especially if one includes the women, who did not vote in church meeting. The church, it should be remembered, was a covenanted body of those admitted to the communion table. In the early decades of Puritan New England, admission to church membership, with the privilege of approaching the Lord's Table, required a confession of religious experience that would indicate that the candidate was probably one whom God had elected and predestinated to eternal salvation. The requirements had lost some of their original rigor with the passage of time, but they were still predicated on a distinction between the regenerate and the unregenerate derived from the Reformed theology. Liberals often found themselves excluded from the communion table, whereas the church was made up for the most part of theological conservatives, comfortable with evangelical doctrine and piety.

The parish, on the other hand, was dominated by those who were critical of Bates. It included all the male inhabitants of the town, excepting only those who had specifically signed off to join some recognized dissenting group, such as the Episcopalians. One hesitates to say they were all religious liberals, since the opposition to Bates must have included political opponents and the religiously apathetic as well as those aroused chiefly by his orthodox doctrine and the policy of exclusion. They were taxed for the support of public worship in the belief that the benign influences of Christianity, more particularly Protestant Christianity, were essential to the well-being of society here and now, in this world. Public worship was an affirmation of a kind of civic religion, common to all citizens, of whatever denomination or theological persuasion. But tax money was not used for the distinctive purposes of the church, which was concerned with the immortal souls of its members, and so administered the sacraments of baptism and communion. Church and parish in Dedham, as generally in Massachusetts communities, were separate organizations, with different purposes and different qualifications for membership.

It had long been the practice to call upon the minister of the church also to be the "public teacher of piety, religion and morality" for the town or parish, as the Massachusetts Constitution of 1780 termed the civic office. He was supported by assessments on all the inhabitants, not because he was the minister of the church, but because he was thought to be performing a public function for the common good. Thus the minister had two roles to play, and two constituencies to satisfy. In earlier times, when the inhabitants of Dedham shared a common religious culture, that had been possible. Bates's ministry to a community divided on many issues, often bitterly so, made it clear that this was no longer the case.[17]

The leaders of the parish were resolved that Bates's successor as its public teacher should be cut from different cloth. They had heard enough preaching from Andover students to know they wanted no more of it, so they turned to the theological institution at Cambridge, which we now know as the Harvard Divinity School. Three men supplied the pulpit as candidates, but Alvan Lamson seems to have been the only one seriously considered.[18] Twenty-five years of age, he was a graduate of Harvard College in 1814 and of the divinity school in 1817. As might have been expected, he failed to please the orthodox, who found him wanting in "spirituality and knowledge of the scriptures," and manifesting little of "that which fixes the attention and reaches the heart." They accused him of being a puppet of the parish committee, which was busy canvassing the parish in support of his candidacy.[19]

On July 13, 1818, a parish meeting authorized the employment of Lamson as a candidate for an additional eight sabbaths, despite protests from the orthodox that "they were desirous to hear some other candidate, which they earnestly requested they might be indulged in."[20] Meetings of both church and parish were held at the end of August. The church met first, in accordance with tradition, and it rejected Lamson by a vote of 17 to 15. One elderly gentleman who was hard of hearing later protested that he had misunderstood, when the question was called, and that he had really intended to vote against Lamson; so it would appear that of the thirty-eight voting members, fourteen were for Lamson, eighteen against, and six absent. The parish nevertheless met and chose Lamson to be its public teacher by a vote of 81 to 44. Later apologists for the parish often made a point of the fact that Lamson's supporters were not only a strong majority in numbers, but also represented four-fifths of the taxable property of the town.[21]

The size of the opposition was a matter of concern to Lamson, and his immediate reaction seems to have been to decline; but the chairman of the parish committee, Jabez Chickering, persuaded him not to do so. The parish next voted to call an ecclesiastical council with a view of ordaining him. Letters missive went out to fifteen churches, requesting their assistance "in the ordination of Mr. Lamson, as a Gospel Minister over the Church and Society constituting said Parish."[22] Thirteen churches responded by sending their ministers, each accompanied by a lay delegate. Some of the most prominent of the local clergy came, among them President John T. Kirkland and Professor Henry Ware of Harvard; William Ellery Channing of the Federal Street Church, with Judge John Davis as delegate; Charles Lowell of the West Church in Boston; and James Walker of Charlestown, later to become Alford professor and then president of Harvard.

The council convened in Dedham at nine o'clock on the morning of October 28, 1818.[23] It chose the Reverend John Reed of Bridgewater as moderator and the Reverend Ralph Sanger of Dover as scribe. It received a report of the action of the parish in calling Lamson, followed in turn by a long and carefully prepared protest from the orthodox, read by Judge Samuel Haven. The main thrust of the protest was that, since the church is a religious community bound by the laws of Christ's kingdom, it must be free to exercise the rights that Christ has conferred. Preeminent among them is "the right and duty of a Christian Church to elect its own pastor." A council may not ordain a gospel minister over a church without its consent.

Furthermore, the practice in New England had always been for the church to act first in the choice of a minister, and then to present its choice to the parish for settlement. The ordination that follows would be an ecclesiastical ceremony, not a secular one, and an ordaining council is summoned by letters missive from a church to other churches, not by secular authority. For the parish, which is a creation of the Commonwealth, to summon an ecclesiastical council to ordain Lamson "as a gospel Minister over the Church and Society" is to confuse ecclesiastical and secular authority and violate the rights of the church. Pending a permanent settlement, to be sure, a parish might employ a preacher from time to time to perform the duties of a public teacher by preaching on Sunday. But he could not be regarded as the gospel minister of the church, with authority to administer the sacraments or share in the discipline of church members.

The reading of the protest must have taken well over an hour. When it was concluded, the chairman of the parish committee backed away from the wording of the letters missive to ordain the candidate "over the Church and Society" and stated that the committee "did not request to have Mr. Lamson ordained over the church."[24] The parish committee nevertheless presented papers purporting to show that if all who communicated regularly with the church had voted, there would have been a majority for Lamson. The council received this assertion with some reluctance, evidently not relishing the notion of an investigation into the views and membership status of those claimed as now making up a majority of the church. Instead it concentrated on examining the qualifications of the candidate.

The council spent the rest of the day in deliberation and finally announced that it would proceed to the ordination the following day, October 29. The report, or "Result," was prepared by William Ellery Channing; was approved by the council when it reconvened in the morning, and was read at the public meeting for the ordination.[25] It fully accepted the argument of the orthodox protest that a minister may not be set over a church without its consent. At the same time the council felt bound to consider the rights and interests of the whole parish, and its members were of the clear opinion "that circumstances may exist, in which a minister may be ordained over a parish without the concurrence of the church connected with it."[26] The parish, furthermore, was under legal obligation to support a public teacher and was exposed to penalty if it failed to do so.

Although the traditional practice of initial choice by the church and settlement by the parish is "in the main wise and beneficial," the Result continued, that procedure is not always possible under changed circumstances and may be dispensed with "when, after serious deliberation, we are persuaded, that adherence to it will create or increase division, or postpone indefinitely the settlement of a christian minister."

> In such a case, we must consult a higher rule, the general spirit of the gospel, and not expose to imminent peril, the best interests of a society, through regard to a usage, which may often operate injuriously in periods like the present, when difference of religious opinion is widely extended, and when the number of church members often bears a small proportion to the whole society.

In short, while the council agreed that concurrence of church and parish is most desirable, they believe that each of these bodies has a right to elect a pastor for itself, when it shall be satisfied that its own welfare and the general interests of religion require the measure; this right being secured to the church by the essential principles of congregational polity, and to the parish by the constitution and laws of the commonwealth, as well as by the free principles of the same polity, and of the gospel of Christ.

The council expressed sorrow over the lack of unanimity but concluded that no other choice was likely to prove any more acceptable. It urged a spirit of conciliation, and Dr. Henry Ware struck the same note in his ordination sermon.[27]

This would have been a good place for the dispute to end. Inasmuch as the orthodox were unwilling to accept Lamson, the Result of the council was opening the way to a separation, each party left free to control its own affairs. The recommendation was not a compromise solution in the interests of harmony; it was a proper interpretation both of the law and of congregational practise. There were ample grounds, legal as well as ecclesiastical, for a separation between church and parish that would have allowed each to maintain its own identity. Once there had been a mutually beneficial relationship between the two; now each faction was claiming that its own organization was the dominant partner.

Yet the traditional connection between church and parish was so firmly fixed in people's minds that few on either side could entertain the notion that any other relationship was possible. Besides, there must have been emotional attachments that would have had to be broken, and that process is never easy. Members of the orthodox group would have felt obliged to leave a meeting-house to which they were endeared by many associations, and in which they felt they had a financial stake. The liberals would have had to gather a new church within the parish and relinquish a claim to the deacons' funds, which in some years had provided an important part of the salary of the minister. In the Dorchester controversy, six years earlier, in an even more bitterly divided congregation, the two factions reached an understanding with respect to the property and so were able to agree to an amicable separation. That should have happened in Dedham.

Instead, Deacon Joseph Swan walked out of the ordination service, followed by his father-in-law, Deacon Samuel Fales, and a number of others of the orthodox party. Judge Haven promptly assailed the legitimacy of the ordination council and attacked its explanation of its decision. "This document and the letter missive which gave rise to it should be preserved as curiosities connected with our ecclesiastical history," he declared. Just because of the prominence of those responsible for it, "it calls more loudly for an exposition of every deviation from principle." His position was simple. The initiative in calling a minister belongs with a church. The parish is to wait until the church presents its chosen candidate for settlement. If the parish does not assent, a second choice may be made, and so on until agreement is finally reached. It was improper for an ecclesiastical council to assemble at the call of the parish; Lamson's ordination was irregular and should not be recognized by other Christian churches. "Here is a young man," Haven expostulated, "who has endeavoured to acquire dominion over one of the congregational churches against her consent . . . and behold! under these circumstances, a dozen of her sister churches are made to say to him, we esteem, and love, and *embrace* you in this very act! To show our *fellowship* for this sister, we take to our arms her despoiler!!!"[28]

Seeking further guidance, members of the church voted to summon an ecclesiastical council to meet on November 18. Letters missive went out to all the churches whose ministers were members of the local ministerial association except those who had participated in the ordination council. Meanwhile the liberals, noting that some of those who had previously voted against Lamson were now inclined to support him, believed that a majority of the church members were now ready to accept him in the interest of conciliation. On Sunday, November 15, a meeting of the church members chose Lamson as minister, twenty-one votes being cast in his favor, and it admitted him to membership by an even larger margin. Those still opposed to Lamson boycotted this meeting and declared it irregular and invalid. But the liberals could now assert that Lamson was the minister in proper standing of both parish and church.[29]

The council convened by the orthodox was dominated by their sympathizers, but it did include such liberals as Dr. Porter of Roxbury, Dr. Harris of Dorchester, and the Reverend John Pierce of Brookline. Not surprisingly, it was unable to come to a unanimous decision. It expressed disapproval in rather restrained language of the procedure of the parish in departing from custom in its choice of a public teacher, though some of the members would have preferred stronger words of condemnation. It concluded rather lamely with an injunction to foster "a spirit of candour and benevolence, of meekness and condescension." Nevertheless, eight members voted against approval of the Result, "some for one reason, and some for another."[30]

Meekness, benevolence, and a spirit of conciliation were not in the air. For the orthodox, Judge Haven prepared an extended Statement of the Proceedings in the First Church and Parish in Dedham, Respecting the Settlement of a Minister, published as a book of 102 pages. It incorporated the full text of the Protest and Remonstrance Judge Haven had presented to the ordination council as well as the texts of the Results of both councils. These were accompanied by extensive historical analysis, which was ably done, but which was uncompromising in its insistence on the traditional initiative of the church in calling a minister, and on the definition of councils as ecclesiastical, not secular, bodies. In his comment on recent events, Haven lost no opportunity to refer to his opponents in derogatory and even insulting language. Their introduction of Lamson to the community was "both disgusting and ridiculous." They had deliberately aroused prejudice and passion; they were guilty of "depreciating misrepresentations" of Joshua Bates, the late pastor; the meeting of July 13, which had extended the period of Lamson's candidacy, was "a farce," marked by "management, intrigue, and deceit"; the agitation over the proceedings of the parish council was the direct cause of the death of Deacon Joseph Swan on November 13; the church meeting on

November 15 that admitted Lamson to membership was a "shocking profanation" exhibiting "scenes of wickedness" characterized by "indecency and barbarity." If the orthodox had any real hope of recovering the church's privileged position, such language was not the way to go about it.[31]

Meanwhile, Deacon Fales and other orthodox members of the church had withdrawn from public worship with the parish. They did not relinquish their claim to be a majority of the church on the basis of the church meeting of August 31, which had rejected Lamson by a vote of 17 to 15. They condemned as invalid and irregular the meeting of November 15, which was the basis for the counterclaim by the liberals, when a majority of the church members had apparently voted for Lamson. There were now two claimants to the church records, the communion silver, and the church funds. Deacon Fales had these in his possession, since the deacons were by law a body corporate to hold title to property on behalf of the church. Title to the meetinghouse was not in question, because that was clearly parish and not church property.

On March 15, 1819, Deacon Jonathan Richards, who had initially not gone with the orthodox group, resigned his office. The church of the liberal faction then voted to dismiss Deacon Fales from office, and to elect two new deacons, Eliphalet Baker and Luther Richards. A few weeks later, the new deacons sued for possession of the church records and other property. After a preliminary legal skirmish, which need not concern us, the matter came to trial before Judge Samuel S. Wilde in the April term of 1820. On referral to the full Supreme Judicial Court at the October term, 1820, the case was argued for the plaintiffs by Daniel Davis, Solicitor General of the Commonwealth, and by Daniel Webster for the defendants. The decision, by Chief Justice Parker, was handed down in February 1821.[32]

The decision would necessarily turn on whether Baker and Richards were the deacons of the church, rather than Fales; and that in turn would depend on a determination of which of two rival bodies was the true First Church. One might have expected the issue to involve a judicial determination of the legality of the meeting of November 15 at which Lamson was chosen minister of the church. If that was a legal meeting, the church controlled by the liberals was a majority and was the true First Church, and its subsequent election of Baker and Richards as deacons made them properly the custodians of the property. Yet it is a puzzling fact that the plaintiffs did not advance this claim. Lawyers ordinarily have no hesitation in developing more than one line of argument, so that if one fails another may be successful. Because counsel for the plaintiffs did not follow this very obvious course, it is hard to avoid the conclusion that they believed the action of that church meeting to be on shaky ground. The explanation Lamson gave twenty years later is hardly persuasive:

> The portion of the church which remained in connexion with the Parish, or their legal advisors, did not consider it as material, in the pending controversy, on which side the majority was. . . .they wished to present the case in its simplest form, and unencumbered by any extraneous questions. They wished to appeal to first principles. They believed that according to these principles the right was with them. . . .[33]

The alternative line of argument, the one Chief Justice Parker actually adopted, was that the connection between the First Parish and the First Church was permanent and indissoluble. Those who left the church associated with the parish forfeited their membership. Even if a majority left in a body, they had no claim to be regarded as the original church. The continuity rested with the minority that maintained its traditional relationship with the parish. If all the members departed, it would be "competent to the members of the parish to institute a new church . . . and this new church would succeed to all the rights of the old, in relation to the parish." In short: "those who withdraw from the [parish] cease to be members of that particular church, and the remaining members continue to be the identical church."[34]

Parker viewed the church as an appendage of the parish, rather than a separate partner in the common enterprise of public worship. To support his conclusion, he first examined the record of grants and bequests made to the church to see if there was any designation of a trust or limitations as to use. One of them, made in 1660, he used as the model for all. It granted land to the church in Dedham, "and *to the use thereof forever* ... being so granted for the use and accommodation of a *teaching church* officer."[35] In the language of seventeenth-century New England, this meant the ordained minister of the church. Parker understood this grant as establishing a trust, and he gave the other grants the same construction, even though no limitation as to use by the church was stipulated. Who, then was the *cestui que trust,* or beneficiary? So far as the grant of 1660 goes, it would plausibly be the "teaching church officer," or minister of the church. But taking all the grants together, Parker subtly broadened the terms by adding language of his own. The words "to the use of the church" meant to him that "the lands, or the proceeds, were to be used for religious purposes; the support of a minister, building or repairing the meeting house, or some other object connected with, and promotive of, the public worship of God"[36]

This was simply legal sleight of hand. It showed no awareness that in New England, both church and parish were concerned for religion, but in different ways, for different purposes, each using means appropriate to its distinctive nature. The church was concerned with the eternal souls of men and women and their translation to the bliss of heaven; for this purpose its membership was restricted to the regenerate, who chose ministers to guide them in their quest, to administer the sacraments, and when necessary to lead in the discipline of church members. The parish was concerned with the behavior in this life of all the inhabitants, regenerate and unregenerate alike, since religious influences promote morality and help to maintain a tolerable civilized community; to this end, the town or parish provided a meeting house and settled a public teacher of morality. Preaching subserved both objectives, and so both church and parish cooperated in the support of public worship. But it hardly follows, as Parker would have it, that "when the donation is to the church, no trust or use being expressed, and no other implied from the nature of the property, the parish must be the *cestui que trust*." By using the general term *religion* to cover both experiential religion, which was at the heart of the church community, and civic religion, which was the concern of the parish, Parker had transformed unrestricted grants to the former into a trust for the benefit of the latter.[37]

Up to this point, Parker had accepted for purposes of argument that when these grants were made "there was a body of men in *Dedham*, known by the name of the *Dedham Church;* distinct from the *society* of Christians usually worshipping together in that town." The next stage of his argument was to deny that there had ever been a real distinction between church and congregation in Dedham, so that a grant to the church was really a grant to all the Christians who gather for worship on Sunday. "Probably there was no very familiar distinction at that time between the church and whole assembly of Christians in the town. We have had no evidence that the inhabitants were divided into two bodies, of church or society or parish—keeping separate records, and having separate interests." This is plainly nonsense. In Dedham, of all places in the Bay Colony, the process by which a church of the regenerate was gathered out of the whole number of the inhabitants was a long, carefully considered, and deliberate process, which is well documented and is the basic theme of the early years of the town's history.[38]

What Parker could not grasp was that for the early settlers of Dedham, the church was not simply—in his words—"an assembly of Christians meeting together in the same place, for the publick worship of God, under the same minister or ministers."[39] It was something more specific: a covenanted community of regenerate Christians, gathered out of the whole body of nominal Christians, in the hope and expectation that on the Day of Judgment, by God's eternal decree they would be found among those who would glorify him through all eternity, rather than those fated to suffer everlasting torment. The distinction between the regenerate and the unregenerate was crucial in the definition of a congregational church. The writings of William Ames, John Cotton, Thomas Hooker, and others discussed this distinction theologically, scripturally, and ecclesiologically. Of all this, Parker took no note whatsoever and seems to have been wholly ignorant. Since the theological distinction between the regenerate and the unregenerate was lost on him, he apparently could not understand that it had once defined the nature of a congregational church, and that it was still important to the evangelical party.

For Parker, the distinction between church and congregation or parish was a product, not of scriptural authority or theological definition, but of legislative enactment:

> there appeared to be little practical distinction between church and congregation, or parish, or society, for several years after our ancestors came here. It was not until the year 1641, that we find any legislative recognition of the right and power of churches to elect ministers. Before that period, without doubt, the whole assembly were considered the church. . . . But in that year the right to gather churches under certain restrictions was established, and the power of electing church officers, comprehending without doubt ministers, was vested in the church.[40]

In Parker's view, the right to choose ministers had originally belonged to the whole congregation, which had, as it were, delegated its authority to a subordinate entity within the parish. The church within the parish has the power "of *divine worship* and *church order* and *discipline*. They still retain, by courtesy, the practice of nominating to the congregation."[41]

Parker's mind-set predisposed him to interpret the historical record in a way the orthodox properly protested, and which we in turn recognize as distorted beyond all belief. Part of the explanation may be that he was a member of the Brattle Street Church in Boston, which he offered as a happy example of the ecclesiology he favored. But the Brattle Street Church had departed from the normative congregationalism of the day when it was gathered in 1699. There were no territorial parishes in Boston, and those who worshiped at Brattle Street supported it voluntarily rather than by assessments. Unlike most of the other congregational churches, it required no confession of an experience of regeneration for admission to communion but simply restricted the ordinance to "persons of visible Sanctity." Finally, Brattle Street did not limit the right to choose the minister to male communicants. Instead, "every Baptized Adult Person who contributes to the Maintenance should have a Vote in Electing." All this was so familiar to Parker, and worked so well in his church, that it shaped his understanding of the New England Way of the churches.[42]

Furthermore, for the liberals, a restriction of access to the Lord's Table to the regenerate was no longer persuasive. They could not defend it on the basis of a required conversion experience, so for them church membership was coming to be no more than a special commitment to a Christian kind of piety. Church discipline, with excommunication as the ultimate sanction, had largely disappeared in the liberal churches. The communion service itself was becoming increasingly problematic, and ministers struggled to encourage people to participate. Only a few years later, Ralph Waldo Emerson left the ministry with the plea that the Lord's Supper had become a meaningless form. In short, for liberals like Parker, the church was no longer the important focus of the religious life that it still was for the orthodox. Their identification with a religious community was with the larger congregation of inhabitants of the parish. For the orthodox, the church was central, surrounded by the lesser community of the Sunday congregation. For the liberals, the church was becoming peripheral; the congregation was the essential religious community; the parish was its legal form.

The result was that when Parker encountered constitutional provisions, legislative enactments, and judicial precedents, he saw them through Brattle Street lenses. The 1780 constitution of the Commonwealth states that "the several towns, parishes, precincts, and other bodies politic, or religious societies, shall, at all times, have the exclusive right of electing their public Teachers, and of contracting with them for their support and maintenance."[43] It very specifically calls them "public teachers of piety, religion and morality," who might be of any sect or denomination and does not refer to them as *ministers*. But a distinction between a public teacher of morality and a minister made no sense to Parker, who rejected it when it was urged by counsel.[44]

Parker's preconceptions likewise colored his interpretation of legislation. On two occasions, the General Court had enacted laws declaring that churches "connected and associated in public worship" with the several towns, parishes, precincts, et cetera, "shall at all times have, use, exercise and enjoy all their accustomed privileges and liberties."[45] Most important of these privileges and liberties was surely the right for churches to order their own affairs and choose their own leaders. But when Parker saw "churches connected in public worship with parishes," he supplied in his own thinking the adverbs *permanently* and *indissolubly*, and read the relationship as one of subordination. A church, Parker stated, is not a corporation and "cannot subsist without some religious community to which it is attached"—that is, without being connected with a parish or incorporated religious society.[46]

If a church exists "unconnected with any congregation or religious society," Parker asserted, "it has no legal qualities."[47] The question whether an unincorporated body of worshipers calling itself a church had any legal standing was a long disputed issue, but one that the Religious Freedom Act of 1811 had sought to put to rest. The question had originally arisen in connection with the claim of members of unincorporated churches to exemption from town or parish assessments on the grounds that they were supporting their own public teachers of piety, religion, and morality. In 1810, Chief Justice Parsons had denied the claim in *Barnes* v. *The First Parish in Falmouth*.[48] The Religious Freedom Act the next year was a prompt and explicit repudiation of that decision, granting legal standing "as well where such teacher or teachers is or are the teacher or teachers of an unincorporated as of a corporate religious society." In *Adams* v. *Howe* (1817), Parker acknowledged that the law was constitutional, though he clearly thought it bad policy.[49] By the time of the constitutional convention of 1820—of which Parker was the presiding officer at the very time the Dedham case was being litigated—legal recognition of unincorporated religious societies was not questioned, though there was extended debate over other aspects of the system of tax support of public worship.

Finally, Parker brushed aside the precedent of *Avery* v. *Tyringham* (1807) in which Chief Justice Parsons had entertained the notion that a distinction should be made between teachers of piety, religion, and morality, and ministers of the gospel. Parsons had written:

If the church, when their election has been disapproved by the town, shall unwisely refuse to make a new election, or the town, for any cause, shall abandon the ancient usages of the country in settling a minister, it may, with or against the consent of the church, elect a public teacher, and contract to support him. And such a teacher will have a legal right to the benefit of the contract, although he cannot be considered as the settled minister of the gospel, agreeably to the usages and practice of the Congregational churches in the state.[50]

This supports the position that in Dedham, Lamson was properly the public teacher of the parish, but not the minister of the church "agreeably to the usages and practice of the Congregational churches." Admittedly, Parsons was not altogether clear as to the usages to which he referred, since on a later occasion, in *Burr* v. *Sandwich* (1812), he stated that a minister "has no peculiar relation to his church, but as a member of it." But he did declare unambiguously that "a parish and church are bodies with different powers," and that the deacons "are made a corporation, to hold property for the use of the church, and that they are accountable to the members." He had no doubt that the public teacher of the parish was a minister in some sense, if not in accordance with

133

ancient usage, and that he was settled by contract with the parish. But in vindicating the right of the parish to settle a minister as its public teacher, he did not—like Parker—take the further step to assert that if a man is settled as the minister of a parish, and if it is convenient and customary to choose the minister of the church for that position, it follows that the church is an appendage of the parish with no independent existence.[51]

The ordination council and Chief Justice Parsons came out at the same point. Both esteemed the ancient usage by which the church elected the minister and the parish gave him a settlement, and regretted departure from it. But times change, and ancient practices may not fit new situations. Parsons said that traditional ways may be abandoned "in cases of necessity"; while the council acknowledged that they "operate injuriously in periods like the present," and so should be dispensed with. When church and parish can no longer cooperate harmoniously, they must go their separate ways.

Why the realistic advice of the council was not followed is hard to determine. One might have supposed that the liberals in the parish would have been disposed to accept the advice of a council made up of the most distinguished liberals of the larger community. Perhaps the factionalism that had plagued the town over both politics and religion made sensible accommodation difficult. Surely the scurrilous tone of Judge Haven's book made a bad situation worse, not only because it angered the liberals, but because its stubborn insistence on procedures once acceptable but now anachronistic made it hard for the orthodox to accept gracefully the inevitable separation. The line of argument Judge Parker adopted had surfaced in earlier litigation, but the Court had never accepted it;[52] Parker must bear much blame for not rejecting it out of hand. The larger Unitarian community bears some responsibility for smugly accepting as law a position that many of them must have known full well was unsound as well as of baneful consequence. There seem to have been too many like George E. Ellis, who called the issue "perplexing" and declared himself not perfectly satisfied with the decision but was silent about the errors

even in the historical part of it, which he was presumably competent to correct.[53]

There is a legal doctrine known as *res judicata*, which means
in English: Don't reopen old sores. The case of *Baker* v. *Fales*
determined the ownership of certain property in Dedham and
unhappily set a precedent for similar cases in other communities.
All that is past and cannot be undone. But historical error, even
when given the sanction of the Supreme Judicial Court of the
Commonwealth of Massachusetts, need not pass unchallenged.
So let the record show that *Baker* v. *Fales* was bad law, based on
very bad history.

Unitarian Beginnings in
Western Massachusetts

Within the span of one generation, from 1805 to 1835, approximately 125 churches of the Massachusetts Standing Order, most of them in the eastern part of the state, became Unitarian. There was controversy and schism in a number of well-publicized cases, but in many more instances the churches became liberal through a gradual drift of opinion. Many of the liberals therefore assumed that the gradual process of liberalization would continue, and that the tendencies of the times were in their favor. Hence they saw no particular reason to promote organized missionary activity; indeed they often argued that a too vigorous assertion of Unitarianism might cause an orthodox backlash. Better far, they thought, to rely on the silent advance of liberalism.

Certain of the younger ministers were not content with this passive posture. The extension of liberal religion, they felt, called for a more active strategy and for organization to promote it. The result was the foundation in May 1825 of the American Unitarian Association. Its mission was to publish tracts and to give support to those who might be attempting to enlarge the influence of Unitarianism by organizing new churches in orthodox territory.

The publication program of the Association is familiar to historians, since it resulted in tracts of high intellectual quality, well written, by capable authors. Less well known is the missionary work carried on by the secretaries and agents of the Association. Some indication of this activity may be found in the annual reports of the Association; but for fuller detail one must go to the

137

correspondence files, long inaccessible but now available at the Andover-Harvard Library for investigation by scholars. They often provide a clearer picture of local developments than survives in local parish records or was reflected in published reports.

On February 22, 1825, three months before the organization of the AUA, a small group of liberals in Northampton left the congregational church there and founded the Second Congregational Society. They needed help, and the AUA tried to respond. The early history of Unitarianism in Northampton, therefore, is not simply a local parish episode. It is revealing as to the penetration of liberal religion into an area still dominated by orthodoxy, and it shows how the new Unitarian Association sought to use its limited resources in support of missionary expansion. The results were meagre. But there is something to be learned from the lack of success of Unitarianism at the boundaries, as well as from its relative success at the center of its sphere of influence.

First we must remind ourselves of the sequence of events leading up to the organization of the Second Congregational Society in February 1825. The Reverend Solomon Williams came to Northampton in 1778 as minister of the church of the town— the church of Solomon Stoddard, who was his great-great-grand-father, and of Jonathan Edwards, with whom his grandfather had disputed. Following the Great Awakening, a liberal reaction against the traditional Calvinism developed in many New England churches, especially in eastern Massachusetts. This liberalism, which Edwards was foremost in condemning, was referred to as Arminianism; it was the forerunner of nineteenth-century Unitarianism. It does not appear that the Reverend Mr. Williams was an Arminian; and so throughout his long ministry, which lasted for almost half a century, the pulpit of the Northampton church may be reckoned to have been orthodox.[1]

In Northampton, as in other towns, there came to be liberals in the pews, if not in the pulpit; and Judge Joseph Lyman was a leader among them from an early date.[2] In 1810, there was a movement led by him for a division of the town into two parishes. Whether this was symptomatic of theological divisions is not clear, but it is possible that some of the inhabitants were becoming restive under Williams's preaching. How a territorial division of the town would have worked out does not appear, since the proposal was rejected in town meeting.

In many towns where a division of opinion on doctrinal issues was emerging, the point of crisis came when an old and widely respected minister died, or at any rate reached an age when it was necessary to settle a colleague. Up to that point, affection for an older man of long and honorable service was enough to assure the support of members of the congregation who might not be in accord with him on matters of doctrine. But when a new minister was to be called, who might be expected to set the tone of the parish for thirty years or more, the question of his theological stance assumed great importance. Even if the candidate under consideration was orthodox, the unity of the congregation could be maintained if he was tolerant and accepting of those whose views were more liberal than his own. The crucial issue then was whether the new minister would be exclusive or broad in his sympathies—whether or not a liberal minority in a predominantly orthodox parish would be made to feel as though they were constantly under condemnation.

In 1824, a colleague and eventual successor to Dr. Williams was sought, and the choice fell on the Reverend Mark Tucker. Tucker was a New Yorker, who had been for more than six years minister of the Presbyterian church at Stillwater, a few miles up the Hudson River above Albany. Presumably the kind of liberalism for which Lyman spoke was something he had not encountered at first hand. He had never been faced with the problem of ministering to a church with that particular range of doctrinal diversity and may not have appreciated what might be involved in living with it. He was accustomed to the stricter discipline of Presbyterianism— indeed, he had tasted it before his ordination, when he had been tried by the Presbytery of Albany on the charge of unchristian conduct in circulating reports against a minister of the presbytery, who had been accused both of plagiarism and of intemperance. It appears that the accusations were true; but in any event, Tucker was acquitted of slander—that is, of disseminating derogatory information with a view to injuring another.[3]

When Tucker candidated in Northampton, the liberals were concerned to know whether he belonged to the "strict party" of those who insisted on doctrinal uniformity, or to the more relaxed and forbearing group among the orthodox who found it possible to live with those whose views were not wholly in accord with their own. In other communities, ever since the outbreak of the Unitarian controversy in 1805, bitter conflict had arisen because of misunderstandings on this score. The most widely publicized controversy was from 1810 to 1812 in the Second Parish in Dorchester, where a large body of liberals, perhaps close to a majority, were dismayed to discover that their newly installed minister, John Codman, refused to follow the long-established custom of pulpit exchanges with the other members of the Boston Association of Ministers, liberals and orthodox alike.[4] The custom of pulpit exchanges was a sort of safety valve. A liberal in a community where the minister was orthodox, or conversely one of the orthodox in a church served by a liberal Christian, could at least hope to be better pleased when one of the neighboring clergy occupied the desk. When Codman decided to exchange only with colleagues with whom he was in agreement, he tied down the safety valve, and the parish exploded.

The Dorchester controversy is a fascinating one, with colorful incidents and dramatic confrontations. Its importance for Northampton is that the liberals were evidently aware of it, and seem to have sought with painstaking care to avoid the kind of situation that had split the Dorchester parish wide open. Not that there are specific allusions to Dorchester in the Northampton record; but local leaders like Judge Lyman could not but have been familiar with the story and be influenced accordingly.

What was at stake in these disputes, and what was to be the central issue in Northampton, was whether the fellowship of Christians was to be drawn so narrowly as to exclude all except those willing to subscribe to the Westminster Confession. The tradition in Northampton had been more generous, more inclusive. A specific vote of the church had declared that "all Christian professors" should be invited to join in the communion service, and it had been understood that this invitation included Unitarians in the parish.[5]

The practical issue, however, focused on the question of exchanges, since the pattern of a minister's exchanges would reveal very quickly whether or not he belonged to the "strict party." So four liberals, themselves among the most prominent citizens of the town, took the opportunity to sound Tucker out, and felt reassured by his response. To Judge Samuel Howe, Tucker replied that his views were those of President Nott of Union College, who refused a call to the Park Street Church in Boston *"because that Church would not suffer him to EXCHANGE with the other ministers in Boston."*[6] The Park Street Church, then as now, stood for orthodox doctrine; indeed, it had been gathered in 1809 as a bastion of orthodoxy in Boston when almost all the other churches there were sliding into liberal control. To Judge Samuel Hinckley, Tucker said that he would not be pressured by members of the ministerial association who might try to make him adopt narrow views.[7] To Judge Lyman, he remarked that he would *pursue such a course here in relation to invitations and exchanges, as would satisfy the expectations of all."* To Dr. Flint he declared: *"I know ... what you and your friends want, and if I should be settled here, you may rest assured that they shall not be disappointed."*[8]

Reassured by such conversations, the liberals were ready to see Tucker settled by vote of the town. But that there should be no chance of misunderstanding, Judge Howe offered a motion in town meeting, affirming that the Society—that is, the town in its ecclesiastical capacity—was willing that the colleague minister about to be settled *"should EXCHANGE with, or invite to preach, in the desk, any pious Clergyman, of any denomination of Christians."* This was to assure Tucker that the policy the liberals thought he espoused would not be undercut by pressure from members of his flock. The vote passed unanimously; and when the results were reported to Tucker, he responded that he cordially approved.[9]

So Tucker was installed as minister of the church and the society, and everything seemed to promise well. But only a few weeks after the installation, a cloud appeared on the horizon. The Reverend William B.O. Peabody of Springfield wrote to Tucker, offering to exchange with him whenever it might seem appropriate to do so. In reply, Tucker gave a series of explanations for not accepting: that he had no horse and chaise, that he had not yet gotten to know his flock, that in Stillwater it had never been his practice to do much exchanging. What was missing from the letter was any indication that he would welcome an exchange at some future time, when his immediate and pressing problems had been solved.[10]

Peabody took the letter to be a clear refusal—a brush-off, as one might say. The liberals in Northampton were much upset and sought renewed assurances from Tucker. It soon became apparent that, while he described himself as a man of peace and thought himself as not illiberal and refused to characterize the Unitarians as unchristian, he nevertheless felt no obligation to exchange with them or anyone else. After a series of letters between Tucker and Judge Lyman, which ended with Tucker refusing to answer, the liberals published the correspondence together with a statement of the controversy, as prepared by Judge Hinckley and Judge Lyman.[11]

What we know of this controversy, it is only fair to note, is mostly derived from the pamphlet prepared by the liberals. It presents their side of the case very ably. If there was another side, it is lost to us; for the sake of the historical record and his own reputation, Tucker really ought to have responded. Whether he had been misunderstood when he apparently gave assurances prior to the installation, or whether he changed his mind, or whether there had been some dissimulation, as the liberals suspected, we shall presumably never know. What we do know is how the liberals felt about it. It seemed to them that they had given their votes for the settlement of Tucker only to have him welch on the prior understanding. So they gave up on the old church and resolved to start a new one.

Sometime in the fall of 1824, Judge Lyman inquired of friends in Boston whether there was a young ministerial candidate who would be interested in coming to Northampton; and Edward Brooks Hall went out. Hall was twenty-four years old, a graduate both of Harvard College and of the Divinity School.[12] Classes at the Divinity School were small in those days, but Hall's contemporaries included men who later achieved considerable distinction. In his own class was Charles W. Upham, who served as minister of the First Church in Salem, wrote extensively on Salem witchcraft, and served a term as a member of Congress. In the class just ahead were William H. Furness and Ezra Stiles Gannett; in the following class was George Ripley. It was young men of this generation, and indeed some of those just mentioned, who provided the energies needed to organize the American Unitarian Association in May 1825.

The liberals began to meet for Sunday worship on December 5, 1824, when William B.O. Peabody of Springfield preached. The numbers were small but grew when Hall arrived. "His preaching has been highly appreciated," Mrs. Howe wrote, "and his character as a man has secured our respect and regard."[13] The liberals sought to reach an amicable agreement with the orthodox for a division of the funds of the old society, but were turned down in town meeting. The Second Congregational Society was then formally organized at a meeting on February 22, 1825, which Judge Lyman described in a letter to Stephen Higginson, Jr., in Boston:

I gave public notice to all who were desirous of organizing a new religious society to meet at the Town Hall yesterday afternoon— forty three persons assembled— The Revd Mr Hall addressed the throne of grace in a fervent & happy manner, & retired— Judge Howe & Mr. Bancroft then addressed the meeting— after which the whole number signed the articles of agreement— thus we are organized under the law of 1811. The people from the west part of the town were necessarily absent, but will sign the articles in the course of the present week— we calculate with certainty upon more

143

than one hundred who now pay a ministerial tax in the old society— to the labours of Mr Hall we are much indebted for our increase of numbers—we appointed a Committee to wait on him & request him to preach for us as a candidate with a view to his future and permanent settlement— three Gentlemen then pledged themselves to be at three fifths of the expense & cost of a house of public worship—two others one fifth & three others the remaining fifth—a Committee was then appointed to procure a plan & fix upon the site &c.[14]

The efforts of the Northampton people were successful in persuading Hall to become their settled minister, though because of ill health it was not until the following year, on August 16, 1826, that he was ordained. Later in 1826, on October 30, he was married by President Kirkland of Harvard to Harriet Ware, daughter of Professor Henry Ware who had been one of Hall's teachers at the Divinity School. By his marriage to Harriet Ware, Hall became the brother-in-law of Henry Ware, Jr., then minister of the Second Church in Boston, and William Ware, the first minister of the New York church, now known as All Souls Church. While we are noting Hall's family connections, perhaps we should mention that his brother Nathaniel was later minister of the First Parish in Dorchester, and his sister Caroline married Francis Parkman, minister of the New North Church in Boston; Francis Parkman the historian was their eldest son. These family ties are not simply of antiquarian genealogical interest; they were significant channels of communication and influence, helping to bind the liberals into a cohesive party.

Hall was never physically strong, and his pastorate in Northampton was more than once interrupted by illness. Indeed only about three years from the time of his ordination, he felt compelled to resign and spend some time in Cuba with his brother Nathaniel in search of renewed health and strength. But illness seems to have been equated with spirituality in those days, and one of his Northampton parishioners described his appearance thus: "We recall with gratitude to-day the pleading of his veiled voice, and the pathos of his invalid appearance; his face glowing with a half-consumptive hectic, round which a halo of light and curling hair played in clusters. Tall and thin, he seemed to us preaching over his own grave, and to bring a solemnity and directness to the work which one soon to pass within the veil might naturally use."[15]

When the AUA was organized in May 1825, its officers had strong personal connections with Northampton. Judge Lyman was named a vice president; but the title was more honorary than significant. The Reverend Aaron Bancroft of Worcester was named president, and he was the father of George Bancroft of the Round Hill School. Lewis Tappan, chosen treasurer, was a Boston merchant who had come from Northampton and had been attracted to the preaching of William Ellery Channing; but his family back home were staunchly evangelical, and about two years later he reverted to the family faith. Ezra Stiles Gannett, as secretary, was the real executive moving force in the new organization, and he was one of Hall's very close friends at the Divinity School. With these connections, together with his family relationships with the Wares and the Parkmans, Hall was not at all out of touch with the doings in the metropolis and was actively drawn into promotion of the work of the AUA.

In the spring of 1827, Gannett wrote to Hall asking for information as to the prospects for Unitarianism in western Massachusetts, to be incorporated into his report for the annual meeting. Hall replied that "the general state of things in this place & all the vicinity is highly encouraging. . . ." There had been an increase in the numbers of his own society greater than he had expected, considering the infancy of the church, and "considering also that an Episcopal society has formed here within that time & taken many who would have come to us." The society was attracting members from a considerable distance—several from as far away as twenty miles—and he was being solicited to preach in remoter towns, like Ware and Northfield. All this was despite considerable hostility aroused by revivals, which had been promoted by the orthodox specifically to counteract Unitarian expansion.[16]

In this letter of May 21, 1827, Hall made a specific suggestion, which the directors of the AUA immediately seized upon, and urged that Hall be the first to try it out:

> One thing I do think of great importance, & wish if the nature of the case admits of it, it might be introduced & urged at this time— I mean, the importance of taking some measures of spreading, *viva voce* the knowledge of our opinions in this & other regions, now in utter ignorance yet ready to be enlightened— the best way of doing this would be, I believe, not to send new preachers directly into these waste places, but to make some provision for the occasional supply of Unitarian pulpits in regions like this, & letting the incumbents— who of course are best acquainted with the wants of the people about them— go out themselves as missionaries— I am persuaded a vast deal might be done in this way— There is little more wanted than to give information respecting Unitarianism & to give it in a prudent earnest way, in order to extend its influence—[17]

When Gannett wrote back to Hall, some weeks later, that the Executive Committee of the AUA would support preaching in Northampton so that he could take the road as a missionary, his enthusiasm cooled somewhat. "As to the request of the AUA," he replied, "I will attempt something—or at least I will think about it—but I fear it will not amount to much—for really I have not the time—I am working too hard, as it is, for my strength—& get actually *no* time for study or even reading—this wont do either for body or mind— But then again somebody must do something in this way, & I am willing to bear my part of the burden—" He went on to note that the local liberal ministers' association—the Franklin Evangelical Association, it was called—would be meeting soon at New Salem, and would discuss the matter. Then he added: "I can see no possible objection to employing members of the [Divinity] School in this way, & think our people would like it."[18]

The Divinity School student who was persuaded to accept the

assignment was Ralph Waldo Emerson.[19] Emerson explained the arrangement to his brother William: "I am going to preach at Northampton, in the service of the Unitarian Assoc., for Mr. Hall, a few weeks, whilst he goes into the adjoining towns to missionize. His church is a small one, & I shall be able to preach all day I suppose without inconvenience. Afterward I am at liberty to do the same for Mr. Willard of Deerfield & send him on the same errand."[20] Actually, it did not work out quite that way: Emerson preached in Northampton on September 9, and then the next four Sundays alternately in Greenfield and Deerfield, and finished up with three Sundays in Northampton. For these services he was paid ten dollars a Sunday.

At Northampton, he lived with Judge Lyman, whose son was a college friend of his brother Charles. "I now live at Judge Lymans," he wrote to Charles on October 10, "who has a monopoly of the hospitality of the town."[21] To Dr. Ezra Ripley, the minister in Concord, he reported that orthodoxy in the area was not as strongly rooted as he had expected. "Intelligent men," he learned, "are of opinion that the majority of this County is unitarian." Then he added, a bit wryly: "I had supposed it must be so, from my acquaintance with the human mind, but feared to be contradicted by acquaintance with the County."[22] To Ezra Stiles Gannett he reported: "The clergymen are very glad to see me, having feared that the mission was indefinitely postponed. They find the better sort of people in most of the towns inquisitive & favorably disposed to views of liberal Christianity. It is a singular fact of which I hear frequent mention made, that in elections, Unitarians are almost universally preferred, when the suffrage is given by ballot, & rejected, when given by hand vote."[23]

Meanwhile, Hall was out on his missionary tour. He went first to Cummington, then Worthington, Chesterfield, Goshen, and Williamsburg; returned to Northampton for a wedding; and finally went to Belchertown—preaching, selling tracts, and encouraging the formation of local auxiliary societies (not churches) related to the AUA. In each case he found small numbers of receptive hearers, eager to listen, but not large enough groups to separate from the established churches. The first circuit took about a week. A month later he started out again, this time going to Berkshire County, stopping at Adams, North Adams, Lenox, Stockbridge, Pittsfield, and Great Barrington. The journal of his travels ended with a paragraph of summary:

As regards my labors in Berkshire— tho' I considered it wholly a voyage of discovery— I think there is reason to be fully satisfied— I found much more liberality than I had supposed— for there is not a unitarian Society in the whole county & their clergy have been determined there never should be— but there is not a town of importance which does not contain some open and resolute Unitarians— Besides those I visited— I heard of several others where there were many— in one (Sandisfield) I was told they had had liberal preaching from an illiterate man springing up in the midst of them— All that is wanted, is that those in different towns and distant parts of the county holding Unitarian opinions, should be brought together, made acquainted with each other, learn their whole strength, & stir one another up— And this I think my mission has in part effected, if it have done nothing more— I have opened their eyes to the fact that they are not alone as they have thought, & need not fear avow their opinions— I have distributed a good many tracts among them, & put them in the way of getting many more— I could have disposed of a great many more than I had taken with me—[24]

Hall forwarded his missionary journal to Gannett with a covering letter, dated October 29, 1827, in which he discussed the problems facing the liberals and the strategy that had been forced on them. Hall was obviously unhappy to see the dissolution of the old order, in which all the inhabitants of a town joined in common worship. He would have much preferred it had mutual forbearance been exercised, so that the old parishes might remain intact. But recent changes in the laws respecting the support of the ministry,

he realized, had completely broken down the old parish boundaries, so that a new situation existed and would have to be
recognized. Alienation from the old parish system was finding
expression in various ways, particularly in the spread of Methodist, Baptist, and Universalist societies. The Universalists, in particular, he asserted, "have occupied ground on which we might
have stood," and done so in a divisive, sectarian manner.[25]

As for himself, Hall would have hesitated to encourage the
separate organization of Unitarian churches had it not been for
widespread complaints he heard from the liberals of the discrimi-
natory treatment they were receiving in the old churches, especially in their exclusion from the communion table, and often the
refusal of orthodox ministers to baptize their children:

> Though they may be members in regular standing of some
> other Chh— tho' indeed they may have been members of this
> Chh before their change of opinions— tho their moral char-
> acter be confessedly without a blemish, & their desire to
> enjoy the benefits of Xn ordinances ever so strong or seri-
> ous— it matters not— they are not allowed to approach the
> communion table— they are not allowed to bring their
> children to the baptismal font— they are not allowed even
> with all these deprivations to enjoy quietly their own opin-
> ions— but must submit to be held up to public odium &
> vulgar prejudice— to hear their opinions grossly misrepre-
> sented, themselves & those they most esteem calumniated,
> & all this by those whom they are helping to support in the
> ministry.[26]

Gannett was so well pleased with the results of Hall's tour that
he urged a quick follow-up; but Hall felt that it was now too late
in the season. His response to Gannett, dated November 13, 1827,
does have a postscript of some interest, which local historians will
have to exegete: "As to Lewis Tappan's defection," it reads, "it
creates no surprise here— they have been expecting & even
wishing it— for they have not faith in any of the Tappan blood—

One man says, he will now declare himself a Unitarian, since the last Tappan has gone over to the other side— You will call this prejudice— & so no doubt much of it is—but it is grounded on a long acquaintance with the whole family—"[27]

In 1828, the Executive Committee of the AUA renewed the suggestion that Hall go on another missionary tour and set aside forty dollars to pay for the supply of the Northampton pulpit for four Sundays; but Hall begged off until later in the year. The most he found time for was a visit to Chesterfield, where the Baptists had had a row and were split between the Calvinist and the Free Will factions; and a brief visit in September to Bernardston and Greenfield, while George Ripley took the Northampton pulpit.[28]

In 1829, Hall hoped to do better, and suggested to Gannett a spring missionary tour, partly as a relief from the burden of parish duties. The AUA assented and once again Ripley was asked to substitute, but a renewed attack of illness intervened. "I have had a violent attack of something like a fever," Hall wrote at the end of April, "checked only by powerful remedies, which has reduced my strength." Though by the time he wrote he was recovered enough to be about as usual, he hesitated to undertake anything involving great exertion.[29] Ill health continued to plague him throughout the year, and in the early fall he left on a trip in hopes of recovering his strength. He went first to Maine, where he found changes in the wind, but the Universalists rather than the Unitarians were in a position to benefit; then across New Hampshire and Vermont, where the Free Will Baptists seemed to be growing; and to Montreal, where he likewise found liberalism appearing among the Scotch Presbyterians. (The Montreal church was not founded until a dozen years had elapsed, however.) Hall was asked to preach there, but his health did not permit. Indeed, as his report makes clear, his health was a constant source of concern, preventing him from doing as much as he wished to promote the cause of liberal Christianity.[30]

Hall resigned his pastorate at the end of 1829. Although he served the church in Cincinnati for several months in the winter of 1830 to 1831, it was not until 1832 that he was able to resume full-time care of a parish. In November 1832, he was settled in Providence, where he remained for thirty-three years, until his death in 1866.

One thing Hall's recurrent illnesses never did was to dampen his optimism with respect to the prospects for Unitarianism in Northampton and the communities round about that he visited. His was an eager generation which, although it deplored the split that was destroying the Standing Order in Massachusetts, was nevertheless prepared to accept the situation for what it was and to bear witness to the principles of liberal Christianity. For a decade or so, the situation seemed very fluid, and the opportunity seemed to exist for the development of a strong liberal movement in the Connecticut Valley as well as in eastern Massachusetts. The Unitarians were trying to seek out their sympathizers, to give them support and encouragement, and connect them with the larger liberal movement. Meanwhile, the orthodox were counter-attacking with revivals, especially under the leadership of Lyman Beecher.

The letters that went from Northampton to the Secretary of the AUA in Boston give a vivid impression of the opportunities that seemed to be opening up, and of the ways the liberals hoped to take advantage of them. But the results were disappointing. The auxiliaries promoted by Hall in 1827 had disappeared by 1832.[31] A listing of Unitarian churches prepared by Ezra Stiles Gannett in 1830 showed only sixteen in all of the four western counties of Massachusetts; only seven of them had ministers.[32] In 1846, when a Unitarian yearbook was published for the first time, the number of churches had shrunk to thirteen, served by ten ministers.[33] That was not what Hall and Gannett had had in mind twenty years earlier.

An attempt to explain the failure was made by A.D. Mayo in 1873. He argued that western Massachusetts had long been more conservative theologically, dominated by "the old Congregational Calvinism of the Puritans." Development within that culture, rather than missionary activity from without, was the way change was coming about, and Mayo pointed to the spread of Methodism and the rise of the New Haven theology as evidences of a process of liberalization. "The Christian religion as preached by the great New Haven divines, by Bushnell, by the Beechers, by the majority of Congregational ministers under forty, in Western Massachusetts today,—is substantially another religion from that preached in the same region half a century ago." His conclusion was that the old Calvinism had been replaced by an "evangelical" Christianity whose "central spirit" was "far more allied to Christian Liberalism than any orthodoxy of the past." The result was a "Liberal Orthodoxy" essentially the same as the earlier Liberal Christianity of William B.O. Peabody, Henry Ware, and William Ellery Channing, though reached by a different path. To this transformation, Unitarianism and Universalism had doubtless made a contribution, but it was not through the spread of Unitarian churches.[34]

The difference between the religious culture of eastern Massachusetts and the Connecticut Valley was of long standing. Eighteenth-century Arminianism had been confined to those areas where the pulpits were filled by Harvard graduates. Until the railroads came, transportation and communication between the river towns and New Haven was much easier than eastward to Boston, and the people looked to Yale for their ministers.[35] At the turn of the century, it was only in the northern third of Old Hampshire County—afterwards separated to become Franklin County—that a cluster of Harvard graduates survived in the pulpits. That helps to explain why in Gannett's compilation in 1830 six of the seven ministers he listed were in Franklin County. None of them were Yale graduates; three were from Harvard, two from Brown, and one from Dartmouth. It was only in Franklin County that old parishes became Unitarian in the course of long ministries, as so often happened in eastern Massachusetts. In (new) Hampshire and Hampden counties, Unitarian churches resulted from liberal departures from the old parish churches. Almost without exception, attempts to plant new Unitarian churches in towns where there had been no overt dissension in the parish came to nothing.[36]

To survive, a new Unitarian church in western Massachusetts evidently required a support system, emotional as much as financial, to reduce the sense of isolation. In Deerfield, where Samuel Willard was installed in 1807, a local support system existed; so although Willard was a graduate of Harvard (Class of 1803), he did not have to rely solely on his eastern connections for his sense of identity. The church had become liberal long before there was an AUA. In Springfield, William B.O. Peabody was the first minister of the Unitarian church, in 1820; but the separation from the orthodox church brought with it the aged minister of the First Church, recently replaced by a younger and more orthodox man.[37]

In Northampton, the striking fact is that the support system depended greatly on the laity who led the departure from the old church, laymen who had strong connections with the Boston Unitarian community. Judge Lyman, Judge Howe, and Judge Hinckley were none of them Harvard graduates, but the marriages of Lyman and Howe to Anne and Sally Robbins of Milton made for strong connections with Boston. Howe, indeed, was still orthodox at the time of his second marriage, and it was two years before his views changed.[38] When Hall arrived, a friend of Gannett and in due course the son-in-law of Henry Ware, the network of interpersonal relationships was strongly reinforced.

The extent to which networks of interpersonal relationships were involved in defining the possibilities of Unitarian success is one of the lessons of the Northampton story. It is an aspect of the early Unitarian development that should not be discounted, since it is apparent that when attempts were made to plant Unitarian churches in more distant parts, such as Baltimore in 1818 or New York in 1819, the nucleus was most often some Boston families who found themselves in alien territory. Unitarianism did not make its way on the strength of its rational and humane theology unless there was a network of interpersonal relations to sustain it; and family relationships were among the strongest of these.

Lacking them, the scattered liberals in the towns Hall visited could not sustain their witness. Doubtless Hall's illness and consequent inability to follow up on his early initiatives are part of the explanation for the failure of the individuals he located to organize and establish firmly rooted institutions. No doubt the AUA was too new and lacking in resources to provide the necessary support. In any case, the opportunities that Hall proclaimed would not last forever. In 1835, the younger Henry Ware published a tract entitled *Sober Thoughts on the State of the Times Addressed to the Unitarian Community*, in which he acknowledged that the period of controversy, of turmoil and unrest, and indeed of massive shifts in religious opinions and allegiances, had come to an end.[39] At about the same time, Oliver Stearns, who was Hall's successor in Northampton, was reaching some sober conclusions about prospects for further Unitarian growth in the Connecticut Valley:

> There is not a prospect of a speedy spread of our views in this place, or just about here. Northampton is dulled into orthodoxy thoroughly, & great pains are taken to put the young in a train to be got into the church in early life, & then they are fixed. . . . Many serious people, who would have found salvation in our views if educated in them, are afraid of us.[40]

The Channing We Don't Know

Many of us are familiar with the portrait of William Ellery Channing by the Italian artist Gambardella, since it has frequently been reproduced and is to be found as the frontispiece of more than one of the biographies. It is the portrait that is always presented as if in its original oval frame. It shows the head only. The deep-set eyes confront you directly; the nose is straight and rather long; the mouth is firm; there is a small untidy lock of hair on the forehead. The impression is of a man of commanding presence.

The portrait dates from 1839, when Channing was fifty-nine years of age. Channing's nephew and first biographer says of it that "in a mellow light it preserves many characteristics of the original not elsewhere to be found." At the same time, he expressed reservations about all the likenesses that had been made of his uncle: "The romantic and tender beauty of his expression," he insisted, "as well as the power of thought in his countenance, has never been adequately given in any portrait." Channing himself was well pleased with the result, however. "Mr. Gambardella has succeeded in his work," he wrote. "My friends are entirely satisfied with the picture. It is not only a good likeness, but a meritorious work of art. After so many unsuccessful attempts, this poor face is faithfully transferred to canvas, and, on the whole, is better worth looking at than I supposed."[1]

Channing's features are thus familiar to us, and even in a portrait they suggest something of his personality. In some measure, at least, we seem to know him. We feel we know him, too, from his writings, so frequently anthologized. There is the Baltimore Sermon of 1819, in which he presented a manifesto of liberal religion in contrast with the prevailing orthodoxy. There is the sermon on "Likeness to God" in 1828, in which the dignity of human nature is asserted in language such as this: "That the soul, if true to itself and its Maker, will be filled with God, and will manifest him, more than the sun, I cannot doubt."[2] There is the election sermon on "Spiritual Freedom" in 1830, whence come the strophes beginning "I call that mind free . . . ," sometimes used as a responsive reading in services of worship. There is the little book on *Slavery*, published in 1835, which did much to advance the antislavery cause even though abolitionists like Samuel Joseph May thought that Channing should have taken his stand much earlier.

That is how Channing has come down to us—the spiritual features of his countenance, with a sort of romantic pallor on account of his persistent ill health; the testimony of his contemporaries as to his eloquence in the pulpit; a personal magnetism that stirred his listeners almost to the point of idolatry; the liberating effect of his concept of human dignity and the infinite capacity of human nature for spiritual growth, so that the younger Transcendentalists called him "our Bishop" even as they complained that he lagged behind them; the spiritual godfather of many reform movements, even though his poor health meant that he often had to leave the burden of advocacy and organization on other shoulders.

It is not my intention to argue that this familiar image of Channing is false in what it asserts. One can quote chapter and verse from his own writings and from the testimony of his contemporaries to support it. But I would like to suggest that it is an incomplete picture of Channing; that there are other aspects of his character, his theological position, and his contribution to the life of his own day, that we have allowed to disappear from sight. The result is that we do not really understand the part of Channing that does survive in our awareness. There is a mythological Channing as well as a historical Channing, though most of us are not conscious of the difference. And so I would like to suggest that there are at least three neglected aspects of Channing's career that need to be brought back to consciousness. Let me state them first, and then elaborate on each in turn. There is, first of all, Channing the evangelical. Next, there is Channing the Christian. And finally, there is Channing the man of affairs.

Channing the evangelical: What does that mean? Does it mean that, at least in the early years of his ministry at Federal Street, he should be ranked among the orthodox ministers rather than among the Liberal Christians who were soon to be called Unitarians? Some scholars have thought so. His understanding of the human predicament, and his emphasis on our sinful nature, seem to us so far removed from later Unitarianism as to raise that question. The sermon Channing delivered at the ordination of John Codman in 1808 was warmly received by the orthodox, of whom Codman was himself one. To whom is the minister sent to preach? Channing asked.

> He is sent to a world of sinners, in whose hearts lurk idolatry, sensuality, pride, and every corruption. . . . He sees immortal beings, committed to his care, advancing with rapid steps to the brink of an abyss, from which they are never to arise. And can he be unconcerned? Can he read of that fire which is never quenched, of that worm which never dies, and yet see without emotion fellow beings, with whom he sustains the tenderest connexions, hastening forward to this indescribable ruin? . . . and is it not a thought unutterably affecting, that these are all trembling on the verge of the grave, that soon, very soon, one or another will be forever removed from the reach of our warning voice, to receive an irreversible sentence from the righteous Judge? Negligent minister, look forward to the tribunal of God, Behold a human being there condemned, whom thy neglect has helped to destroy.[3]

This is pretty strong stuff, coming from a Unitarian. Yet the evidence is plain that even as he spoke, Channing did not regard himself as belonging to the orthodox or Calvinist party; that he was speaking as one of the Liberal Christians.[4] If you go through the sermon very carefully, you will find none of the distinguishing doctrines of the Calvinists, such as election, the derivation of sin from Adam's fall, predestination, the Trinity, or the dual nature of Christ. There is emphasis on the actual sinfulness of human beings but not on original sin; there is emphasis on the need for human beings to be awakened, to turn from their corruption, but there is no doctrine of election or predestination that says they lack the capacity to do so.

This sermon tells us a lot, both about Channing and the party to which he belonged. With respect to Channing, it is a reminder that the congregation to which he came in 1803 was a mixed congregation, containing both liberals and orthodox. How should one minister to a congregation in such circumstances? Some men would have done it by the kind of doctrinal preaching that would lay down an unambiguous party line, so that those who were discomforted by it would sooner or later go elsewhere. But Channing seems to have taken another tack. He preached liberal doctrine with evangelical fervor. There was something there for both elements in the congregation. Caught up in the glow of the rhetoric, the evangelicals may hardly have noticed the absence of evangelical doctrine. The combination was working as late as 1825, when a young man named Lewis Tappan was recruited from Channing's congregation to be the first treasurer of the American Unitarian Association. He came from a staunchly orthodox background in Northampton and was attracted by Channing's eloquence. Two years later, he repudiated the Unitarians and all their works, reasserted his ancestral Calvinism, and moved to New York where, in association with his brother, he became one of the mainstays of the evangelical associations for the promotion of benevolent causes, such as the American Tract Society and the Home Missionary Society. Once beyond Channing's magnetism, he found he was orthodox after all.

As Channing's career progressed, the rhetoric he used was transformed. By the time he prepared the introductory remarks for the collected edition of his works in 1841, he declared: "The following writings will be found to be distinguished by nothing more, than by the high estimate of human nature."[5] Yet it must not be forgotten that Channing's concept of the dignity of human nature is based on an assertion of the potential capacity of human beings to achieve spiritual greatness, not on their actual condition. We sometimes overlook the qualification that Channing makes, even as he asserts a doctrine of human dignity: "When we look merely at what it now is, at its present development, as what falls under present consciousness, we see in it much of weakness and limitation, and still more, we see it narrowed and degraded by error and sin."[6] It did not seem necessary to Channing, in his later preaching, to emphasize that part of his doctrine of human nature; there were plenty of other voices then to do that. But the somber side of his doctrine so prominent in the Codman ordination sermon was never repudiated, however much it was muted; and it needs to be kept in the picture, if only as a shadow that gives depth to the whole.

It needs to be kept in the picture also, if we are not to misunderstand Channing in relationship to his contemporaries; for a somber view of human nature was characteristic of that whole generation of liberals. We do not read the writings of Channing's contemporaries any more—preachers like the Henry Wares, senior and junior, or Orville Dewey, or Ezra Stiles Gannett—so Channing seems much more like an isolated mountain peak than he should. To see Channing in context is both to understand him better, and to understand better the movement of which he was the most widely known leader.

One reason why so little is known of the evangelical side of Channing is that it is scarcely represented in his collected works. Although there are generous excerpts in the memoir by Channing's nephew, we have almost no complete texts of Channing's Sunday sermons in the first two decades of his ministry, when he was preaching most often and making his reputation.[7] The collected works include only sermons preached on special occasions, as at ordinations, or at the dedication of Divinity Hall, which were first published in pamphlet form, and later collected along with review articles from the *Christian Examiner* and pamphlets dealing with public issues like the annexation of Texas. There is a whole aspect of Channing's career, which was crucial in the creation of his contemporary reputation, that is unavailable to us.

But that is not the problem with the second aspect of Channing's career to which we remain oblivious, namely, his Christian commitment. Here is a part of him readily accessible in his public works, which we choose to disregard. I myself know how easy that is. In anticipation of the bicentennial celebration of Channing's birth, I was asked to help in choosing brief selections from Channing's writings for a special issue of the journal KAIROS. We had chosen passages illustrating his views on the human soul and its tendencies toward infinity; on the trinity; on the church; on the social issues of war, slavery, and the poor. We were just about to congratulate ourselves on the completion of our task, when it occurred to us that there was no mention of Jesus Christ, despite the fact that the collected works include five items on the character of Christ or love to Christ, and even more than that on Christianity and the means to promote it. We should not forget that the Baltimore Sermon, so-called, is properly entitled *Unitarian Christianity*. Channing seldom if ever referred to Unitarianism; he more often used the term Unitarian Christianity.

We quickly turned to the sermon, "The Imitableness of Christ's Character," and picked out the following passage:

Christ came to give us a religion,—but this is not all. By a wise and beautiful ordination of Providence, he was sent to show forth his religion in himself. He did not come to sit in a hall of legislation, and from some commanding eminence to pronounce laws and promises. He is not a mere channel through which certain communications are made from God; not a mere messenger appointed to utter the words which he had heard, and then to disappear, and to sustain no further connection with his message. He came not only to teach with his lips, but to be a living manifestation of his religion,—to be, in an important sense, the religion itself.[8]

There was a time when people used to speak of "Channing Unitarianism." Ordinarily they were trying to dissociate themselves from the radicalism of the Free Religious Association, in the latter part of the nineteenth century, which allotted Christianity no special place among the religions of the world and was sometimes explicitly and abrasively non-Christian in its stance. It is of course possible to read Channing selectively, to pick out those pages that the modern-day liberal finds congenial and forget the rest. In this process, Channing's Christian commitment and his concern for the spread of true Christianity easily disappear, partly because Christianity as a cultus no longer holds the sway it once did, and partly because Channing's Christology and his Christian apologetics no longer appeal even to many members of the Unitarian Universalist Christian Fellowship.

It is inevitable that as we explore the past, and even as we explore our own roots, there will be parts of it to which we still resonate and parts that have wholly lost their vitality. It is to be expected that some things that were important to Channing will be of small consequence to us. But once again, if we are to do justice to that part of Channing that we still find to be alive, we must see it in the context of the whole man and the whole career. Instead, we tend to shrink the substance down, until little is left except a name invoked on ceremonial occasions, and a few passages chopped up into responsive readings for the back of the hymnbook.

The third aspect of Channing's career of which I wish to speak is that of Channing as a man of affairs. Here I am talking about the first twenty years of Channing's professional career, from 1803 when he became the minister of the Federal Street Church until 1822 when he went abroad for his health. Soon after his return the next year, Ezra Stiles Gannett was ordained as a colleague at the Federal Street Church, and so at the age of forty-four Channing was able to give over the major responsibility for the running of the church to him. Thereafter he preached less frequently, indeed quite infrequently in the closing years of his life.

Channing's withdrawal to a limited ministry, dictated largely by problems of health, was matched by a withdrawal from much that had earlier occupied him in the larger community. What were some of the things Channing had been involved in during the first two decades of his ministry? Here are some of them.

For thirteen years, from 1813 to 1826, he was one of the Fellows of Harvard College—that is to say, a member of the small governing board, generally referred to as the "Corporation," that runs the University. He was an active member of the Board. According to the memoir by Channing's nephew, "During this period he took an efficient part in all plans for the improvement of the courses of instruction and discipline in the College. Voluminous notes remain to prove with what comprehensive and minute attention he made himself acquainted with the condition, wants, dangers, opportunities of the students, and with what discriminating sympathy he lent his aid to every proposed reform.[9]

Secondly, he was much involved in shaping the Harvard Divinity School in its early years. In 1816, he was one member of a committee of three of the Corporation "to digest and report a plan of Instruction and a course of exercises for Theological Students at the University."[10] In 1826, he delivered the address at the dedication of Divinity Hall. Channing's nephew says, in connection with the Divinity School, that Channing was "one of its most active guardians, as is conclusively shown in many letters and manuscripts."[11]

Thirdly, he participated actively in crucial episodes of the Unitarian Controversy. One thinks first of all, to be sure, of the Baltimore Sermon in 1819, which was no casual affair, but a carefully planned occasion deliberately intended to attract notice and present a manifesto of liberal Christianity. But Channing had earlier engaged in controversy over the publication of a pamphlet that accused the liberals of deceit in refusing to acknowledge openly, so the accusation went, their true views with respect to the nature of Christ. Channing was so deeply involved in ecclesiastical politics at that time it is no wonder that it was taken for granted that he should be the first president of the American Unitarian Association, when that organization was formed in

1825. He declined, to be sure, partly because of health and partly because he thought the scheme premature. But he was known then as one actively involved in community organizations.

Fourthly, his early ministry at the Federal Street Church involved much more than preaching and some minimal parish calling. In 1817, he was busy shaping plans for the erection of a vestry for the church, and persuading the Prudential Committee to accept them. A singing school, a charity school, a Sunday school, a place for parish meetings, a library with the minister as librarian—these were some of the activities that he was promoting as part of the life of the church, for which the new building was needed.

For eight years, from 1812 to 1820, he headed the Executive Committee of the Massachusetts Bible Society, and in that capacity prepared its annual reports. One suspects that the duties of the office were not onerous; but that is not the point. The point is rather that he was asked to assume, and did assume, his share of responsibility in the operation of the charitable, religious, and educational organizations of Boston.

In cooperation with the Reverend Noah Worcester, he was one of the leaders of the American Peace Society—the Reverend John Pierce says that he was "its life and soul." For years, according to his biographer, "he devoted himself to the work of extending its influence with unwavering zeal, as many of his papers of that period attest."[12]

Finally—though the biographer does not mention it—he was one of the founders of the Provident Institution for Savings, which still exists as one of the savings banks of Boston.

We have paid little attention to this side of Channing's career, and there are a number of reasons for that neglect. The most salient is that only briefest mention is made of it in the biography by Channing's nephew, the Reverend William Henry Channing. The younger Channing had a huge mass of manuscript materials—sermons, letters, memoranda—to work with, and so was forced to pick and choose what was most relevant for his purpose. But the process of making extracts is a process of interpretation, and so the final result bears the marks of the younger Channing's perceptions, and indeed of his eccentricities. William Henry Channing was an idealist, given to abstract speculation, whose career in the ministry was a long succession of brave dreams and abortive practical ventures. As a biographer, he was interested above all else in the spiritual principles for which his uncle stood, the timeless truths that were his legacy. Hence material of certain types was deliberately set aside. In the private papers, the biographer acknowledged, "are many passages of deeper interest than any that we have felt at liberty to publish."[13] Among those discarded papers were all those that would reveal Channing interacting on mundane matters with the leaders of his own church, or exercising practical responsibilities as a member of the Harvard Corporation, or organizing the Provident Institution for Savings. Clearly, Channing, at least in the first decades of his ministry, was by no means as much a disembodied spirit as his nephew makes him out to be.

One would ordinarily expect such a memoir to be rewritten in a later day, by a biographer with different perspectives and concerns, who might extract a different kind of ore from the manuscript treasure. Unfortunately, most of the Channing papers were destroyed in a railroad accident some sixty years after his death. It is no longer possible to go back to the documents that William Henry Channing used—to verify the quotations, to restore omitted names, to recover information once set aside as irrelevant or presumed to be trivial. Every biographer since W.H. Channing has had to take his memoir as though it were primary source material, since it remains the most important single source of information. But in this way, we are left with an etherealized and spiritualized Channing, while Channing as a man of affairs remains unknown.

Some may wonder whether it makes any difference, after all, to be reminded that Channing as a young minister preached with evangelical zeal about the fire which is never quenched and the worm which never dies; or that he believed that Jesus Christ was a superangelic being created before the world began whose mission to reveal God's will to sinful creatures was attested by miracles, as we know from the New Testament; or that he once shared responsibility for seeing that the salaries of professors in Harvard College were paid. In the winnowing process of time and history, all that has gone by the board; and if the result is a mythological Channing instead of a historical one, nevertheless we live in myths.

That response might be persuasive if the remaining myth were a vital one. But my hunch is that the myth itself has become lifeless; and that all that remains for most Unitarian Universalists is a name, usually invoked in association with those of Emerson and Parker. Channing, Emerson, and Parker: how often have we heard those names invoked; but how much do we discover behind them? Of the three, Channing is perhaps the least well known and least accessible. We know he was important in his day, and we are assured that he is still an important part of our tradition; but the image of him is insubstantial at best.

Part of the trouble, I am convinced, is that we have inherited an impression of Channing that mythologizes only a part of the man. A myth is but the shadow of a man; but let it at least be the shadow of the whole man. Channing is more complex, and I think a more interesting figure when we are aware of the Channing that, up to now, we haven't known.

Nineteen eighty marked the bicentennial of Channing's birth. The exact day of the anniversary was April 7th. Doubtless there were dozens of commemoration sermons preached from Unitarian Universalist pulpits. How many of them got beyond a summary of the life, on the order of the *Dictionary of American Biography*, along with a reference to the Baltimore Sermon? One shudders at all the conventional things that were said, and the pale cliches that were resorted to. But there really was a live man there once, a charismatic preacher whose deep-set eyes suggested hidden resources of spiritual experience and meaning, and who participated actively in the life of the day. Can we bring the myth to life again, full-bodied, not shrunken? This is the time to try.

165

The Theological World of Samuel Gilman

In recent decades, scholars have begun to explore a problem in Unitarian history that had long been neglected. What happened to those Unitarians of the second generation who chose not to go the way of the Transcendentalists? They were, actually, a majority of the denomination in the 1840s and 1850s, and yet little attention has been paid to them. The Transcendentalists make a big splash in our historical accounts; they are lively and interesting people, whose contributions to American literature and involvement in social reform attract the attention of students who may not be primarily concerned with religious issues. As soon as Emerson and Parker appear on the scene, the attention shifts to them; and the image of non-Transcendentalist Unitarianism becomes stereotyped and fixed, as though Andrew Norton's "Latest Form of Infidelity" represented the final point beyond which no further movement took place. It then becomes easy to assume that Transcendentalism represented the mainstream of Unitarian development, while the older generation gradually died out.

The validity of this emphasis on the Transcendentalists, to the neglect of their conservative contemporaries, is now being seriously questioned. Some years ago, Perry Miller noted that a revolution was in the making with respect to the "Transcendental" period of New England history. Somewhat to his dismay, younger historians were beginning to have a good word to say for the conservative Unitarians, even for Andrews Norton, whom the Transcendentalists had made a special object of attack. The suggestion was made that Boston Unitarianism was something more than the "pale negations" of Emerson's deprecatory comment; and it no longer seemed as obvious as Parker's partisans had always proclaimed that the Unitarian clergy were base hypocrites for advocating toleration while rejecting Parkerism. "What a revolution in our historiography is adumbrated, let alone executed," Miller exclaimed, "by the very raising of this consideration."[1]

In the course of the nineteenth century, the Unitarians moved a long way from the theological verities of the first generation. The old Unitarianism, of Christianity as a supernatural revelation attested by miracles, completely disappeared. It does not follow that what happened was that Transcendentalism replaced a moribund Unitarian orthodoxy. If Unitarianism had been transformed, the Transcendentalist challenge was only one of many intellectual influences that had transformed it. If the generation after the Civil War saw the development of new expressions of radicalism, it also saw the emergence of a new kind of conservatism. "We have all been on the move," John White Chadwick testified in 1894. "The most conservative today would have been radicals among us fifty, forty, even thirty years ago."[2] When something like a new consensus was achieved, it contained the residues of Transcendentalism, but much else besides. By the end of the century, the prevailing motif was evolutionary optimism, which found classic expression in James Freeman Clarke's phrase: "the progress of mankind onward and upward forever." The popularizers of Darwin, like John Fiske, may well have contributed more to this triumphant result than did Theodore Parker.

Not only has this transformation never been analyzed in detail, but we have hardly a plausible account of it. One way of opening up the problem would be by way of a series of intellectual biographies of a number of Unitarians, representing various points of view within the denomination: conservatives, radicals, evangelicals, and Broad Church men—to use Bellow's scheme of classification in 1865.[3] This essay on Samuel Gilman (1791–1858), theologically a conservative, may be regarded as a fragment of such a larger plan of investigation.

The Theological World of Samuel Gilman

The material available enables us to focus on two phases of Gilman's career. The first is the period beginning in 1811, including the years of theological study and the early part of his ministry in Charleston. Gilman's manuscript reading notes from these years have survived, and they show him mastering the conventional Christian supernaturalism of the first generation of American Unitarians. The second phase finds a focus in Gilman's Dudleian Lecture in 1848, in which, among other things, he was involved in a critique of the theological ideas of Theodore Parker. In this second phrase, therefore, we may not only see how a conservative responded to the rise of Transcendentalism, but also become aware of the way in which Gilman's ideas were changing at mid-century.

Phase One: Supernatural Rationalism

A passage from a letter written by Gilman to Caroline Howard in March 1812 provides a convenient starting point for the exploration of the first phase. Gilman was twenty-one years of age; he had graduated from Harvard College the previous year and was well launched on his theological studies. Caroline, then seventeen, was spending the winter in Savannah. Seven years would elapse before they would be married, but Gilman was much in love, and felt obliged in his letters not only to communicate gossip and trivia, but also to improve Caroline's mind. This particular passage is an overall assessment of the state of religion in 1812, in which Gilman was expressing the accepted attitudes of the religious liberals of that time and place:

The age of speculative infidelity, Dear Caroline, is no more. The enemies of Christ have been driven from argument to argument, till every inch of the ground is won by his faithful and unwearied disciples. All the doubts and conjectures about the chronology of scripture, all the contradictions of the Mosaic history, all the disputes respecting miracles, all the objections to a revealed religion, and all the arguments against the revelation by Jesus Christ, are at length chased by the overwhelming light of reason. The idle cavillers at our religion thought that by attacking its supporters on the ground of reason they would surely overthrow them. They imagined that our only castle was faith. But they were fatally mistaken. The very weapons they laid hold of for the destruction of that beautiful fabric have recoiled with destructive force upon themselves. There is now scarcely to be known a man of science and learning, who pretends to doubt of the religion of Jesus. Those who railed are now abashed by argument, those who hesitated are convinced by demonstration, and those who believed, are confirmed by an accumulated and complicated mass of evidence that [defies] opposition. The principal difficulty at present is, how this bible which we all receive as genuine shall be explained. An immense *desideratum* is, a concurrence of opinion, and an union of faith in the whole body of Christians. When this happy state of things shall arrive, it is impossible to predict; but there surely seems to be an appearance of a tendency towards it, however remote the event may be. Toleration is now almost universal. There is no martyrdom for opinion. All sects appear to be studying the scriptures principally for the love of truth. People of different persuasions are seen uniting to promote the cause of Christianity, by missions, Bible Societies, and other institutions, and the sword of controversy, though it is yet unsheathed, and wielded with a hostile ardour, which the peaceful spirit of Christianity does not allow,—yet is at least no more defiled with blood, and is blunted of its cruel sharpness.[4]

In this passage, there are at least five themes that need to be identified and separated out for examination. There is, first of all, a rejection of what Gilman called "speculative infidelity." Then there is the assertion that this infidelity has been destroyed, and revealed religion established, by "the light of reason," by "demonstration," and by "an accumulated mass of evidence." This suggests, in the third place, an attachment to a particular philosophical tradition, which we shall identify in due course. Then there is an indirect assertion that it would be considerations arising from biblical interpretation and criticism that would shape the next stage of theological development: "The principal difficulty at present is, how this bible which we all receive as genuine shall be explained." Finally, the confidence is expressed that Christians will be able to unite—to find a "concurrence of opinion"—on the simple truths of the religion of Jesus, which is both scripturally grounded and rationally vindicated. These themes were commonplaces of the time and the place and the group with which Gilman was identified. They represent in compact form a rather complex intellectual tradition that was one of the main strands of the eighteenth-century Age of Reason.

(1) *Speculative infidelity.* "The age of speculative infidelity," Gilman declared, "is no more." Infidelity here means Deism, or "freethinking," as it was sometimes called. The deist argued that the Creator has endowed us with the faculty of Reason; and that by its use, unassisted by any revelation of God's will, as in the Bible, we may know of his existence and of our duties of piety to Him and benevolence to our fellows. God's universal revelation of Himself in the creation is all that is required to establish religious truth and moral obligation:

> The spacious firmament on high
> And all the blue ethereal sky
> And spangled heavens, a shining frame,
> Their great Original proclaim.

Deism, in short, was an assertion of the sufficiency of Natural Religion; that is to say, those principles of religion that can be established by the Reason alone. Christianity, as revealed religion, was either dismissed as superfluous or attacked as the product of designing priestcraft.

In the 1790s, Christian believers had thought the threat of

infidelity to be very great. The first part of Tom Paine's *Age of Reason* appeared in 1794, while the French Revolution brought not only disorder and the guillotine but an attempt to establish a Religion of Reason supplanting Christianity. Gilman doubtless had Paine in mind as he wrote to Caroline; for when he made a courtesy call on Professor Henry Ware some weeks earlier, the conversation had largely turned on Paine's infidelity. In 1813, Gilman read James Cheetham's *Life of Thomas Paine*, in which the wretched closing years of Paine's life were described, and commented, "I presume the account is substantially true; for I have never heard its veracity impeached. If it be true, oh that all infidels would read the history of the last years of the life of Thomas Paine."[5]

(2) *The light of Reason.* Gilman thus shared the prevailing adverse judgment on Deism and on Tom Paine as a notorious advocate of it. But, positively, he also shared the prevailing view that Christianity may be demonstrated to be a divinely authorized revelation of God's will. He took particular satisfaction in showing that Christianity is validated, not by blind faith, or dogmatism, or emotional excess, but by Reason itself, which the deists had too readily taken for granted worked to their advantage: "All the objections to a revealed religion, and all the arguments against the revelation by Jesus Christ, are at length chased by the overwhelming light of reason."

The position Gilman had adopted is one that modern historians sometimes refer to as "Supernatural Rationalism." It begins with the proposition of the deists that there is such a thing as Natural Religion, which can be established by the unassisted intellect. But it denies the sufficiency of Natural Religion. On Natural Religion as a foundation there must be built a structure of Revealed Religion, to supply additional guidance, beyond what the unassisted reason could ever discover, as to the way by which salvation is to be attained. Furthermore, Christianity is such a revealed religion, as may be demonstrated by the evidence of history, especially the fact that Christ fulfilled prophecies and worked miracles.[6]

Gilman surely heard these propositions expounded many times from the pulpit, and he encountered them in theological books at every turn. One such book was George Campbell's *Lectures on Systematic Theology*, which he read at the very beginning of his theological studies, no doubt in the edition reprinted at Boston in 1810.[7] Before Gilman was done, he had read all of Campbell's major works, in church history, criticism, and biblical interpretation, as well as in theology. He shared his enthusiasm for Campbell with Caroline in an early letter:

> I am highly pleased with Campbell's Lectures in Theology. Dr. George Campbell was a celebrated Scotch divine, who flourished in the last century, and maintains a high rank on the list of its literary men. He died in 1796, at the advanced age of 76, having a little before resigned the office of professour of Divinity in the University of Aberdeen. But the work which will establish his fame with posterity, is the "Philosophy of Rhetoric" of which I have heard the most exalted encomiums, and which I shall commence immediately after completing the Theological Lectures. Both of these works I own, and hope that one day you will derive from them the same pleasure which I now have the opportunity of enjoying.[8]

Gilman did indeed go on to read the *Philosophy of Rhetoric*, which he found to be "a noble work."[9] Some time later he turned to the "Preliminary Dissertations" prefixed to Campbell's translation of the Gospels. Then, in November, 1814, he turned to Campbell's *Lectures on Ecclesiastical History* with eager anticipation:

> It was with impressions of no ordinary delight that I resolved on reading another work of the calm, the clear, the candid, the learned, the amiable George Campbell. Three years ago, I set out in my theological career, by reading his lectures on systematic Theology. The same winter, I perused nearly the

whole of his Philosophy of Rhetoric. A year ago, I read the most of his preliminary dissertations to the N.T.—How important are the subjects on which he chose to employ his labors! The mind that cannot be taught by every page of his writings, is either too stupid to learn, or too far advanced beyond the reach of instruction. I set no bounds on my anticipation of what I shall find in these lectures.[10]

Gilman read with approval other exponents of Supernatural Rationalism as well. In October, 1813, he noted that in the course of the previous year, he had been reading "three great writers." Campbell was one of them; the others were Nathaniel Lardner and William Paley. Gilman was especially impressed with Paley's *Horae Paulinae* (1790), in which the inner consistency between the Epistles of Paul and the Book of Acts is adduced as evidence of the authenticity of the New Testament. Paley has "convinced me by this work of the truth of the Christian Religion,"[11] Gilman declared. But even greater than these three, in his mind, was Samuel Clarke, whose Boyle Lectures on Natural and Revealed Religion, preached as long ago as 1705, he still found to be among the best:

> . . . to me it seems to contain one of the most condensed, complete, and satisfactory defenses of Christianity, that can well be devised. The subject is treated with the hand of a master. Every page is deep, yet every page is clear. Original thought, acute criticism, enthusiastic love of virtue, are every where conspicuous. . . . How much do Lardner and Campbell sink beneath him. I will not say Paley, too, for I believe that with as much study and energy, Paley would have been as great a man as Clarke. He had the advantage of a century's new discoveries and new ideas.[12]

Although deists and supernatural rationalists argued bitterly over the truth of the Christian revelation, it should be noted that their philosophical assumptions were the same. Both accepted the psychology of John Locke and agreed that knowledge is based on sensation and reflection. Religious truths are no different from any other in this respect. Hence the deists argued that the human intellect, as it experiences the world of Nature through the evidence of the senses, will be irresistibly drawn to the conclusion that all this is the product of an intelligent and all-powerful Creator. The Christian apologists insisted in addition that a special revelation of God's will, attested by historical evidence such as the miracles of Christ which were witnessed by multitudes, is as firmly established as any propositions that ever depended on the testimony of eyewitnesses. So Gilman could write with vast satisfaction, as noted above, that the very weapons the deists laid hold of for the destruction of Christianity "have recoiled with destructive force upon themselves."

(3) *The Scottish Philosophy and the response to skepticism.* But supernatural rationalists were sensitive to another danger to Christian truth. Deists might batter at the outworks of the citadel of Christian faith, but the skepticism of the acute and subtle Hume threatened to undermine its very foundations. Hume argued that if you start with the assumption of John Locke that knowledge is based on the evidence of the senses, then the structure of knowledge will disintegrate because no sensations can be found to account for certain concepts that tie our experiences together. Take the notion of causality, for example. There is no sensation to correspond with the idea of cause. Our notion of cause and effect derives from the fact that we have become accustomed to the sequence of event *A* followed by event *B*. But just because we have observed this sequence many times in the past, we have no assurance from the evidence of the senses, which Locke declared was the ultimate source of all knowledge, that it is inherent in the scheme of things and will happen in the future. Since deists and supernatural rationalists alike argued that the universe was the effect of which God was the cause, skepticism as to the concept of causality threatened the entire theological structure of the Age of Reason.

Hume's skepticism was felt at another sensitive point as well.

For the supernatural rationalist, the New Testament miracles were a crucial link in their argument. The deists had rejected the miracle stories as fables, since there can be no break in the uniformity of natural law. Hume was even more subtle in his attack, for in his "Essay on Miracles" (1747) he argued that even if one allowed the possibility of miracles, they would still be useless as evidences of a divine revelation. The Christian apologists relied on the evidence of witnesses; but "no testimony is sufficient to establish a miracle, unless the testimony be of such a kind, that its falsehood would be more miraculous than the fact which it endeavors to establish. . . ."[13] Or, to put it another way, the chances that the testimony is in error are much greater than the chances that a miracle had occurred.

Gilman found in his reading answers to the skepticism of Hume, just as he did answers to the infidelity of the deists. For that generation, the most effective response was considered to be that of the Scottish common-sense realists, of whom Thomas Reid and Dugald Stewart were leading figures. George Campbell, indeed, was a member of the circle that gathered around Reid. The Scottish philosophers argued that Locke had been in error in supposing that knowledge was a matter of the agreement or disagreement of ideas in the mind. That position would mean that we would be hard put to explain whether there is any correspondence between the idea in the mind and the external reality of which the senses take account. Our awareness of the external world as being what we experience it to be, the Scottish philosophers insisted, is a basic intuition, which is self-validating and not dependent on argument. Before they were done, the Scottish realists had elaborated the number of such intuitive judgments so as to restore all the connective concepts, like cause and effect, and personal identity, that seemed necessary to tie the structure of knowledge together again.

That the New England liberals—and not they alone—accepted the Scottish revision of the Lockean philosophy is no new discovery; but some important recent scholarship has underlined the significance of that fact and explored its implications.[14] Scottish authors, as might have been expected, loom large on Gilman's reading lists. Campbell we have already encountered. Dugald Stewart was read in 1816, and Gilman apostrophized him thus: "If I were allowed to say but one single observation to Dugald Stewart, it would be—keep on writing—keep on writing. Every moment of time which you devote to anything else is robbing the world of so much instruction and delight."[15] Thomas Brown, third in line of the Scottish mental philosophers after Reid and Stewart, attracted Gilman's attention in the early 1820s, and he spent many weeks preparing assessments of Brown's works for publication in the *North American Review*.[16] On one occasion, he referred to him as "the closest analytical reasoner of modern times."[17]

As for Hume's skeptical "Essay on Miracles," Gilman found a wholly persuasive refutation in Campbell's "Dissertation," appended to the *Lectures on Ecclesiastical History*:

At the conclusion of this volume of lectures is appended the author's celebrated essay on miracles. I have read it. The most prominent reflection which strikes the reader from the beginning to the end of the essay, is, that Mr. Hume is *killed*—killed too by a thousand stabs. The slain is slain more than thrice. . . . Oh, what a writer Hume had been, could his mind have taken a less metaphysical turn. The same acuteness, which has now been preempted in the cause of sophistry and error, would have then been employed for the maintenance and establishment of the truth.

Perhaps no controversialist ever received a more complete overthrow than this far-famed miracle hero. On the first view, one would hardly imagine it possible, [that] any writer of reflection, or jealousy for his literary reputation, would commit himself to such a degree as he has here done. It almost appears to be a concert between Campbell and Hume, that the latter should have taken a subject and written so carelessly and vaguely upon it as he possibly could, that the former might have the glory of combatting and discrediting it. Must not this answer have secretly embittered the latter days of Hume, much as he professed never to be ruffled or anxious? Must not his reputation have severely suffered under the blow? And if he had anything which he valued, if he had a tender point, if he had an object of adoration, was it not his literary reputation? Oh, I know he writhed under this lash much and often. His pride, which he was as full of as his own blood, never suffered him to confess how far he felt himself wounded. But if his heart would have been inspected, I would lay my intellect, that it was wrung by torture on many occasions, and that the name of Campbell particularly was a talisman which should throw him into a fit of inconceivable desperation. But I think he was a deep hypocrite, and his hypocrisy could conceal his agony—[18]

This passage has been quoted at length to remind us that an earlier generation saw the controversy over Hume's essay on miracles in a very different light than we are likely to do. Campbell's "Dissertation" had been published in 1762; here was Gilman, more than fifty years later, referring to it as a "celebrated" essay, and finding its reasoning conclusive. Most modern historians of the Enlightenment will give the impression that Hume had the better of the argument. After all, we know enough not to believe in miracles, or suppose that they would be of any value to validate religious truth; and besides, the fact that Hume is remembered while his critics are not creates a presumption in his favor. We need to be reminded that there was a time when it was generally taken for granted that men like George Campbell and Hugh Farmer—now so obscure that they scarcely rate mention in a footnote—were acclaimed as having effectively answered him.

(4) *Biblical interpretation.* The fourth theme to be found in Gilman's letter to Caroline Howard is the stress on the importance of the critical study of the Bible. If one is convinced that Christianity is a divinely authenticated revelation, then it becomes a matter of the highest urgency to arrive at a correct understanding of the documents by which that revelation is transmitted to us. This

means both a detailed study of the manuscripts, to be sure that errors have not crept into the text, and careful analysis of the contents, to make sure that theologians and commentators and creedmakers have not distorted the pure revelation of God's will.

It has been altogether too common for liberals of a later generation to suppose that the issue in the days of the Unitarian Controversy was the use of reason in religion, as opposed to biblical orthodoxy. But Unitarianism on these shores began as a biblical religion. As Channing put it in the Baltimore Sermon (1819): "Whatever doctrines seem to us to be clearly taught in Scripture, we receive without reserve or exception." Granted, our rational powers are not to be despised. Reason must establish the principles of Natural Religion, and verify the evidences of Revealed Religion. The use of reason is necessary in order to clarify the obscurities of Scripture and understand its doctrine aright; and Channing had a sublime confidence that the Bible, properly understood, will never be found to sanction irrationalities in doctrine. The recurrent complaint of the early liberals was not that the orthodox were too much bound by the Bible in their statement of Christian doctrine, but that they were not biblical enough. The great attraction of biblical criticism to the liberals was that they were convinced that it would enable them to demonstrate that orthodox views of the Trinity, or the dual nature of Christ, or the Atonement, were unscriptural.

The work of Biblical criticism that impressed Gilman most, as he began his theological study, was—not surprisingly—by a Scotsman. It was Gilbert Gerard's *Institutes of Biblical Criticism* (1806), of which Gilman wrote, in November, 1813:

A more interesting book, on a subject apparently so repulsive, I cannot conceive. . . . I could not have imagined how much light it would throw into my mind. Biblical criticism is not the dangerous weapon which I had once apprehended it. Instead of its having a tendency to overthrow any of the vital articles of our faith, it is on the contrary rather calculated to confirm and establish them. Indeed, I almost tremble, when I see with what an intrepid and undaunted hand some of these ingenious dissectors open up those writings which have so long engaged the implicit and reverent assent of millions. I never experienced so strongly the necessity of studying the scriptures with redoubled diligence, as I do now. Never was my ignorance so pressed home upon me, as by perusing this book. . . . It has excited a curiosity to know something more of these invaluable Sacred writings.[19]

Gilman's reading of Gerard came at a time of rapid change in methods of biblical study in this country. Heretofore, Americans had confined their reading almost entirely to the works of British scholars. Now their horizons were widening to include the riches of German critical scholarship. Joseph Stevens Buckminster of Boston traveled abroad in 1806 and brought back a whole library of books, including many items of German biblical criticism not previously available on this side of the Atlantic. An edition of Griesbach's New Testament was published in Cambridge in 1809. George Ticknor, Edward Everett, Joseph Cogswell, and George Bancroft in due course were on their way to German universities to study. Other New England Unitarians began to study German, so that they could read Eichhorn, Michaelis, Wetstein, Rosenmüller, and De Wette in the original.

Gilman became aware that the field of biblical criticism was undergoing radical transformation, but he came along just a bit too early to become wholly master of the new scholarship. His early studies were under the direction of the elder Henry Ware, who represented an older generation, and who never did keep up with changing trends. Gilman himself struggled with the German language in order to be able to read Eichhorn; but by that time he was already settled in Charleston, South Carolina, where the burdens of the parish interfered with ambitious plans for study. Gilman and Jasper Adams, then president of Charleston College, resolved to study German together; but the only time they could manage to find was from five to six o'clock in the morning. "Accordingly," Gilman recalled, "as he lived in my neighborhood,

I visited his house every morning at that hour, summer and winter, for about two years. I always found him at his post, awaiting my arrival, with his fire glowing and his candle burning, in the short and gloomy mornings." They resolved to read Eichhorn, whose many-volumed works Gilman had purchased. "But long periods of indisposition or of absence from Charleston, on the part of one or the other, and then of enforced removal of residences, dissipated these fond dreams, and we conquered comparatively but a few volumes of the learned Eichhorn."[20]

(5) *A concurrence of opinion*. In the short run, the importance of biblical criticism for the liberals was that it seemed to provide support for a unitarian concept of the nature of God and an Arminian (rather than Calvinistic) view of human nature. It gave the liberals, they thought, an immediate advantage in the doctrinal controversies of the day. Its value in the long run lay in the hope that a rigorously critical appeal to scripture would heal disagreements, remove grounds for controversy, and promote unity in the Christian fold. Already, as they saw it, liberals and orthodox held much in common. The principles of Supernatural Rationalism were commonplace among trinitarian Calvinists. Liberals and orthodox agreed on the chief doctrines of Christianity, even though they differed on particular points of interpretation. Both believed in the unity of God even while they disagreed on the doctrine of the Trinity; both regarded us as accountable beings under God's moral government, even if they disputed over our natural state and our power to do the will of God; they agreed that our hopes rest in the divine mercy, and that Jesus Christ is the instrument of our salvation, even if they were not of one mind as to the terms of salvation. The disagreements, the liberal repeatedly declared, were over issues that were either peripheral or clouded in obscurity. To the extent that the obscurity derived from confusion over the meaning of Scripture, biblical criticism would promote agreement. So Gilman wrote to Caroline Howard: "An immense *desideratum* is, a concurrence of opinion, and an union of faith in the whole body of Christians."

In Charleston, however, Gilman found himself in a situation in which such a concurrence of opinion seemed more remote than it had in Boston. To be sure, the separation between the Circular and the Archdale Street churches had been managed in such a way as not to arouse ill will. But the two churches were launched on divergent courses, and the liberals encountered a good deal of odium in the community at large. "Bitter speeches," Gilman recalled in 1852, "were daily circulated against us with the activity of current coin."[21] He was particularly exercised over the attacks printed in a local weekly paper, the *Southern Intelligencer*. "Epithets the most odious, associated ideas the most loathsome, and a spirit and language the most vulgar have been employed against Unitarians," he complained, "which were as entirely unwarranted by the rules of Christian feeling and good breeding, as they were unprovoked by the party assailed."[22]

Gilman was reluctant to get involved in sectarian wrangling, partly because he was confident that the spirit of the age was working to his advantage and would ultimately assure a liberal triumph; but he did feel an obligation to respond when the liberals were unfairly attacked and their views misrepresented. In 1822 he and Martin L. Hurlbut, one of his parishioners, undertook to reply. They began publication of a biweekly paper entitled, significantly, the *Unitarian Defendant*. It included articles such as: "Unitarians Defended by Their Opponents," and "On the Attempt to Deprive Unitarians of the Name of Christians." Even this mild kind of polemical writing was not congenial to Gilman, however, and after eleven issues, the publication was dropped. The circulation of tracts in which religious truths might be stated positively, without polemics, was more to his taste; and he preferred to put his efforts into the Charleston Unitarian Book and Tract Society, founded in 1821, which lasted for thirty years or more.

Gilman's theological study and early ministry fell within the period of controversy that saw the division of the congregational churches into two separate denominations. This controversy is often understood in narrow doctrinal terms, with major emphasis on the pamphlet debate between Andrews Norton and Moses Stuart over the doctrine of the Trinity, and between Henry Ware,

Sr., and Leonard Woods over human nature. It is doubtless inevitable that the attention of historians should be attracted to matter of disagreement and episodes of controversy and should slide casually over areas of agreement. The experience of someone like Gilman reminds us that most of what liberals stood for was not in dispute, and it clarifies for us the perspective from which it was possible to argue, in all sincerity, that the orthodox were insisting on drawing a line where none was necessary. That is to say, the difference between orthodox and liberals was quite as much a question of the usefulness of those particular theological debates as it was a question of the correctness of the doctrines debated. The most basic disagreement between the parties was over the question as to what they should be debating about. That difference in priorities sheds more light on the controversy that developed than all the pages that scholars have devoted to theological and scriptural analysis of the rival Christologies of the two factions.

Phase Two: The Twilight of Supernatural Rationalism

Having examined the intellectual milieu that shaped Gilman's early theological studies and first years as a preacher, a milieu that he found wholly congenial, we are now confronted with the question: How much did his early views change in the course of a ministry of almost forty years? To what extent did doctrines that seemed axiomatic in the year 1819 still have vitality in the 1850s? Did Gilman adjust his own doctrinal position in response to intellectual changes in the world about him? If Gilman's views in 1811 through 1819 represent a wholly typical expression of the liberal Christianity of the day—as they surely did—to what extent did his own intellectual odyssey parallel that of the denomination to which he belonged? What was his response, quite specifically, to the Transcendentalist revolt within Unitarianism, which agitated the denomination for about a generation, beginning in the mid 1830s?

Transcendentalism eludes simple summary or tidy definition.

But whatever else it may have involved, in the realm of religion it meant a rejection of the entire scheme of apologetics we have referred to as Supernatural Rationalism, and indeed of the empirical philosophy on which it rested. The long undisputed sway of the commonsense realists came under explicit attack. The great truths of religion, said the Transcendentalists, are not grounded in logical argument or induction from observed facts of the world of matter. They are primal intuitions[23]; they are expressions of the "religious sentiment," which is part of our essential constitution. Man is by nature a religious being, wrote Theodore Parker:

> The existence of God is a fact given in our nature: it is not something discovered by a process of reasoning; by a long series of deductions from facts; nor yet is it the last generalization from phenomena observed in the universe of mind or matter. But it is a truth fundamental in our nature; given outright by God; a truth which comes to light as soon as self-consciousness begins.[24]

Once the Transcendentalists had shifted the ground of religious truth from external evidences to inner consciousness, revolutionary consequences followed all down the line. The argument for miracles as evidence for the divine origin of revealed religion now suddenly seemed trivial. Christianity does not rest on miracles, Parker wrote, but on "the truth of its doctrines, and its sufficiency to satisfy all the moral and religious wants of man."[25] The very distinction between natural religion and revealed religion no longer seemed to be a useful one. It is the direct, immediate intuition of the divine that is the primary fact of spiritual consciousness; religious doctrines are secondary or derivative; and historic religions, including Christianity, are simply particular expressions of the universal religious element.

When Emerson gave poetic expression to views such as these in his Divinity School Address (1838), he seemed to many Unitarians to be undermining the supernatural claims of Christianity. Andrews Norton characterized Emerson's position—though without mentioning him by name—as the "latest form of infidelity." Younger Unitarian ministers, George Ripley and Theodore Parker among them, replied to Norton. Themselves the product of an earlier controversy, the Unitarians discovered that a rebellious younger generation was producing a new controversy within their midst; while the orthodox smugly remarked that they had known all along that Unitarianism would decline into infidelity and irreligion.

Gilman was not a conspicuous participant in the controversies that swirled around Emerson and Parker. That his sympathies were with the conservatives of the day, however, is clear both from the Dudleian Lecture he delivered at Harvard in 1848, and from incidental comments in other addresses and sermons. He preached on one occasion, probably in the 1850s, for George W. Burnap in Baltimore, and declared:

> I am further happy in professing on this occasion full theo-logical sympathy with your present and former Pastors. Those views of Christianity which I imbibed from the Kirklands, the Channings, and the Wares of my earlier life, only inspire me with increasing confidence and reverence as I advance in years. The supernatural element in the character of Christ and his religion, mingled with, elevating, and strengthening that human reason to which it is addressed, seems to me to meet all the wants and capacities, the aspirations and the destiny of man. It is such a system that I wish to live and die by. . . .[26]

Elsewhere he spoke of "the fundamental error of those who reject the idea of a special revelation," and refuted the notion that "the soul of man is naturally sufficient for its own religious necessi-ties."[27]

At first glance it may look as though Gilman's doctrinal views had not changed at all in thirty years, and that he was simply perpetuating the patterns of thought he had so thoroughly mas-tered earlier. But a closer look at Gilman's later writings will suggest that more is happening than appears on the surface.

Although the structure of his thoughts did remain the same, the argumentation on which he relied was changing in a significant way. He did not live long enough for the new concepts he was assimilating to force a major restructuring of his theological position. But his later writings reveal a conservative Unitarian in the process of assimilating certain new ideas, only some of which were Transcendentalist, which would eventually transform the outlook of the denomination.

Gilman's Dudleian lecture in 1848 is especially significant in this connection. The lectureship had been established a century earlier by Chief Justice Paul Dudley, who prescribed four topics to be treated in annual rotation. Two of them were Natural Religion and Revealed Religion; that is to say, for one hundred years the lectures on this foundation had been expounding the principles of Supernatural Rationalism for the benefit of successive generations of Harvard undergraduates. The established framework of the lectureship was exactly right to show the extent to which later lecturers like Gilman were adhering to a tenacious intellectual tradition, or were modifying it, or were diverging from it. What Gilman said in 1848, therefore, can be measured directly against familiar standards.

Gilman began his lecture, which was on Revealed Religion, with a summary of current trends in American religion, intended to show that the lectureship was not obsolete, and that there was still a job for Dudleian lecturers to do. Then he declared: "I propose confining myself to a single line of argument, defending merely the fact of a positive, special supernatural revelation, in accordance with all but universal belief of the religious portion of mankind."[28] To which the shade of Chief Justice Dudley doubtless nodded assent. But the interesting thing is that Gilman did not then turn for proof to the Bible, or, indeed, to the religious experience of mankind. Instead he turned to science, particularly to geology. Perhaps he had been reading the Bridgewater Treatises,[29] more likely he had encountered a summary in one of the quarterly reviews, which were his chief reliance for keeping up with trends in philosophy, religion, and public policy. In any event, what geological science seemed to be saying was quite clear. It was that fossil remains are to be found in different layers of the earth's surface, showing that quite different species and genera of animals have existed at different times in the past. No one can read the reports of geologists, he declared, "without an irresistible conviction, that new, specific, and original impulses of designing and creating power have from time to time interposed to change the pre-existing order of things, and substitute another in its place."[30]

Gilman understood this geological evidence to mean that the uniformity of Nature, often urged as an argument against miracles, does not preclude special intervention by God in the workings of his creation. What is true in the domain of Natural History must equally be true in human history. There, Gilman discerned three successive religious eras, the transition from one to the next being explicable only in terms of "some kind of special, Divine interposition, entirely extraneous to the ordinary workings and principles of human nature."[31] He identified the three eras as those of Idolatry, Pure Theism—i.e., Jewish Monotheism—and Christianity. He devoted the middle part of the lecture to a series of arguments designed to prove that Theism could not have arisen out of Idolatry, or Christianity out of Theism, solely on the basis of natural forces operative in the culture without special intervention. The gist of the conclusion is found in this sentence:

As the Deity had specially interposed to repair, arrange, and extend the material creation by the introduction of successive classes of organized bodies, there is a commanding presumption that he would also specially interpose to elevate, educate, and transform the moral agents on whom he has conferred a being.[32]

From the perspective of today, this pre-Darwinian natural theology seems so very naive that we may easily fail to recognize the element of novelty in it and the extent to which it prepared the way for later developments. But it suggests that important changes were in the making. The familiar framework of Natural Religion, Revealed Religion, and miraculous intervention had not yet collapsed; and Gilman probably would have clung to them even if he had lived a decade longer than he did. But the argumentation under each head was very different from what he had mastered under the tutelage of Kirkland and Ware. Formerly, it had been the Newtonian cosmology that had provided deists and supernatural rationalists alike with rational proofs for the existence of God. Now it was the record of fossil remains in the rocks. The scientific model appropriated by theologians for the construction of Natural Theology was shifting from physics to biology, thereby underlining the concept of historical development and making it possible for a concept of biological evolution to seem plausible.

The nineteenth century became historically minded in a way the eighteenth had never been; it found it necessary to give genetic, developmental explanations for all sorts of phenomena that the eighteenth century had handled in nonhistorical, rational terms. For the eighteenth century, God's revelation through Jesus Christ was a historical event, to be sure; but it was one in which the emphasis was on the miraculous interruption of historical continuity, so that Revealed Religion was an arbitrary intrusion into history, rather than something to be understood as the product of historical development. But Gilman's three religious eras were stated as stages of historic development, even though special intervention was acknowledged at particular points in the historic process. One could not pass from Idolatry to Christianity without passing through an intermediate stage. The New Testament miracles, once the keystone in the structure of Christian apologetics, now appeared to be no more than a kind of incidental byproduct of the notion that God may intervene in his creation. When Gilman could write that "the miraculous events recorded in the Scriptures are but harmonious appendages to the very idea of a special revelation,"[33] it is evident that the old supernatural rationalist apologetics was obsolescent.

But what was taking its place was not Transcendentalism, even if Gilman's later sermons sometimes contain what seem to be verbal echoes of Theodore Parker. What was taking its place was a philosophy of developmentalism, and eventually of evolutionary progress. Many intellectual currents were drawn into a new synthesis: the eighteenth century idea of progress; the Arminian doctrine of salvation by gradual reformation of character; the material advances of the young republic; scientific work in geology and paleontology; the rise of historical studies; Hegelianism; and eventually Darwinism. But if Transcendentalism made a contribution to this rather incongruous mixture, it was not the most important one. Parker's Absolute Religion, after all, was no more historically conditioned than the Natural Religion of the supernatural rationalists had been.

Historians have often argued that it was the Transcendentalists who destroyed the philosophical presuppositions of the first generation of Unitarians by their attack on Lockean sensationalism and the substitution for it of an intuitional epistemology. That is what actually did happen for some people, and to that extent it is a sound analysis. But it is far from being the whole story. There were many paths from the nonhistorical rationalism of the first generation to the developmentalism of the third, and they did not necessarily pass through Transcendentalism. Nor was the outcome the acceptance of the intuitional epistemology that the Transcendentalists had used to undermine the philosophical presuppositions on which the old version of Christian apologetics had rested. There now begin to open before us a whole new range of questions about the course of American Unitarian history in the mid-nineteenth century that heretofore have not even been raised.

But I think we have discovered enough already to indicate that when the story is fully told, Gilman will be found contributing to the earliest phase of one of the main lines of development. In view of his growing awareness of scientific thought, how would he have responded to the *Origin of Species*, I wonder!

Ministers Serving Boston Churches
1791–1815

In both appendices, the affiliations are given in order: first, service as an officer (point score 3), next, service as trustee or comparable duty, or incorporator (point score 2); finally, ordinary membership (point score 1).

Congregational

John L. Abbott (1783–1814). AB, HC '05. First Church, 1813–1814.

0–0–0 = 0.

Jeremy Belknap (1744–1798). AB, HC '62. Federal Street, 1787–1798.

MHS, Corr. Sec., 1791–1798; Cong. Charitable Soc., Council, 1796; AAAS; Humane Soc.; SPG Indians, 1788; Fire Soc., 1794. 1–1–4 = 9.

Joseph Stevens Buckminster (1784–1812). AB, HC '00. Brattle Street, 1805–1812.

Fire Soc., Corr. Sec., 1807–1812; Humane Soc., Trustee, 1811–1812; AAAS; MHS, 1811. 1–1–2 = 7.

Samuel Cary (1785–1815). AB, HC '04. King's Chapel, 1809–1815.

AAAS; Humane Soc. 0–0–2 = 2.

The Unitarian Controversy

William Ellery Channing (1780–1842). AB, HC '98. Federal Street, 1803–1842.

Harvard College, Fellow, 1813–1826; AAAS; Humane Soc.; Cong. Charitable Soc., 1814; SPG Indians, 1804–1842. 1–0–4 = 7.

John Clarke (1755–1798). AB, HC '74. First Church, 1778–1798.

Humane Soc., Corr. Sec., 1786–1788, 1797; AAAS, Inc.; SPG Indians, Inc.; MHS, 1796; Fire Soc., 1794. 1–2–2 = 9.

Joseph Eckley (1750–1811). AB, Coll. NJ '72. Old South, 1779–1811.

Cong. Charitable Soc., Sec. 1805–1810; Immigrant Soc., Inc., Treas., 1793; SPG Indians, Inc., 1787; Humane Soc.; Fire Soc., 1794. 2–1–2 = 10.

John Eliot (1754–1813). AB, HC '72. New North, 1779–1813.

Harvard College, Fellow, 1804–1813; Humane Soc., Treas., 1805–1813; Cong. Charitable Soc., Sec. 1811–1812; MHS, Libr., 1791–1793, 1795–1798, Cabinet Keeper, 1791–1793, Corr. Sec. 1798–1813; SPG Indians, Inc.; Fire Soc., Trustee, 1796–1813; Immigrant Soc., Inc.; AAAS 4–3–1 = 19.

William Emerson (1769–1811). AB, HC '89. First Church, 1799–1811.

Fire Soc., Corr. Sec., 1804–1807, Trustee, 1807–1811; Humane Soc., Trustee, 1807–1810; MHS, Standing Comm., 1803–1809; AAAS 1–2–1 = 8.

Edward Everett (1794–1865). AB, HC '11. Brattle Street, 1814–1815.

0–0–0 = 0.

Oliver Everett (1752–1792). AB, HC '79. New South, 1782–1792.

AAAS, Humane Soc. 0–0–2 = 2.

Appendix A

James Freeman (1754–1835). AB, HC '77. King's Chapel, 1782–1835.

AAAS, Treas., Council; Fire Soc., Inc., Corr. Sec., 1794–1804; MHS, Rec. Sec., 1793–1812, Standing Comm., 1812–1826; Humane Soc. 3–0–1 = 10.

Edward D. Griffin (1770–1837). AB, YC '90. Park Street, 1811–1815.

0–0–0 = 0.

Horace Holley (1781–1837). AB, YC '03. Hollis Street, 1809–1818.

AAAS; Humane Soc. 0–0–2 = 2.

Simeon Howard (1733–1804). AB, HC '58. West Church, 1767–1804.

Harvard College, Fellow, 1780–1804; Humane Soc., Treas., 1786–1796, 2nd VP, 1797–1798, 1st VP, 1799–1804; Cong. Charitable Soc., Inc., 1786, Treas., 1786–1804; AAAS, Council; SPG Indians, 1792–1804; Immigrant Soc., 1793. 3–1–2 = 13.

Joshua Huntington (1786–1819). AB, YC '04. Old South, 1808–1819.

Humane Soc.; SPG Indians, 1814–1819. 0–0–2 = 2.

John T. Kirkland (1770–1840). AB, HC '89. New South, 1794–1810.

Harvard College, Pres., 1810–1828; AAAS; Humane Soc.; Cong. Charitable Soc., 1814; SPG Indians, 1804–1842. 1–0–4 = 7.

John Lathrop (1739–1816). AB, Coll. NJ '63 (HC '63 *ad eund*). Second Church, 1768–1816.

Harvard College, Fellow, 1778–1815; AAAS, Libr., Council; Humane Soc., Trustee, 1786–1797, Corr. Sec. 1798, 2nd VP 1799–1804, Pres., 1805–1816; SPG Indians, 1792–1816, VP, 1806–1816; Fire Soc., 1794; Immigrant Soc., 1793. 4–0–2 = 14.

Charles Lowell (1782–1861). AB, HC '00. West Church, 1806–1861.

Humane Soc., Trustee, 1814–1816; Cong. Charitable Soc., 1813; SPG Indians, 1814–1861; MHS, 1815–1856, 1859–1861. 0–1–3 = 5.

Francis Parkman (1788–1852). AB, HC '07. New North, 1813–1849.

Fire Soc., Trustee, 1815–1816; Humane Soc. 0–1–1 = 3.

John Snelling Popkin (1771–1852). AB, HC '92. Federal Street, 1798–1802.

AAAS; MHS, 1801. 0–0–2 = 2.

Peter Thacher (1752–1802). AB, HC '69. Brattle Street, 1785–1802.

SPG Indians, Sec. 1790–1802; Humane Soc., Trustee, 1786–1802; Cong. Charitable Soc., Inc., 1786; MHS, Publications Comm., 1791; AAAS; Fire Soc.; Immigrant Soc. 1–3–3 = 12.

Samuel Cooper Thacher (1788–1818). AB, HC '04. New South, 1811–1818.

Humane Soc.; AAAS. 0–0–2 = 2. Later (1816–1818) Fellow of Harvard College.

Samuel West (1738–1818). AB, HC '61. Hollis Street, 1789–1808.

AAAS, Inc., 1780; Humane Soc.; SPG Indians, 1792–1808; Fire Soc., 1795. 0–1–3 = 5.

Episcopalian

John S. J. Gardiner (1765–1830). AM (Hon.) HC '03. Trinity, 1792–1829.

Humane Soc. 0–0–1 = 1.

Appendix A

Samuel Parker (1744–1804). AB, HC '64. Trinity, 1771–1804.

Humane Soc., Rec. Sec., 1786–1788, Corr. Sec., 1789–1796, Treas., 1797–1804. 1–0–0 = 3.

William Walter (1737–1800). AB, HC '56. Christ Church, 1792–1800.

Humane Soc.; Fire Soc., 1794; Immigrant Soc., 1793. 0–0–3 = 3.

Baptist

Thomas Baldwin (1753–1826). Second Baptist, 1790–1825.

Fire Soc., Trustee 1811–1820; Humane Soc. 0–1–1 = 3.

Caleb Blood (1754–1814). Charles Street, 1807–1810. 0–0–0 = 0.

Joseph Clay (1764–1811). First Baptist, 1807–1808. 0–0–0 = 0.

Thomas Gair (1755–1790). Second Baptist, 1787–1790. 0–0–0 = 0.

Daniel Sharpe (1783–1853). Charles Street, 1812–1853. 0–0–0 = 0.

Isaac Skillman (1740–1799). Coll. NJ '66. Second Baptist, 1773–1787. 0–0–0 = 0.

Samuel Stillman (1737–1807). AM, HC '61 *ad eund.* First Baptist, 1765–1807.

Fire Soc., Trustee, 1796–1807; Humane Soc., 1794. 0–1–1 = 3.

James Manning Winchell (1791–1820). First Baptist, 1814–1820. 0–0–0 = 0.

Methodist

Jesse Lee (1758–1816). Methodist, 1790–? 0–0–0 = 0.

Thomas F. Sargeant (1776–1833). Methodist, 1800–?
0–0–0 = 0.

Universalist

Paul Dean (1783–1860). First Universalist, 1813–1823.
0–0–0 = 0.

Edward Mitchell (d. 1834). First Universalist, 1810–1811.
0–0–0 = 0

John Murray (1714–1815). First Universalist, 1793–1815.
Humane Soc.; Fire Soc., 1795. 0–0–2 = 2.

Roman Catholic

John Cheverus (1768–1836). Catholic, 1796–1823.
Humane Soc. 0–0–1 = 1.

Francis A. Matignon (1753–1818). Catholic, 1792–1818.
Fire Soc., 1794. 0–0–1 = 1.

John Thayer (1758–1815). Catholic, 1790–1792?
0–0–0 = 0.

Boston Men of Affairs, 1791–1815

James Bowdoin (1752–1811). AB, HC '71. Brattle Street.

Harvard College, Fellow, 1792–1799; Fire Soc., Trustee, 1794–1796; AAAS, Humane Soc. 1–1–2 = 7.

Joseph Coolidge (1747–1820). King's Chapel.

Humane Soc., Trustee, 1807–1821; Fire Soc. 0–1–1 = 3.

Theophilus Cushing. 0–0–0 = 0.

John Davis (1761–1847). AB, HC '81. Federal Street.

Harvard College, Fellow, 1803–1810, Treas., 1810–1827; AAAS, Rec. Sec., 1804; MHS, Standing Comm., 1798–1818, [Pres., 1818–1835]; Humane Soc.; SPG Indians; Fire Soc. 2–1–3 = 11.

Thomas Dawes, Sr. (1731–1809). Old South.

AAAS; Humane Soc.; SPG Indians; Fire Soc. 0–0–4 = 4.

Aaron Dexter (1750–1829). AB, HC '76. King's Chapel.

Humane Soc., 2nd VP. 1805–1813; AAAS, Counsellor, 1814; Immigrant Soc., Inc., 1794; MHS; Fire Soc. 1–2–2 = 9.

Samuel Eliot (1739–1820). West Church.

Cong. Charitable Soc., VP, 1807–1813; AAAS; Humane Soc.; Immigrant Soc. 1–0–3 = 6.

Christopher Gore (1758–1827). AB, HC '76. King's Chapel.

Harvard College, Fellow, 1812–1820; MHS, Pres., 1806–1818; AAAS. 2–0–1 = 7.

Benjamin Greene (1747–1807). Trinity.

0–0–0 = 0.

John Coffin Jones (1750–1829). AB, HC '68. King's Chapel and Brattle Street.

Humane Soc. 0–0–1 = 1.

Benjamin Joy (1757–1829). First Church.

Humane Soc. 0–0–1 = 1.

Thomas Kast (1750–1820). AB, HC '69. Christ Church.

Humane Soc. 0–0–1 = 1.

John Lowell (1743–1802). AB, HC '60. Brattle Street.

Harvard College, Fellow, 1784–1802; AAAS, Counsellor; Immigrant Soc., Inc., 1794; Humane Soc. 1–2–1 = 8.

Mungo Mackay (1740–1811). West Church.

Immigrant Soc., Inc.; Humane Soc. 0–1–1 = 3.

Jonathan Mason, Sr. (1725–1798). Old South.

Humane Soc., 1st VP, 1791–1796, Pres. 1797; SPG Indians, Treas. 1787–1790; Cong. Charitable Soc. 2–0–1 = 7.

Jonathan Mason, Jr. (1756–1831). AB, Coll. NJ '74. Old South.

Humane Soc. 0–0–1 = 1.

Ebenezer Oliver (1752–1826). King's Chapel.

Humane Soc. 0–0–1 = 1.

William Payne (1764–1827).

Humane Soc. 0–0–1 = 1.

William Phillips, Sr. (1722–1804). Old South.

Cong. Charitable Soc., Inc.; SPG Indians. 0–1–1 = 3.

William Phillips, Jr. (1750–1827). Old South.

SPG Indians, Pres. 1806–1827; Humane Soc., Trustee, 1805–1813; Cong. Charitable Soc., Councillor, 1813–? 1–2–0 = 7.

William Spooner (1760–1836). AB, HC '78. Brattle Street.

AAAS, Vice Treas., 1804; Humane Soc., Trustee, 1799–1804, Corr. Sec. 1805–1813, 2nd VP, 1814–1823 [1st VP, 1824–1827, Pres. 1828]. 2–0–1 = 7.

Ebenezer Storer (1730–1807). AB, HC '47. Brattle Street.

Harvard College, Fellow (Treas.), 1777–1807; AAAS, Treas.; SPG Indians, Treas., 1790–1796; Humane Soc. 3–0–1 = 10.

James Sullivan (1744–1808). AM, HC (Hon.) '80. Brattle Street.

Cong. Charitable Soc., VP, 1786–1804; SPG Indians, Pres., 1800–1806; MHS, Pres., 1791–1806; AAAS, Inc.; Humane Soc. 3–1–1 = 12.

David Tilden (1744–1814). First Church.

Humane Soc.; Fire Soc. 0–0–2 = 2.

William Tudor, Jr. (1799–1830). AB, HC '96. King's Chapel.

Humane Soc. 0–0–1 = 1.

John Warren (1753–1815). AB, HC '71. Brattle Street.

Humane Soc., Pres. 1799–1813; AAAS, Counsellor, 1804; Fire Soc. 1–1–1 = 6.

John Collins Warren (1778–1856). AB, HC '97. Brattle Street.

AAAS, Vice Treas., 1814; Humane Soc. [later Councillor and VP]. 1–0–1 = 4.

Oliver Wendell (1733–1812). AB, HC '53. Brattle Street.

Harvard College, Fellow, 1788–1812; SPG Indians, Pres. 1787–1793; Humane Soc.; Cong. Charitable Soc.; Fire Soc. 2–0–3 = 9.

APPENDIX C

Remarks Introductory
to "Ministers, Churches, and the Boston Elite, 1791–1815"
Bicentennial Conference, Massachusetts Historical Society
May 18–19, 1990

I suspect that the substance of this paper comes as no surprise. There has been enough anecdotal material about the relationship between leading Boston merchants, lawyers, and men of affairs in the early nineteenth century, and the churches that ended up being Unitarian, that what we have here simply confirms what people have long assumed. Perhaps it is useful to have more specific demonstration of what has long been suspected, and it may be that there is an unexpected detail here and there. But such novelty as there is, is to be found not in the substance but in the method of analysis—and about that I wish to say a few words.

What kind of a paper is this intended to be? It is not an exercise in collective biography, though there are two groups of individuals examined. It is not a historical study of the Boston elite in all its various aspects. It is most akin to sociological or anthropological studies of smaller communities that can be observed directly, rather than past communities whose inhabitants cannot be interviewed. For examination of a past society, other methods of analysis must be chosen. Quantitative history is one such method, which has come into favor of late. This paper suggests that there is another and very fruitful method.

When I was in graduate school, the Yankee City studies under the direction of Lloyd Warner were new, and attracted considerable attention. Warner's team of almost twenty associates interviewed hundreds of inhabitants of Newburyport, where they discovered a well-defined class structure, imaginatively described as Upper-Upper, Lower-Upper, Upper-Middle, Lower-Middle, Upper-Lower, and Lower-Lower. I suspect that one reason for our interest in Warner's work was that it lent encouragement to poking fun at the quaint behavior of the comfortable and smug representatives of old New England Upper-Upper families. We relished the late George Apley; but so too we enjoyed the little fictional vignettes of life in Yankee City. Thus:

> Mr. Breckenridge was thumbing through a fat genealogical record of his family when his dinner guest arrived—a New York painter who was staying for a few weeks at the Yankee City Inn.
> "I was checking a point in the family history," he said to his guest. "I had an argument at tea about it with Caleb Marshall." He put a marker in the book and placed it on the library table.
> "My children say I think more of that book than I do of my Bible—and you know I think they're right."

Whether or not this was verifiable evidence and good social science, we young whippersnappers thought it was great.

Given the sixfold social structure Warner thought he had found in Newburyport, considerable attention was devoted to figuring out who in Yankee City belonged in each category. His interviewers went about inquiring who were the people in town considered to be of high status and who was looked down upon. His definition of social class was neither based on wealth nor occupation, though such elements could be factored in, but on reputation, on the perception in people's minds. "By social class," Warner wrote, "is meant two or more orders of people who are believed to be, and are accordingly ranked by the members of the community, in socially superior and inferior positions."

In the year 1940, I did not find this sort of thing, however interesting of itself, of particular value in writing a dissertation dealing with eighteenth-century intellectual history—even though the question was a live one as to whether the Arminians I was writing about were of a different social class than the evangelicals who flocked to hear George Whitefield. After all, I was not in a position to interview the Bostonians of 1750. But when it came time to turn the dissertation into a book, I had the benefit of wider experience. I was teaching at MIT in the English and History Department, where a number of young instructors were concerned with problems of what sort of "general education" was appropriate for engineering students. General education was the concept of the day in the late 1940s. We devised two alternative programs. One was a hop, skip, and jump from fifth-century Athens to the present, focusing on just a few key periods and places, where we hoped to study particular societies as social wholes; the other was a study of contemporary society drawing on the various social sciences. The frame of reference was very much in line with the personality, society, and culture construct associated with Clyde Kluckhohn. I worked on this second program, along with such colleagues as Tom O'Dea and Arthur Mann. Tom had been involved in Kluckhohn's cross-cultural survey of Mormons, Indians, and conventional palefaces in the Mormon empire and its fringes, from which resulted his book entitled *The Mormons*. Arthur had just completed the dissertation that was the basis for his first book, on Yankee reformers. Another member of the staff was Robert K. Lamb; and in lunchtime conversation with him and Tom O'Dea, I got clues as to how to add some sociological depth to what had been a rather pure exercise in intellectual history.

Bob Lamb was in his mid-forties when he was appointed Lecturer in Humanities at MIT. He was a Harvard graduate, class of 1928, *magna cum laude* in economics. He received the PhD in Economics in 1935, with a dissertation on the history of entrepreneurship in Fall River. He was close friends with a number of those who were field workers with Lloyd Warner, specifically Eliot Chapple and Conrad Arensberg. But where the Newburyport studies by Warner had gone the route of extensive interviewing, which meant that the identity of informants had to be protected by fictitious names, Lamb's study of Fall River could deal openly and directly with the Bordens and Chaces whose decisions had shaped that community. What resulted was an analysis of the way in which the decisions of such entrepreneurs not only served their own interests, but also largely determined the economic, political, and social development of the whole community. I read the unpublished dissertation after Bob's death and learned more about the social dynamics of Fall River in the nineteenth century than Warner's field workers could discover in Newburyport by interviewing people to find out about the public reputations of representatives of Upper-Upper families.

Bob had had a varied experience after completing his dissertation in 1935. He taught for a couple of years at Williams. During the war he was on the staff of one, perhaps more than one, congressional committee in Washington. Later he was the executive secretary of the CIO legislative committee—his work with the steelworkers gave him a taste for Irish whiskey, which remained his preference. At MIT he was returning to academic life after much practical involvement in political and economic problems. As I see it, he never lost a basic sense of society as made up of individuals interacting with one another and was not tempted to think of social classes as categories, or of social structure as a classification scheme. But if social structures are viewed as the product of myriads of patterned interactions among individuals, one has to have a way to get a handle on a situation of almost infinite complexity. This he did by suggesting the construction of a "living model." By focusing on representative individuals at key points of decision-making and exploring how they interact with one another, one can develop a model of the whole, to be followed through time, so that it is sensitive to the alterations that changing circumstances produce.

Bob's method was applicable both to the study of contemporary communities and to ones in the past. How to do the former was outlined in his "Suggestions for the Study of Your Hometown," which set me to work in the City of Cambridge, an exercise that convinced me that he was onto something. He was working on a historical study at the time of his untimely death from cancer at the age of forty-eight. It was to be a study of family connections at the time of the American Revolution, to see how such networks affected the decision-making that led up to the war.

The book on revolutionary families was not far advanced at the time of his death, and not publishable. And the concept of the living model, with an example of how it could be fruitful, lacked full-fledged development and classic statement. Hence a valuable insight into the way to study community social structures never made its way into the awareness of social historians. It deserves to be rediscovered. The present paper is a very limited use of it; a much richer and more varied construction of a living model of Boston in the 1790s is possible, and would be a vindication of Bob Lamb's vision, as well as a recognition of the very great loss to scholarship from his early death, before he could himself show more of the possibilities he was opening up to investigators.

Notes

The Election of Henry Ware

1. Samuel Eliot Morison, *Three Centuries of Harvard* (Cambridge, Mass., 1936), p. 187.

2. See, for example, such various authorities as: William B. Sprague, *The Life of Jedidiah Morse, D.D.* (New York, c. 1874), p. 59; Earl Morse Wilbur, *A History of Unitarianism in Transylvania, England, and America* (Cambridge, Mass., 1952), p. 405; James King Morse, *Jedidiah Morse: A Champion of New England Orthodoxy* (New York, 1939), p. 94; Joseph W. Phillips, *Jedidiah Morse and New England Congregationalism* (New Brunswick, N.J., c. 1983), pp. 133-136.

3. Jedidiah Morse, *The True Reasons on Which the Election of a Hollis Professor of Divinity in Harvard College, Was Opposed at the Board of Overseers, February 14, 1805* (Charlestown, Mass., 1805), p. 27.

4. The commonplace book of Ephraim Eliot, formerly belonging to Professor Samuel Eliot Morison, is now in the library of the Boston Athenaeum. Another transcript of the same diary entries was made by the Reverend John Pierce in his manuscript "Memoirs," now in the Massachusetts Historical Society, Boston, Mass.

5. Pearson's narrative account was prepared for polemical purposes and with a view to publication, but events apparently moved too fast for him. Both a first draft and a fair copy are in the Harvard University Archives, together with the handwritten ballots and other memoranda saved by Pearson.

6. "Memoirs" of the Reverend John Pierce of Brookline, Vol. 1, p. 125 (August 27, 1803). MS, Massachusetts Historical Society.

7. Boston, *Columbian Centinel* (November 21, 1804).

8. Clifford K. Shipton, *Sibley's Harvard Graduates*, Vol. 12, p. 24. A leaning towards liberalism in theology is suggested by the fact that Storer owned a copy of the Philadelphia edition of Richard Price, *Sermons on the Christian Doctrine* (1787), now in the Andover-Harvard Library.

9. William B. Sprague, *Annals of the American Pulpit* (New York, 1856–1865), Vol. 8, pp. 65–72.

10. Shipton, *Sibley's Harvard Graduates*, Vol. 13, pp. 367–374.

11. Pierce, "Memoirs," Vol. 7 (1837–1838), p. 308. MS, Massachusetts Historical Society. For a more contemporary comment on Pearson's personality, see Samuel Cary to Mrs. Sarah Atkins, March 19, 1806, in *Publications of the Colonial Society of Massachusetts*, Vol. 6 (1900), pp. 177–179.

12. Pierce, *loc. cit.*

13. Josiah Quincy, *The History of Harvard University* (Cambridge, Mass., 1840), Vol. 2, pp. 286–288.

14. Sprague, *Annals*, Vol. 2, pp. 126–131; Claude M. Fuess, *An Old New England School* (Boston, 1917), Ch. 5; Leonard Woods, *History of Andover Theological Seminary* (Boston, 1885), pp. 51–53, 145–147; John Pierce, "Memoirs," Vol. 7 (1837-1838), pp. 308–309; New Series, Vol. 3 (1845), pp. 222-223, MS, Massachusetts Historical Society.

15. Convers Francis, "Memoir of Hon. John Davis, LL.D.," *Collections of the Massachusetts Historical Society*, 3rd Ser., Vol. 10, pp. 186–203; Ezra Stiles Gannett, *A Good Old Age* (Boston, 1847).

16. Sprague, *Annals*, Vol. 8, pp. 92–99; Joseph McKean, "Memoir Towards a Character of Reverend John Eliot, S.T.D.," *Collections of the Massachusetts Historical Society*, 2nd Ser., Vol. 1, pp. 211–251; [James Freeman], *The Character of Rev. John Eliot, D.D.* (Boston, 1813).

17. A memorandum in the Pearson Papers in the Harvard University Archives seems to be Pearson's outline for the remarks he made on this occasion.

18. "Megalonyx" is a reference to the prehistoric beast whose bones

were found in western Virginia, which interested Thomas Jefferson as casting light on Buffon's assertion that animals in the Western Hemisphere were smaller and doubtless more degenerate than those in the old world. Jefferson wrote: "I will venture to refer to him by the name of the Great-Claw or Megalonyx, to which he seems sufficiently entitled by the distinguished size of that member." Thomas Jefferson, "A Memoir on the Discovery of Certain Bones of a Quadruped of the Clawed Kind in the Western Parts of Virginia," *Transactions of the American Philosophical Society*, Vol. 4 O.S. (1799), p. 248. See also Julian P. Boyd, "The Megalonyx, the Megatherium, and Thomas Jefferson's Lapse of Memory," *Proceedings of the American Philosophical Society*, Vol. 102, No. 5 (1958), pp. 420–435.

19. These slips of paper are now in the Harvard University Archives. They are not dated, and it is not possible to say for sure at which meeting they were used. But it is not probable that they date from the meeting of February 1, 1805, since the trial ballots of that date were on different paper, and variations in the handwriting suggest a different occasion and different pens. This procedure of nomination was also used on December 11, 1805, when the Corporation was attempting to elect a president, the chief difference being that instead of listing two names, each of the Fellows listed four.

20. Sprague, *Annals*, Vol. 2, p. 210. There is a sketch of Payson in the *Dictionary of American Biography* (New York, 1938–1947).

21. Cf. George H. Williams, ed., *The Harvard Divinity School* (Boston, 1954), pp. 39–41, and the sources cited there.

22. Joseph Lathrop to John Lathrop, November 12, 1804, as extracted by Eliphalet Pearson. MS, "Pearson Papers," Harvard University Archives.

23. There is a sketch of Appleton in the *Dictionary of American Biography*; see also Sprague, *Annals*, Vol. 2, pp. 380–389.

24. The meeting was attended by nine clerical and six lay members, but the lieutenant governor presided and did not vote. Lathrop, Eliot, and Wendell are all listed in the minutes as being in attendance. It should be noted that Pearson was very critical of the two members of the Corporation who voted with the majority, but says nothing of the third member, who apparently did not disqualify himself either.

25. That Wendell was the author of the compromise is the testimony of Sidney Willard, the son of President Willard. See Sidney Willard, *Memories of Youth and Manhood* (Cambridge, Mass., 1855), Vol. 2, p. 174.

26. The identification of Pearson's choice as Dr. Samuel Stanhope Smith is at best an inference, but one that now seems to be more plausible than my earlier suggestion that it might have been Dr. John Smith of Dartmouth. (See Conrad Wright, *The Beginnings of Unitarianism in America* [Boston, 1955], p. 279 note.) Pearson and Morse were the closest of collaborators at this time, and Morse was eager to cultivate contacts with Presbyterians from the middle states. Furthermore, Pearson's list of nominees for the presidency at the meeting of December 11, 1805 strongly suggests an interest in Presbyterians from outside New England. He named, in order, "Dr. Smith," "Dr. Green," "Dr. Cutler," and "Mr. Mellen." If Smith was probably Samuel Stanhope Smith, Green was surely Dr. Ashbel Green, who became president of Princeton in 1812 when Smith resigned. Cutler was Dr. Manasseh Cutler, minister in Beverly and prominent in Federalist party politics. Mellen was doubtless the Reverend John Mellen, a former Tutor, a Dudleian Lecturer, and a member of both the Historical Society and the American Academy, who had recently resigned his pastoral charge at East Barnstable because of his wife's ill health and had moved to Cambridge.

27. Morse's activities in trying to rally the orthodox in opposition to Ware are revealed in a letter to Dr. Joseph Lyman of Hatfield, dated December 27, 1804. This letter must have been occasioned by the meeting of the Corporation the day before, and it points to the close collaboration between Morse and Pearson, as well as the active part the former was playing even while the matter was still in the hands of the Corporation. The original letter is in the Houghton Library at Harvard; selections made from a copy in the Morse Papers at Yale may be found in Morse, *Jedidiah Morse*, p. 90.

28. Morse, *True Reasons*, p. 19.

29. Quincy, *History of Harvard University*, Vol. 1, p. 248.

30. See John Pierce, "Memoirs," N.S. Vol. 3, p. 224. MS, Massachusetts Historical Society. There is a sketch of Dexter in the *Dictionary of American Biography*. He was the son of the Samuel Dexter who gave to the University the endowment for the Dexter Lectureship on

Biblical Criticism. A lawyer and an exceptionally capable advocate, he had been a Congressman, United States Senator, Secretary of War, and Secretary of the Treasury. In 1805 he was a member of the Governor's Council. He was to cross Morse's path on later occasions, most notably as one of the referees in the dispute between Morse and Miss Hannah Adams, by which Morse's reputation was largely destroyed. See "The Controversial Career of Jedidiah Morse," in this volume.

31. Quincy, *History of Harvard University*, Vol. 1, p. 538.

32. *Monthly Anthology*, Vol. 2 (1805), pp. 152-157. The final completed form of the liberal case may be found in Quincy, *op. cit.*, Vol. 1, pp. 230-264. Quincy had been a member of the Senate in 1805 and therefore on the Board of Overseers; he had attended the small meeting on January 3, 1805 as well as the full meeting on February 14. His analysis of the issues carries special authority because of his personal involvement. By thorough investigation of the College Papers he added one significant point to the earlier case presented by the liberals, *viz.*, that the so-called statutes of the Founder were not of Hollis's devising but had been prepared in New England; and that although Hollis had no difficulty in accepting them, when he did so in what seems to have been a deliberate attempt at clarification of the wording of others, he added the provision, in the form of a declaration to be made by the professor, that the Scriptures were to be accepted as the only rule of faith. Quincy also offered evidence to show that the initial inquisition of Dr. Wigglesworth was done to satisfy a conservative Board of Overseers, rather than to meet any requirement of Hollis.

33. *Monthly Anthology*, Vol. 2, p. 152.

34. Minutes of the Board of Overseers, Feb. 14, 1805. Harvard University Archives.

35. Morse, *True Reasons*, p. 27. The Governor presided and presumably did not vote.

36. A fair copy of this Declaration is in the "Henry Ware Papers," Harvard University Archives.

37. Invitation from the Corporation to Pearson, March 28, 1806, and the draft of his reply. "Pearson Papers," Harvard University Archives.

38. *Monthly Anthology*, Vol. 2, pp. 78-79.

Piety, Morality, and the Commonwealth

1. The most recent significant treatment of the Standing Order is William G. McLoughlin, *New England Dissent, 1630–1833: The Baptists and the Separation of Church and State*, 2 volumes (Cambridge, Mass., 1971). Earlier studies are: Susan M. Reed, *Church and State in Massachusetts, 1691–1740* (Urbana, Ill., 1914), and Jacob Conrad Meyer, *Church and State in Massachusetts from 1740 to 1833* (Cleveland, Ohio, 1930). The interpretation in the present essay differs in significant respects from these studies, but finds support in Charles H. Lippy, "The 1780 Massachusetts Constitution: Religious Establishment or Civil Religion?" *Journal of Church and State*, Vol. 20 (1978), pp. 533–549.

2. "Cambridge Platform," Ch. XI, paragraph 4, in Williston Walker, *The Creeds and Platforms of Congregationalism* (Boston, 1893), p. 221.

3. Province Laws, Ch. 26, Session of 1692–1693, in *Acts and Resolves, Public and Private, of the Province of the Massachusetts Bay* (Boston, 1869), Vol. 1, pp. 62–63.

4. The act was amended the following year to leave the initiative in the choice of the minister to the church, whose decision would then be referred to the town for its concurrence and legal settlement. But in a town where no church had yet been gathered, the town meeting would have full authority to "choose and call an orthodox, learned and pious person to dispense the word of God unto them." Province Laws, Ch. 46, Session of 1692–1693, *op. cit.*, Vol. 1, p. 103. It is to be noted that the "pious person" was not referred to in ecclesiastical language as a "minister."

5. Article III of the Declaration of Rights in the Constitution of the Commonwealth of Massachusetts.

6. John Tucker, *Remarks on a Discourse of the Rev. Jonathan Parsons, of Newbury-Port* (Boston, 1774), p. 14.

7. Enos Hitchcock, *A Discourse Delivered at the Dedication of the New Congregational Meetinghouse in Providence* (Brookfield, Mass., 1795), p. 6.

8. *Barnes* v. *First Parish*, 6 Mass. 401 (1807).

9. Cotton Mather, *Ratio Disciplinae Fratrum Nov-Anglorum* (Boston, 1726), p. 21.

10. Jonathan Mayhew, *A Defence of the Observations on the Charter and Conduct of the Society for the Propagation of the Gospel* (Boston, 1763), p. 60.

11. Reed, *Church and State*, Chs. 5, 6.

12. Charles Chauncy, *The Appeal to the Public Answered* (Boston, 1768), pp. 152–153.

13. Theophilus Parsons, *Memoir of Theophilus Parsons* (Boston, 1859), p. 201.

14. James B. Conant, *Education in a Divided World* (Cambridge, Mass., 1949), pp. 1, 108.

15. *Minersville School District* v. *Gobitis*, 310 US 586 (1940).

16. For discussion of the problem of religious teaching in the public school see: Raymond B. Culver, *Horace Mann and Religion in the Massachusetts Public Schools* (New Haven, Conn., 1929); Sherman M. Smith, *The Relation of the State to Religious Education in Massachusetts* (Syracuse, N.Y., 1926); William Kailer Dunn, *What Happened to Religious Education?* (Baltimore, Md., 1958).

17. Culver, *Horace Mann*, p. 22.

18. Dunn, *What Happened*, pp. 131–132.

Ministers, Churches, and the Boston Elite, 1791–1815

1. Winthrop S. Hudson, *Religion in America* (New York, 1965), p. 162; Merle Curti, *The Growth of American Thought* (New York, 1943), p. 163; James Truslow Adams, *New England in the Republic, 1776–1850* (Boston, 1926), p. 355.

2. Barbara M. Cross, ed., *Autobiography of Lyman Beecher* (Cambridge, Mass., 1961), Vol. 2, p. 81; Jedidiah Morse, *An Appeal to the Public* (Charlestown, Mass., 1814), p. vi; William Henry Channing, *Memoir of William Ellery Channing* (Boston, 1848), Vol. 3, p. 41.

3. Robert S. Rich, "Politics and Pedigrees: The Wealthy Men of Boston, 1798–1852" (PhD Dissertation, UCLA, 1975), p. 277.

4. Exemplary of the way these matters should be handled is John W. Tyler, *Smugglers and Patriots: Boston Merchants and the Advent of the American Revolution* (Boston, 1986), in which the Appendix lists by name the more than 425 overseas merchants on whom the study was based, giving their ages, the value of their real estate in 1771, their church affiliations, the type of business engaged in, whether they were loyalist or patriot, their participation in one or more organizations, and their support of various petitions.

5. In a memorial sketch of Robert K. Lamb (1904–1952), Margaret Mead commented: "Nothing that Bob wrote begins to give an adequate picture of the work he might have produced had he lived longer." That is certainly true of his concept of the "living model" as a tool for the analysis of social structure, which Dr. Mead regarded as "his most important contribution to the social sciences." In the last months before his death from cancer, he published a group of papers indicating the direction his ideas were moving. The usefulness of the concept of the living model as applied to the investigation of present day communities is indicated in "Suggestions for a Study of Your Hometown," *Human Organization*, Vol. 11 (1952), pp. 29–32. Its application to historical investigation is seen in "The Entrepreneur and the Community," in William Miller, ed., *Men in Business* (Cambridge, Mass., 1952), pp. 91–119, and "Productivity and Social Structure," in *Industrial Productivity* (Industrial Relations Research Association, 1951), pp. 50–75. In both historical and modern cases, social structures are defined through identified persons. In historical studies, this means that the adequacy of the scholarship is not hidden in statistical compilations that must be taken on faith and cannot easily be checked. In the case of living societies, essential data is in the public domain, so that it is not necessary to use pseudonyms to protect the privacy of the inhabitants of "Yankee City," or "Jonesville," or "Regional City." See Margaret Mead, "Robert K. Lamb: 1904–1952," *Human Organization*, Vol. 12 (1954), pp. 33–37.

6. Family connections among one group of merchants are spelled out in Kenneth W. Porter, *The Jacksons and the Lees: Two Generations of Massachusetts Merchants, 1765–1844* (Cambridge, Mass., 1937), Vol.

1, pp. 88–98. See also Ferris Greenslet, *The Lowells and Their Seven Worlds* (Boston, 1946), especially the chart between pages 422 and 423, and Peter Dobkin Hall, "Family Structure and Class Consolidation Among the Boston Brahmins," PhD Dissertation (SUNY-Stony Brook, 1973).

7. John Lathrop, *A Discourse Before the Massachusetts Charitable Fire Society* (Boston, 1796), pp. 15–16.

8. The period after the American Revolution also saw a rapid growth of mutual and fraternal charitable societies—as, for example, the Freemasons. See Conrad Edick Wright, *The Transformation of Charity in Postrevolutionary New England* (Boston, 1992).

9. The Massachusetts Historical Society, incorporated 1794: *Massachusetts Acts and Laws*, 1793, Ch. 36; the American Academy, incorporated 1780: *Massachusetts Acts and Laws*, 1780, Ch. 16.

10. See Appendix A in this volume.

11. Limitations on the number of members, as stipulated in the charters of incorporation, were: Congregational Charitable Society, 30; Historical Society, 60; Indian Society, 50.

12. Chief sources: *Historical Register of Harvard University, 1636–1936* (Cambridge, Mass., 1937); *Memoirs of the American Academy of Arts and Sciences*, Vol. 1 (1785), pp. xx–xxi; Vol. 2 (1793, 1804), pp. 162–164; Vol. 3 (1809–1815), pp. 542–522; M.A. DeWolfe Howe, *The Humane Society of the Commonwealth of Massachusetts: An Historical Review, 1785–1916* (Boston, 1918), pp. 283–304; *The Act of Incorporation, Regulations, and Members of the Massachusetts Congregational Charitable Society* (Boston, 1815), pp. 9–10; Richard D. Pierce, ed., *Handbook of the Society for Propagating the Gospel Among the Indians and Others in North America, 1787–1964* (Boston, 1964), pp. 16–31; *Proceedings of the Massachusetts Historical Society*, 1 Ser., Vol. 1, pp. xli–xliv, 1–1i; [Massachusetts Charitable Fire Society], *Proceedings at the 125th Anniversary of the Granting of the Society's Charter, November 14, 1919* (Boston, 1920), pp. 1–18; [Society for the Information and Advice of Foreigners], broadside dated Boston, Dec. 30, 1793.

13. See "Piety, Morality, and the Commonwealth" in this volume.

14. Richard D. Brown, "The Emergence of Urban Society in Rural Massachusetts," *Journal of American History*, Vol. 61 (1974-75), pp. 38–39.

15. *Historical Register of Harvard University*, pp. 8–10.

16. N.S.B. Gras, *The Massachusetts-First National Bank of Boston, 1784–1934* (Cambridge, Mass., 1937), pp. 530–531.

17. Christopher Roberts, *The Middlesex Canal, 1793–1860* (Cambridge, Mass., 1938), p. 222.

18. *Triennial Catalogue of the Massachusetts Medical Society* (Boston, 1875), pp. 4–7.

19. Members of the General Court were listed at the beginning of the published volumes of the *Acts and Laws* of each annual session.

20. See Appendix B in this volume. Those listed in the *Dictionary of American Biography* were James Bowdoin, John Davis, John Lowell, Jonathan Mason, Jr., William Phillips, Jr., James Sullivan, William Tudor, Jr., John Warren, and John Collins Warren.

21. It is of some importance that the Harvard graduates in the group were more involved in the societies than the others. They were less than half of the total (13 of 28), but they accounted for more than two-thirds of the officers chosen from among the men of affairs (16 or 23). Listed in order of point scores for total participation, James Sullivan, not a graduate, is in first place, but the next four were all Harvard men.

22. Joseph T. Buckingham, comp., *Annals of the Massachusetts Charitable Mechanic Association* (Boston, 1853), p. 10.

23. Buckingham, *Massachusetts Charitable Mechanic Association*, p. 13. A full analysis of the church connections of the eighty-three members of the Charitable Mechanic Association remains to be done. But we do know that seven of them were members of John Murray's First Universalist Society. (See Charles W. Howe, "How Human an Enterprise: The Story of the First Universal Society in Boston During John Murray's Ministry," *Proceedings of the Unitarian Universalist Historical Society*, Vol. 22, Pt. 1 [1990–1991]). Other known affiliations include two at Brattle Street and one each at First Church, Second Church, New North, New South, and Christ Church.

24. William Phillips, Jr., for example, a life-long supporter of the Old South, is listed for pew 19 at Hollis Street in 1827. George Leonard Chaney, *Hollis Street Church from Mather Byles to Thomas Starr King, 1732–1861.* (Boston, 1877), p. 67.

25. Chief sources: Richard D. Pierce, ed., *The Records of the First Church in Boston 1630–1868. Publications of the Colonial Society of Massachusetts,* Vols. 39–41 (Boston, 1961); Chandler Robbins, *A History of the Second Church, or Old North, in Boston* (Boston, 1852), pp. 226–291; *An Historical Catalogue of the Old South Church* (Boston, 1883); Hamilton Andrews Hill, *History of the Old South Church* (Boston, 1890); Henry Wilder Foote, *Annals of King's Chapel* (Boston, 1896), Vol. 2; *Records of the Church in Brattle Square* (Boston, 1902); "List of Occupants of Pews in Federal Street Church, December, 1814," *Proceedings of the Unitarian Historical Society,* Vol. 5, Pt. 2 (1937), p. 36; "Records of the West Church, Boston, Mass." *New England Historical and Genealogical Register,* pp. 91–94 (1937–1940), passim.

26. [William Henry Channing], *Memoir of William Ellery Channing* (Boston, 1848), Vol. 1, p. 166.

27. Joseph H. Jones, *The Life of Ashbel Green* (New York, 1849), p. 225.

28. William B. Sprague, *Annals of the American Pulpit* (New York, 1857–1869), Vol. 2, p. 139.

29. Hill, *Old South Church,* Vol. 2, pp. 339, 421.

30. See "The Controversial Career of Jedidiah Morse" in this volume; Joseph W. Phillips, *Jedidiah Morse and New England Congregationalism* (New Brunswick, NJ, 1983).

31. See "The Election of Henry Ware" in this volume.

32. The original officers and trustees of the Massachusetts Missionary Society were: the Rev. Nathanael Emmons, YC '67, Franklin; the Rev. Samuel Austin, YC '84, Worcester; Deacon John Simpkins, HC '86, Boston (Old South); the Rev. David Sanford, YC '55, Medway; the Rev. Daniel Hopkins, YC '58, Salem; the Rev. Ezra Weld, YC '59, Braintree; the Rev. Samuel Spring, Coll. NJ, '71, Newburyport; the Rev. Joseph Barker, YC '71, Middleborough; the Rev. Samuel Niles, Coll. NJ, '69, Abington; the Rev. John Crane, HC '80, Northborough; the Rev.

Jonathan Strong, Dartmouth '87, Randolph. *Massachusetts Missionary Magazine*, Vol. 1 (1803), pp. 7, 77–80.

33. Leonard Woods, *History of the Andover Theological Seminary* (Boston, 1885); *General Catalogue of the Theological Seminary, Andover
Massachusetts, 1808–1908* (Boston, n.d.), pp. 1-4.

34. George H. Williams, ed., *The Harvard Divinity School: Its Place in
Harvard University and in American Culture* (Boston, 1954), pp. 21-28.

35. See "Institutional Reconstruction in the Unitarian Controversy" and
"The Dedham Case Revisited," both in this volume.

36. Thomas Dawes, Sr., was a deacon of Old South for twenty-three years;
Thomas Dawes, Jr., moved to Federal Street. William Phillips, Jr., was
a deacon there even longer; meanwhile his son Jonathan was an
intimate friend of Channing and a member of his church.

37. *The Influence and History of the Boston Athenaeum* (Boston, 1907),
pp. 115–118; Robert W. Greenleaf, *An Historical Report of the Boston
Dispensary* (Brookline, Mass., 1898), p. 44; N.I. Bowditch, *A History of
the Massachusetts General Hospital* (Boston, 1851), pp. 405–408. See
also Ronald Story, *The Forging of an Aristocracy: Harvard and the
Boston Upper Classes, 1800–1870* (Middletown, Conn., 1980), in
which the Athenaeum and the Massachusetts General Hospital are
taken to be key points of influence for the Boston elite.

The Controversial Career of Jedidiah Morse

1. William B. Sprague, *The Life of Jedidiah Morse, D.D.* (New York,
c. 1874), p. 57.

2. Jedidiah Morse, *An Appeal to the Public, on the Controversy Respecting the Revolution in Harvard College, and the Events Which Have
Followed It* (Charlestown, Mass., 1814), p. x.

3. Morse to Belknap, January 18, 1788. *Collections of the Massachusetts
Historical Society*, Ser. 6, Vol. 4, pp. 381–384.

4. Hazard to Belknap, November 15, 1788; Belknap to Hazard, May 2,
1789. *Collections of the Massachusetts Historical Society*, Ser. 5,
Vol. 3, pp. 73, 122.

5. Joseph H. Jones, *The Life of Ashbel Green* (New York, 1849), p. 225.

6. Sprague, *Morse*, p. 74.

7. *The Diary of William Bentley, D.D.*, 4 vols. (Salem, 1905), Vol. 1, p. 187.

8. Sprague, *Morse*, p. 50.

9. Boston, *Columbian Centinel*, November 17, 1790.

10. Sprague, *Morse*, pp. 54–55, where citation is made to the *Columbian Centinel*, November 19, 1790. This citation seems to be in error, since the *Centinel* was not published on that day, but the correct source is yet to be located.

11. Morse, *Appeal*, p. x.

12. Sprague, *Morse*, pp. 51–53.

13. [James Freeman], *Remarks on the American Universal Geography* (Boston, 1793); see also Conrad Wright, *The Beginnings of Unitarianism in America* (Boston, 1955), pp. 272–273.

14. Morse, *Appeal*, p. x.

15. Jedidiah Morse, *A Sermon, Delivered . . . May 9th, 1798* (Boston, 1798). For a general account of the Illuminati scare, see Vernon Stauffer, *New England and the Bavarian Illuminati* (New York, 1918); for detailed treatment of Morse's involvement, see also Joseph W. Phillips, *Jedidiah Morse and New England Congregationalism* (New Brunswick, NJ, c. 1983), pp. 73–102.

16. William Bentley, *A Charge Delivered Before the Morning Star Lodge* (Worcester, Mass., 1798), p. 31.

17. Boston, *Massachusetts Mercury*, August 3 and 10, 1798.

18. Boston, *Massachusetts Mercury*, July 28, 1798. Wells was the son of the Reverend William Wells of Bromsgrove, Worcestershire, who migrated to America in 1793 because, like his friend Priestley, he had been threatened with mob violence. Ironically, when considering emigration, it was Morse to whom he wrote for advice. See Wells to Morse, January 27, 1792, New York Public Library. The younger Wells graduated from Harvard in 1796. Ill health interfered with his plans to enter

the ministry, and from 1805 to 1826 he was a bookseller and publisher in Boston. Beginning in 1827, he was the proprietor of a school of high reputation in Cambridge. His daughter married the Reverend William Newell, minister of the First Parish in Cambridge from 1830 to 1868. See Andrew P. Peabody, *Harvard Graduates Whom I Have Known* (Boston, 1890), pp. 58–65; see also Mrs. James Lowell Moore, "The Fayerweather House," Cambridge Historical Society, *Publications*, Vol. 25 (1938/39), pp. 86–94.

19. Boston, *Massachusetts Mercury*, August 21, 1798. Morse's reference to Bentley was roughly equivalent to calling an ardent New Dealer a Communist agent.

20. Jedidiah Morse, *A Sermon, Exhibiting the Present Dangers, and Consequent Duties of the Citizens of the United States of America* (Charlestown, Mass., 1799), p. 15.

21. Phillips, *Morse*, pp. 86–89; Stauffer, *Bavarian Illuminati*, pp. 287 ff. This curious episode has been cited as evidence that Bentley was none too scrupulous (Stauffer, p. 317). But it is not true, as Stauffer declared, that Ebeling had instructed Bentley that his letter was not to be given to the public (Stauffer, p. 318n). Ebeling's letter specifically states: "You are at liberty to communicate the contents of my letter to your friends and even print what you think worth[y] of public knowledge. . . ." See Ebeling to Bentley, March 13, 1799, Harvard College Library, reprinted in William C. Lane, "Letters of Christoph Daniel Ebeling to Rev. Dr. William Bentley," *Proceedings of the American Antiquarian Society*, N.S., Vol. 35 (1925), p. 333.

22. Stauffer, *Bavarian Illuminati*, pp. 319–320.

23. Charlestown, Mass., 1805; Morse repeated the whole text of the pamphlet in 1814 in his *Appeal*, pp. 37–54.

24. Morse, *Appeal*, p. 36. Morse's *True Reasons* was reviewed by William Wells, Jr., in the *Monthly Anthology* for March 1805, and Morse responded with a long communication in the April issue. *Monthly Anthology*, Vol. 2 (1805), pp. 152–157, 206–216.

25. *Harvard College Records, Part IV*, in *Publications of the Colonial Society of Massachusetts*, Vol. 49 (1975), p. 372. A full discussion of the issue from the point of view of the liberals is in Josiah Quincy, *The*

History of Harvard University (Cambridge, 1840), Vol. 1, pp. 230–264.

26. Quincy, *History*, Vol. 1, p. 538.

27. See "The Election of Henry Ware" in this volume.

28. Morse to Leonard Woods, October 21, 1806. Leonard Woods, *History of the Andover Theological Seminary* (Boston, 1885), p. 463.

29. Hannah Adams to W.S. Shaw, [August 8, 1805], in Morse, *Appeal*, p. 22. Morse printed only two key paragraphs; the letter from which they were excerpted may be found in Joseph B. Felt, *Memorials of William Smith Shaw* (Boston, 1852), pp. 191–201. There is a sketch of Adams in Edward T. James, ed., *Notable American Women, 1607–1950* (Cambridge, Mass., 1971); Vol. 1, pp. 9–11.

30. Morse to Adams, September 25, 1804, in Hannah Adams, *A Narrative of the Controversy Between the Rev. Jedidiah Morse, D.D. and the Author* (Boston, 1814), pp. 34; also in Morse, *Appeal*, pp. 19–20.

31. Adams, *Narrative*, pp. 5–6; Morse, *Appeal*, pp. 57–63.

32. Morse, *Appeal*, pp. 32–33. Seven years earlier, Morse had himself brought suit against a rival author on the grounds of plagiarism. One may surmise that his adversaries were ready to relish the notion that the same charge could be brought against him. The earlier case was *Morse* v. *Reid* in the U.S. Circuit Court for the District of New York, 1797. What appears to be the transcribed text of the findings of the masters appointed by the court, favorable to Morse's claims, is in the Massachusetts Historical Society.

33. Morse to Higginson, December 7, 1808, in Morse, *Appeal*, pp. 65–66.

34. Stephen Higginson, Jr., "Some Notice of the Remarks . . ." in Adams, *Narrative*, separately paged, p. 3.

35. Unsigned memorandum, Hannah Adams Papers, Massachusetts Historical Society. The Charlestown Vital Records show an intention of marriage between Sarah Fayerweather and Aaron Putnam published on November 19, 1805, but no marriage followed. Miss Fayerweather, then 46 years of age, was the daughter of Captain Thomas Fayerweather (1724–1805), a prominent resident of Cambridge, the owner of the Fayerweather house still standing on Brattle Street. Miss Fayerweather was married in 1807 to John Appleton, sometime U.S. consul to France,

the grandson of the Reverend Nathaniel Appleton. See John B. Carney, "In Search of Fayerweathers: The Fayerweather Family of Boston," *New England Historic Genealogical Register*, Vol. 145 (1991), pp. 65–66. Fairweather was the original spelling of the family name. It is now standardized as Fayerweather.

36. The *Dictionary of American Biography* contains sketches of Dawes and Dexter.

37. Morse, *Appeal*, pp. 104–05.

38. *Ibid.*, pp. 105–106.

39. *Ibid.*, p. 109.

40. *Ibid.*, pp. 22–23; Felt, *Shaw*, pp. 191–201.

41. Morse, *Appeal*, p. 123.

42. *Ibid.*, p. 127.

43. *Ibid.*, p. 155.

44. Charlestown: Printed for the Author, 1814.

45. Dr. David Osgood to Morse, July 8, 1814, Rare Books and Manuscript Division, New York Public Library, Astor, Lenox and Tilden Foundations, Jedidiah Morse Papers. Others who wrote back to Morse critical of his behavior were Dr. Elijah Parish, his former collaborator; Samuel Etheridge, a member of his parish; and Sereno E. Dwight, son of Dr. Timothy Dwight, president of Yale, citing also the opinions of his brother Timothy, and his father-in-law, Senator David Daggett.

46. [John Lowell], "Review of Dr. Morse's Appeal to the Publick, Principally with Reference to That Part of It, Which Relates to Harvard College," in Adams, *Narrative*, separately paged, p. 4.

47. [Sidney E. Morse], *Remarks on the Controversy Between Dr. Morse and Miss Adams*. 2nd ed. (Boston, 1814), pp. 27, 29.

48. Phillips, *Jedidiah Morse*, pp. 196–99.

49. *History of the Harvard Church in Charlestown, 1815–1879* (Boston, 1879), pp. 54–55, 60–64.

50. Lyman to Morse, March 27, 1815, New York Public Library.

51. Samuel Whiting (New York) to Morse, October 10, 1814; December 26, 1814; January 28, 1815; March 22, 1815, New York Public Library.

52. Parish to Morse, December 29, 1814, New York Public Library.

53. [Thomas Belsham], *American Unitarianism; or a Brief History of The Progress and Present State of the Unitarian Church in America* (Boston, 1815); [Jeremiah Evarts], "Review of American Unitarianism," *Panoplist and Missionary Magazine*, Vol. 9 (1815), pp. 241–72.

Institutional Reconstruction in the Unitarian Controversy

1. Conrad Wright, *The Beginnings of Unitarianism in America* (Boston, 1955).

2. George H. Williams, ed., *The Harvard Divinity School: Its Place in Harvard University and in American Culture* (Boston, 1954), pp. 44–53; Jerry Wayne Brown, *The Rise of Biblical Criticism in America, 1800–1870* (Middletown, Conn., 1969).

3. Lawrence Buell, "The Unitarian Movement and the Art of Preaching in 19th Century America." *American Quarterly*, Vol. 24 (1972), pp. 166–190.

4. The primary printed sources are: *Proceedings of the Second Church and Parish in Dorchester* (Boston, 1812); *The Memorial of the Proprietors of the New South Meeting-House in Dorchester to the Ministers of the Boston Association* (Boston, 1813); and [Jeremiah Evarts], "Review of the Dorchester Controversy," *Panoplist and Missionary Magazine*, Vol. 10 (1814), pp. 256–281, 289–307, afterwards published as a pamphlet. See also William Allen, *Memoir of John Codman, D.D.* (Boston, 1853).

5. John Pierce, *A Sermon, Delivered at the Gathering of the Second Congregational Church, in Dorchester . . . with an Appendix* (Boston, 1808), pp. 31–38.

6. W.B. Sprague, *Annals of the American Pulpit*, 9 vols. (New York, 1857–1869), Vol. 8, pp. 215–222.

7. Eliphalet Porter, "The Right Hand of Fellowship" in Pierce, *Sermon at the Gathering*, p. 25.

8. *Proceedings*, pp. 9–10.

9. Allen, *Memoir*, pp. 22–25; [John Codman], "Review of Cooper's Sermons on Predestination Unto Life," *Panoplist*, Vol. 1 (1805), pp. 23–25.

10. *Proceedings*, pp. 11–13.

11. *Ibid.*, pp. 14–21; William Ellery Channing, *A Sermon Delivered at the Ordination of the Rev. John Codman* (Boston, 1809).

12. *Memorial of the Proprietors*, pp. 42–44.

13. *Ibid.*, pp. 6 ff.

14. *Proceedings*, pp. 22–24.

15. *Ibid.*, pp. 25–44.

16. Allen, *Memoir*, pp. 188–189, 190–191; *Proceedings*, pp. 82–83, 76–78.

17. *Proceedings*, pp. 44–103.

18. *Ibid.*, pp. 105–109; Allen, *Memoir*, pp. 87–91, 202–214. The ministers who, with their delegates, supported Codman were: Thomas Prentiss of Medfield, Joseph Lyman of Hatfield, William Greenough of Newton, Samuel Austin of Worcester, Jedidiah Morse of Charlestown (the delegate being Jeremiah Evarts), and Samuel Worcester of Salem. Those who voted against him were: John Reed of Bridgewater, Richard R. Eliot of Watertown, Thomas Thacher of Dedham, Aaron Bancroft of Worcester, Samuel Kendall of Weston, and Nathaniel Thayer of Lancaster. Of these only Morse was a member of the Boston Association.

19. *Proceedings*, pp. 110–124; Allen, *Memoir*, pp. 91–92, 220–225.

20. The ministers who, with their delegates, supported Codman at this time were: Thomas Prentiss of Medfield, Daniel Dana of Newburyport, Samuel Stearns of Bedford, and Samuel Worcester of Salem. Those who voted to dismiss him were: Thomas Barnard of Salem, John Reed of Bridgewater, John Allyne of Duxbury, and Nathaniel Thayer of Lancaster. By agreement, each party was allowed to select no more than two of the churches represented in the first council to participate in the second. Allen, *Memoir*, p. 93; Evarts, Review, Vol. 10, p. 294.

21. *Proceedings*, p. 124; Allen, *Memoir*, pp. 93–94, 225–227; Evarts, Review, Vol. 10, pp. 295–297.

22. Evarts, "Review," Vol. 10, pp. 298–300.

23. *Ibid.*, Vol. 10, pp. 300–302.

24. *Ibid.*, Vol. 10, pp. 302–305; *Memorial*, passim.

25. *Memorial*, p. 4.

26. Evarts, "Review," Vol. 10, p. 257.

27. For Bentley, see a memorandum in the Bentley Papers, Vol. 4, American Antiquarian Society, Worcester; for Allen, the source is his Journal, privately owned; for Prentiss, *History of the Harvard Church in Charlestown, 1815–1879* (Boston, 1879); for Brazer, Abigail Phippea West, "Record of Preaching at North Church, Salem, Massachusetts, 1822–1826," Andover-Harvard Library.

28. Allen, *Memoir*, pp. 102–103.

29. *A Statement of Facts, in Relation to the Call and Installation of the Rev. Mark Tucker, over the Society in Northampton* (Northampton, Mass.,1824), pp. 5, 13.

30. Richard Holmes, *Communities in Transition: Bedford and Lincoln, Massachusetts, 1729–1880* (Ann Arbor, Mich., 1980), p. 136.

31. Richard Sykes, "Massachusetts Unitarianism and Social Change: A Religious Social System in Transition, 1780–1870" (PhD dissertation, University of Minnesota, 1966), pp. 101–102.

32. Holmes, *Communities in Transition*, p. 139.

33. [First Church in Cambridge], *An Account of the Controversy in the First Parish in Cambridge* (Boston, 1829); [First Parish in Cambridge], *Controversy Between the First Parish in Cambridge and the Rev. Dr. Holmes, Their Late Pastor* (Cambridge, Mass., 1829).

34. Asa Cummings, *Memoir of the Rev. Edward Payson, D.D.* (Portland, 1830), pp. 186–189.

35. *An Address to the Christian Public* (Greenfield, Mass. 1813), p. 13.

36. [Jeremiah Evarts], "Review of American Unitarianism," *Panoplist*, Vol. 11 (1815), p. 265.

37. William E. Channing, *Remarks on the Rev. Dr. Worcester's Second*

Letter to Mr. Channing, on American Unitarianism (Boston, 1815), pp. 26–27.

38. Samuel Worcester, *A Letter to the Rev. William E. Channing* (Boston, 1815), p. 28.

39. *Proceedings*, pp. 22, 119.

40. Channing, *Dr. Worcester's Second Letter*, p. 42.

41. *The Works of William E. Channing, D.D.* (Boston, 1841), Vol. 3, p.197.

42. Williston Walker, *The Creeds and Platforms of Congregationalism* (New York, 1893), p. 230.

43. *Ibid.*, p. 488.

44. Charles W. Akers, *Called Unto Liberty: A Life of Jonathan Mayhew, 1720–1766*, (Cambridge, Mass., 1964), pp. 48–53.

45. Walter D. Kring, *The Fruits of Our Labors* (Worcester, Mass., 1985), p. 26.

46. *The Results of Two Ecclesiastical Councils* (Greenfield, Mass., 1813), pp. 9–10.

47. See note 33.

48. [Lyman Beecher], *The Rights of the Congregational Churches of Massachusetts* (Boston, 1827).

49. *Report of the Committee of the Proprietors of the Meeting House in Hollis Street, Upon the "Result" of the Late Mutual Ecclesiastical Council* (n.p., n.d.), p. 20.

50. Province Laws, Ch. 26, Session of 1692–1693, in *Acts and Resolves, Public and Private, of the Province of the Massachusetts Bay* (Boston, 1869), Vol. 1, pp. 62–63.

51. Province Laws, Ch. 46, Session of 1692–1693, ibid., Vol. 1, p. 103.

52. See "Piety, Morality, and the Commonwealth" in this volume; Charles Lippy, "The 1780 Massachusetts Constitution: Religious Establishment or Civil Religion?" *Journal of Church and State*, Vol. 20 (1978), pp. 533–549.

53. *Avery* v. *Tyringham*, 3 Mass. 180–181 (1803).

The Dedham Case Revisited

1. George E. Ellis, *The Church and Parish in Massachusetts Usage and Law* (Boston, 1888), p. 3.

2. Ellis's address was also printed in the commemorative volume prepared by the two celebrating churches. But it is most conveniently available as one paper of the Channing Hall series of lectures in 1888–1889, and citation is therefore made to this publication: *Unitarianism: Its Origin and History* (Boston, 1889), pp. 147–148.

3. Leonard W. Levy, *The Law of the Commonwealth and Chief Justice Shaw* (Cambridge, Mass., 1957), p. 38.

4. William W. Fenn, "The Unitarians," in *The Religious History of New England: King's Chapel Lectures* (Cambridge, Mass., 1917), p. 110. For careful scrutiny of the decision it is necessary to go back to a persuasive article in 1829 in Lyman Beecher's anti-Unitarian journal: "Examination of Some Laws and Judicial Decisions in Relation to the Churches of Massachusetts," *Spirit of the Pilgrims*, Vol. 2 (1829), pp. 128–140. By indirection, Chief Justice Charles Doe of New Hampshire did the same thing by rejecting the precedent of *Baker* v. *Fales* in deciding a similar case in 1877. See *Holt* v. *Downs*, 58 N.H. 170 (1877).

5. William W. Sweet, *The Story of Religion in America*, rev. ed. (New York, 1950), p. 242.

6. Clifton E. Olmstead, *History of Religion in the United States* (Englewood Cliffs, N.J., 1960), p. 297.

7. Sydney E. Ahlstrom, *A Religious History of the American People* (New Haven, 1972), p. 397.

8. Joshua Bates, *A Discourse, Delivered February 15, 1818, Being the Sabbath Preceding the Dissolution of the Pastoral Relation Between the Author and the First Church in Dedham* (Dedham, 1818).

9. *Covenant of the First Church in Dedham* (Dedham, 1878), p. 3; Charles Warren, *Jacobin and Junto: or Early American Politics as Viewed in the Diary of Dr. Nathaniel Ames, 1758–1822* (Cambridge, Mass., 1931), p. 288.

10. Warren, *Jacobin and Junto*, p. 289.

11. Alvan Lamson, *A History of the First Church and Parish in Dedham* (Dedham, 1839), p. 68.

12. A brief biographical sketch of Bates is in William B. Sprague, *Annals of the American Pulpit*, 9 vols. (New York, 1857–1869), Vol. 2, pp. 465–471.

13. See "Institutional Reconstruction in the Unitarian Controversy" in this volume.

14. Lamson, *History*, pp. 68–69. The reference is to the Andover Theological Seminary.

15. Erastus Worthington, *The History of Dedham* (Boston, 1827), p. 77.

16. *Ibid.*, pp. 110–111.

17. See "Piety, Morality, and the Commonwealth" in this volume; also Charles H. Lippy, "The 1780 Massachusetts Constitution: Religious Establishment or Civil Religion?" *Journal of Church and State*, Vol. 20 (1978), pp. 533–49.

18. One of the others was Samuel Gilman, author of "Fair Harvard," who was called the following year to the Unitarian church in Charleston, SC, where he served until his death almost forty years later.

19. Samuel Haven, *A Statement of the Proceedings in the First Church and Parish in Dedham, Respecting the Settlement of a Minister, 1818* (Cambridge, Mass., 1819), p. 10.

20. *Ibid.*, p. 12.

21. Haven, *Statement*, pp. 11, 14–16; *Covenant of the First Church*, p. 22.

22. *Covenant of the First Church*, p. 21.

23. The Result of the council was appended to Henry Ware, *A Sermon, Delivered October 29, 1818, at the Ordination of the Reverend Alvan Lamson, as Minister of the First Parish in Dedham* (Dedham, 1818), pp. 33–39; it was printed in full in Haven, *Statement*, pp. 45–50. The protest presented to the council by Judge Haven is in his *Statement*, pp. 24–42.

24. Haven, *Statement*, p. 42.

25. That Channing prepared the Result is revealed in a letter from Lamson

to John Langdon Sibley, Dedham, Mass., Jan. 12, 1857. Houghton Library, Harvard University.

26. Haven, *Statement*, p. 47.

27. *Ibid.*, pp. 48–49.

28. *Ibid.*, pp. 51, 79.

29. Haven, *Statement*, p. 83; *Covenant of the First Church*, pp. iv, 23, 25. See also Lamson, *History*, p. 101.

30. Haven, *Statement*, p. 91.

31. *Ibid.*, pp. 10, 11, 12, 85, 86, 88. Haven's publication was the occasion for a suit for libel brought on behalf of Lamson by Jabez Chickering. It is generally understood that the grand jury for Norfolk County declined to indict, but since the book had been published in Cambridge, Chickering had better success in Middlesex County. Lamson described the outcome many years later: "The author was indicted for a libel by the Grand Jury of Middlesex County, and had his trial at Lechmere Point, as it was then called, before the Supreme Court, Judge Jackson presiding. But in the agitated state of public feeling, the controversy between the religious parties running high, it was hardly to be expected that a jury of twelve men would convict. There was one *stiff* fellow who would not yield & the verdict was one of acquittal." Lamson asserted that the booklet "contains some of the most barefaced & outrageous falsehoods ever uttered." Actually, where the strictly factual content of Haven's narrative can be tested against other sources, it stands up pretty well. Lamson may have been right, however, in his assertion: "Its very bitterness, however, in a great measure disarmed it of its power to injure, the venomous tooth was too apparent." Lamson to J. L. Sibley, Dedham, Mass., Jan. 12, 1857.

32. The preliminary skirmish was concerned with the question whether a writ of replevin was appropriate in the case in question. See *Eliphalet Baker and Another* v. *Samuel Fales*, 16 Mass. 146 (1819). The important case is *Eliphalet Baker and Another* v. *Samuel Fales*, 16 Mass. 487 (1820).

33. Lamson, *History*, p. 101.

34. 16 Mass. 503–504 (1820).

35. 16 Mass. 489 (1820).

36. 16 Mass. 496 (1820).

37. 16 Mass. 496 (1820).

38. 16 Mass. 497–498 (1820). The story of the gathering of the Dedham church is retold in Kenneth A. Lockridge, *A New England Town, the First Hundred Years: Dedham Massachusetts, 1636–1736* (New York, 1970).

39. 16 Mass. 498 (1820).

40. 16 Mass. 514 (1820).

41. 16 Mass. 520 (1820).

42. Samuel Kirkland Lothrop, *A History of the Church in Brattle Street* (Boston, 1851), pp. 22, 23, 25. Parker's definition of a church, cited above, is very similar to paragraph 13 of the Manifesto of the Brattle Street Church. See Lothrop, *Church in Brattle Street*, p. 24.

43. Article III of the Declaration of Rights of the Constitution of the Commonwealth of Masssachusetts.

44. 16 Mass. 508 (1820).

45. Chap. 87, Statutes of 1799, reprinted in Edward Buck, *Massachusetts Ecclesiastical Law* (Boston, 1866), pp. 252–253.

46. 16 Mass. 505 (1820).

47. 16 Mass. 503 (1820).

48. 6 Mass. 401 (1810).

49. 14 Mass. 340 (1817).

50. *Avery* v. *Tyringham*, 3 Mass. 160 at 180, 181 (1807).

51. *Burr* v. *First Parish in Sandwich*, 9 Mass. 277 at 299, 297 (1812).

52. It was advanced by counsel in 1812 in *Boutell* v. *Cowdin* (9 Mass. 254) but Judge Sedgwick refused to address the issue and the decision rests on quite different grounds. It was also advanced in *Deacons of the First Parish in Sandwich* v. *Tilden*, a case that Parker refers to in *Baker* v. *Fales* (p. 502) as though it were a controlling precedent. The assertion

is disingenuous, to say the least. The Tilden case was being litigated contemporaneously with *Baker* v. *Fales*, and it is reported that Lamson's friends watched the proceedings with interest as revealing the leaning of the court. But counsel for the defendant was unable to be present so the case was never tried, and judgment was entered for the plaintiffs by default. *Sandwich* v. *Tilden* must not be confused with *Burr* v. *Sandwich* (1812) which deals with a quite different issue. In addition to the footnote to *Baker* v. *Fales* in the Massachusetts Reports, see *Spirit of the Pilgrims*, Vol. 2 (1829), p. 139n.

53. George E. Ellis, *A Half-Century of the Unitarian Controversy* (Boston, 1857), p. 426.

Unitarian Beginnings in Western Massachusetts

1. Franklin Bowditch Dexter, *Biographical Sketches of the Graduates of Yale College*, 6 vols. (New York, 1885–1912), Vol. 3, pp. 396–398.

2. Joseph Lyman, born 1767, graduated from Yale in 1783. In 1824, he was Sheriff of Hampshire County, but had earlier been Judge of the Court of Common Pleas and Judge of Probate. His second wife, whom he married in 1811, was Anne Jean Robbins of Milton, daughter of Edward Hutchinson Robbins, sometime Lieutenant Governor of the Commonwealth. (In that capacity, Robbins presided over the meeting of the Board of Overseers of Harvard College in 1805 that confirmed the election of Henry Ware as Hollis Professor of Divinity.) See Dexter, *Yale Graduates*, Vol. 4, pp. 291–293; Edward B. Hall, "Obituary," *Christian Examiner*, Vol. 44 (1848), pp. 319–320; and especially Susan I. Lesley, *Recollections of My Mother, Mrs. Anne Jean Lyman of Northampton* (Boston, 1899).

3. *Official Documents of the Presbytery of Albany, Exhibiting the Trials of the Rev. John Chester & Mr. Mark Tucker* (Schenectady, 1818).

4. *Proceedings of the Second Church and Parish in Dorchester; Exhibited in a Collection of Papers* (Boston, 1812). See also "Institutional Reconstruction in the Unitarian Controversy" in this volume.

5. *A Statement of Facts, in Relation to the Call and Installation of the Rev. Mark Tucker, Over the Society in Northampton, Together with His Correspondence on the Subject of Exchanges* (Northampton,

1824), p. 31.

6. *Ibid.*, p. 4. Samuel Howe, born 1785, graduated from Williams in 1804. He was a cousin of Judge Lyman, and his second wife, Sally, was a sister of Mrs. Lyman. In 1821, he was appointed associate justice of the Court of Common Pleas. There is a sketch in the *Dictionary of American Biography*; see also Edward B. Hall, "Sketch of the Life and Character of the Hon. Samuel Howe," *Christian Examiner*, Vol. 5 (1828), pp. 185–202; and Rufus Ellis, *Memoir of the Hon. Samuel Howe* (Boston, 1850).

7. *Ibid.*, pp. 4–5. Samuel Hinckley was born in 1757 and graduated from Yale in 1781. He served as Judge of Probate from 1818 to 1835. See Dexter, *Yale Graduates*, 4:188.

8. *Statement of Facts*, pp. 5–6.

9. *Ibid.*, pp. 12–13.

10. *Ibid.*, pp. 13–14.

11. *Ibid.*, pp. 14–35.

12. Samuel A. Eliot, ed., *Heralds of a Liberal Faith*, 3 vols. (Boston, 1910), Vol. 3, pp. 150–153; "Memoir," pp. ix–xviii in Edward B. Hall, *Sermons* (Boston, 1867).

13. Sarah Howe to Eliza Cabot, Feb. 23, 1825, in Lesley, *Recollections*, p. 183. Mrs. Howe's friend, Eliza Cabot, was active in Channing's Federal Street Church where she organized the Sunday School. She later was married to Charles Follen, the German refugee scholar.

14. Joseph Lyman to Stephen Higginson, Jr., Feb. 23, 1825, AUA Letterbooks, MS, Andover-Harvard Library. (References in the notes to manuscripts in the Andover-Harvard Library [A-H] are all in this collection.) Higginson was the Steward of Harvard College, active in the organization of the Harvard Divinity School, and deeply involved in Unitarian affairs; Thomas Wentworth Higginson was his son. "Mr. Bancroft" was George Bancroft, who had recently started the Round Hill School in Northampton; he was the son of the Reverend Aaron Bancroft of Worcester, the first president of the AUA. The Religious Freedom Act of 1811 had made it easier for those supporting a dissenting religious society to secure exemption from taxation on

behalf of the Standing Order. The meetinghouse was constructed in time to be dedicated on December 7, 1825, the preacher on that occasion being Henry Ware, Jr.

15. Hall, *Sermons*, p. x.

16. Hall to Gannett, May 21, 1827. MS, A-H.

17. *Ibid.*

18. Hall to Gannett, July 31, 1827. MS, A-H.

19. It appears that Gannett first approached Emerson with the proposal that he serve for three months as missionary in western Massachusetts, but that appointment was declined. Ralph L. Rusk, ed., *The Letters of Ralph Waldo Emerson*, 6 vols. (New York, 1937), Vol. 1, p. 203n.

20. Rusk, *Letters*, Vol. 1, p. 210.

21. *Ibid.*, Vol. 1, p. 215.

22. *Ibid.*, Vol. 1, p. 213.

23. Emerson to Gannett, October 9, 1827, MS, A-H. The body of the letter, though not transcribed with scrupulous accuracy, may be found in George W. Cook, *Unitarianism in America* (Boston, 1902), p. 151n.

24. Missionary journal to Berkshire County, entry for October 23, 1827. MS, A-H.

25. Hall to Gannett, Oct. 29, 1827. MS, A-H.

26. *Ibid.*

27. Hall to Gannett, Nov. 13, 1827, MS, A-H.

28. Gannett to Hall, April 15, 1828; Hall to Gannett, April 24, 1828; Oct. 28, 1828. MS, A-H.

29. Hall to Gannett, March 31, 1829; April 16, 1829; April 29, 1829. MS, A-H.

30. Hall, "Report to the Executive Committee of the A.U.A." [October, 1829]. MS, A-H.

31. Auxiliaries in Cummington, Chesterfield, Williamsburgh, and

Belchertown were duly listed in the *Third Annual Report to the American Unitarian Association* (Boston, 1828), p. 67. None of them appear in: [American Unitarian Association], *The Reports... Presented at the Seventh Anniversary, May 29, 1832* (Boston, 1832), pp. 89–91.

32. "Unitarian Congregations & Ministers. May 1830. Of the Congregational Order," compiled by Ezra Stiles Gannett. MS, A-H.

33. *The Unitarian Annual Register for the Year 1846* (Boston, 1845), pp. 16–17.

34. A.D. Mayo, "Liberal Christianity in Western Massachusetts," *Religious Magazine and Monthly Review*, Vol. 50 (1873), pp. 65, 66.

35. Conrad Wright, *The Beginnings of Unitarianism in America* (Boston, 1955), pp. 256–259.

36. The Franklin County ministers listed in 1830 by Gannett were: Timothy F. Rogers (H.C., 1802), Bernardston; John Fessenden (HC, 1818, Divinity School, 1821), Deerfield; Winthrop Bailey (HC, 1807), Greenfield; Alpheus Harding (Dartmouth, 1805), New Salem; Preserved Smith (Brown, 1786), Rowe; Preserved Smith, Jr. (Brown, 1812), Warwick. In Hampden County, William B.O. Peabody (HC, 1816, Divinity School, 1819) was in Springfield. The Northampton pulpit (Hampshire County) was vacant.

37. William B. Sprague, *Annals of the American Pulpit*, 9 vols. (New York, 1859–1869), Vol. 8, p. 182.

38. Ellis, *Samuel Howe*, p. 22.

39. Henry Ware, Jr., *Sober Thoughts on the State of the Times Addressed to the Unitarian Community* (Boston, 1835).

40. Stearns to Charles Briggs, Nov. 7, 1838. MS, A-H.

The Channing We Don't Know

1. William Henry Channing, *Memoir of William Ellery Channing*, 3 vols. (Boston, 1848), Vol. 3, pp. 492, 494.

2. William Ellery Channing, *Works*, 6 vols. (Boston, 1841), Vol. 3, p. 239.

Notes to Pages 157-168

3. William Ellery Channing, *A Sermon Delivered at the Ordination of the Rev. John Codman* (Boston, 1809), pp. 16–17.

4. For a survey of the evidence, see Conrad Wright, *The Liberal Christians* (Boston, 1970), pp. 22–40.

5. Channing, *Works*, Vol. 1, p. vi.

6. *Ibid.*, Vol. 1, p. vii.

7. A few sermons or sermon fragments survive in manuscript; for two that have been edited and published, see *Unitarian Universalist Christian*, Vol. 35, No. 1 (Spring, 1980), pp. 24–47; also David Lyttle, *Studies in Religion in Early American Literature* (Lanham, Md., 1983), pp. 142–50.

8. Channing, *Works*, Vol. 4, p. 135.

9. Channing, *Memoir*, Vol. 2, p. 129.

10. George Huntston Williams, ed., *The Harvard Divinity School* (Boston, 1954), p. 25.

11. Channing, *Memoir*, Vol. 2, p. 125.

12. *Ibid.*, Vol. 2, p. 111.

13. *Ibid.*, Vol. 2, p. 165.

The Theological World of Samuel Gilman

1. Perry Miller, "Theodore Parker: Apostasy Within Liberalism," *Harvard Theological Review*, Vol. 54 (1961), pp. 275–276. Miller had doubtless been reading the chapters by Sydney E. Ahlstrom and myself in George H. Williams, ed., *The Harvard Divinity School* (Boston, 1954); he had also read William R. Hutchison, *The Transcendentalist Ministers* (New Haven, 1959). Later products of the continuing historiographical revolution to which he referred were the special Bellows issue of the *Proceedings of the Unitarian Historical Society*, Vol. 15, Part 2 (1965 issue, published 1968); and Daniel Walker Howe, *The Unitarian Conscience* (Cambridge, Mass., 1970). For an assessment of revisionist tendencies in scholarship, see David M. Robinson, "Unitarian Historiography and the American Renaissance," *ESQ*, Vol. 23 (1977), pp. 130–37.

235

2. John White Chadwick, *Old and New Unitarian Belief* (Boston, 1894), p. 231.

3. Conrad Wright, *The Liberal Christians* (Boston, 1970), pp. 86–87.

4. Gilman to Caroline Howard, March 8, 1812. Gilman Papers, Harvard University Archives (HUA).

5. Gilman's reading notes for October 10–17, 1813. HUA.

6. Supernatural Rationalism is explored in greater detail in Wright, *Liberal Christians*, pp. 1–21.

7. Campbell's *Lectures* were originally given in 1772–1773. The book was regularly used at the Divinity School throughout the whole period down to the Civil War. See Williams, *Harvard Divinity School*, p. 129.

8. Gilman to Caroline Howard, December 23, 1811. HUA.

9. Gilman to Caroline Howard, December 24, 1811. HUA.

10. Reading notes for November, 1814. HUA.

11. Reading notes for October 17–24, 1813. HUA.

12. Reading notes for November, 1814. HUA.

13. *The Philosophical Works of David Hume* (Boston, 1854), Vol. 4, p. 131.

14. See Sydney E. Ahlstrom, "The Scottish Philosophy and American Theology," *Church History*, Vol. 24 (1955), pp. 3–18; and Daniel Walker Howe, *The Unitarian Conscience*, especially pp. 27–44.

15. Reading notes for May 14, 1816. HUA.

16. Samuel Gilman, "Cause and Effect," *North American Review*, Vol. 12 (1821), pp. 395–432; "Brown's Philosophy of Mind," *op. cit.*, Vol. 19 (1824), pp. 1–41; "Character and Writings of Dr. Brown," *op. cit.*, Vol. 21 (1825), pp. 19–51. All reprinted in Samuel Gilman, *Contributions to Literature* (Boston, 1856).

17. Samuel Gilman, *A Sermon on the Introduction to the Gospel of St. John*. Second edition (Boston, 1828), p. 13n.

18. Reading notes, November, 1814. HUA.

19. Reading notes, November, 1813. HUA. Gilman presumably used the second edition of Gerard (Edinburgh, 1808). Andrews Norton's copy of

this edition, inscribed late in life to his protégé , Ezra Abbot, is in the library of the Harvard Divinity School. An American edition was published in Boston in 1823.

20. Gilman to W.B. Sprague, in Sprague, *Annals of the American Pulpit*, 9 vols. (New York, 1856-1869), Vol. 5, pp. 643–44.

21. Samuel Gilman, "Farewell to the Old Church" in *The Old and the New* (Charleston, 1854), p. 21.

22. *Unitarian Defendant*, (Charleston, SC), No. 1 (June 22, 1822), p. 2.

23. It should be noted that while both the Scottish philosophers and the Transcendentalists used the word "intuition," they used it in different ways. For the former, intuition was understood as a direct apprehension by the intellect of aspects of the material world. For the latter, it had reference to an immediate apprehension of the wholeness of things that lies behind the phenomena experienced through the senses. This difference parallels the difference in the use of the term "Reason," with which students of New England Transcendentalism are thoroughly familiar.

24. Theodore Parker, "The Previous Question Between Mr. Andrews Norton and His Alumni . . ." in John E. Dirks, *The Critical Theology of Theodore Parker* (New York, 1948), pp. 140–141.

25. *Ibid.*, p. 157.

26. Samuel Gilman, *Contributions to Religion* (Charleston, 1860), pp. 21, 22.

27. Samuel Gilman, "Revealed Religion," *Christian Examiner*, Vol. 45 (1848), pp. 77, 80. For a contrasting Transcendentalist affirmation, see Emerson's letter to Solomon Corner, 1842: "the powers of the Soul are commensurate with its needs, all experience to the contrary notwithstanding." Willard Reed, ed., *A Letter of Emerson* (Boston, 1934), p. 18.

28. *Ibid.*, p. 63.

29. At his death in 1829, the 8th Earl of Bridgewater left £8000 to the Royal Society to commission a series of treatises "On the Power, Wisdom and Goodness of God, as manifested in the Creation." Among them was one by William Buckland, DD, "Geology and Mineralogy considered with reference to Natural Theology."

30. Gilman, *Revealed Religion*, p. 65.

31. *Ibid.*, p. 67.

32. *Ibid.*, p. 76.

33. *Ibid.*, p. 80.

Index

Index

BX 9833.5 .M4 W75 1994
Wright, Conrad.
The Unitarian controversy

DATE